DEC 0 4 2021

P9-CME-601

When America Chavez's super hero mothers sacrificed their lives to home dimension, the Utopian Parallel, young America knew she needed to live up to their example. America fell to Earth and became the portal-punching, dimension-shattering, superstrong hero she was born to be.

As a Young Avenger, an Ultimate and (most recently) a West Coast Avenger, America knows what she's doing, where she's going and who she is.

Doesn't she?

AMERICA CHAVEZ
★ MADE IN THE USA ★

Kalinda Vazquez
WRITER

Carlos Gómez
ARTIST

Jesus Aburtov
COLOR ARTIST

VC's Travis Lanham
LETTERER

**Sara Pichelli &
Tamra Bonvillain**
COVER ART

Annalise Bissa
EDITOR

**Jordan D. White
& Sana Amanat**
SUPERVISING EDITORS

DISCARD

Jennifer Grünwald COLLECTION EDITOR **Daniel Kirchhoffer** ASSISTANT EDITOR
Maia Loy ASSISTANT MANAGING EDITOR **Lisa Montalbano** ASSISTANT MANAGING EDITOR
Jeff Youngquist VP PRODUCTION & SPECIAL PROJECTS **Jay Bowen** BOOK DESIGNER
David Gabriel SVP PRINT, SALES & MARKETING **C.B. Cebulski** EDITOR IN CHIEF

AMERICA CHAVEZ: MADE IN THE USA. Contains material originally published in magazine form as AMERICA CHAVEZ: MADE IN THE USA (2021) #1-5. First printing 2021. ISBN 978-1-302-92445-4. Published by MARVEL WORLDWIDE, INC., a subsidiary of MARVEL ENTERTAINMENT, LLC. OFFICE OF PUBLICATION: 1290 Avenue of the Americas, New York, NY 10104. © 2021 MARVEL No similarity between any of the names, characters, persons, and/or institutions in this magazine with those of any living or dead person or institution is intended, and any such similarity which may exist is purely coincidental. Printed in Canada. KEVIN FEIGE, Chief Creative Officer; DAN BUCKLEY, President, Marvel Entertainment; JOE QUESADA, EVP & Creative Director; DAVID BOGART, Associate Publisher & SVP of Talent Affairs; TOM BREVOORT, VP, Executive Editor; NICK LOWE, Executive Editor, VP of Content, Digital Publishing; DAVID GABRIEL, VP of Print & Digital Publishing; JEFF YOUNGQUIST, VP of Production & Special Projects; ALEX MORALES, Director of Publishing Operations; DAN EDINGTON, Managing Editor; RICKEY PURDIN, Director of Talent Relations; JENNIFER GRÜNWALD, Senior Editor, Special Projects; SUSAN CRESPI, Production Manager; STAN LEE, Chairman Emeritus. For information regarding advertising in Marvel Comics or on Marvel.com, please contact Vit DeBellis, Custom Solutions & Integrated Advertising Manager, at vdebellis@marvel.com. For Marvel subscription inquiries, please call 888-511-5480. Manufactured between 8/20/2021 and 9/21/2021 by SOLISCO PRINTERS, SCOTT, QC, CANADA.

10 9 8 7 6 5 4 3 2 1

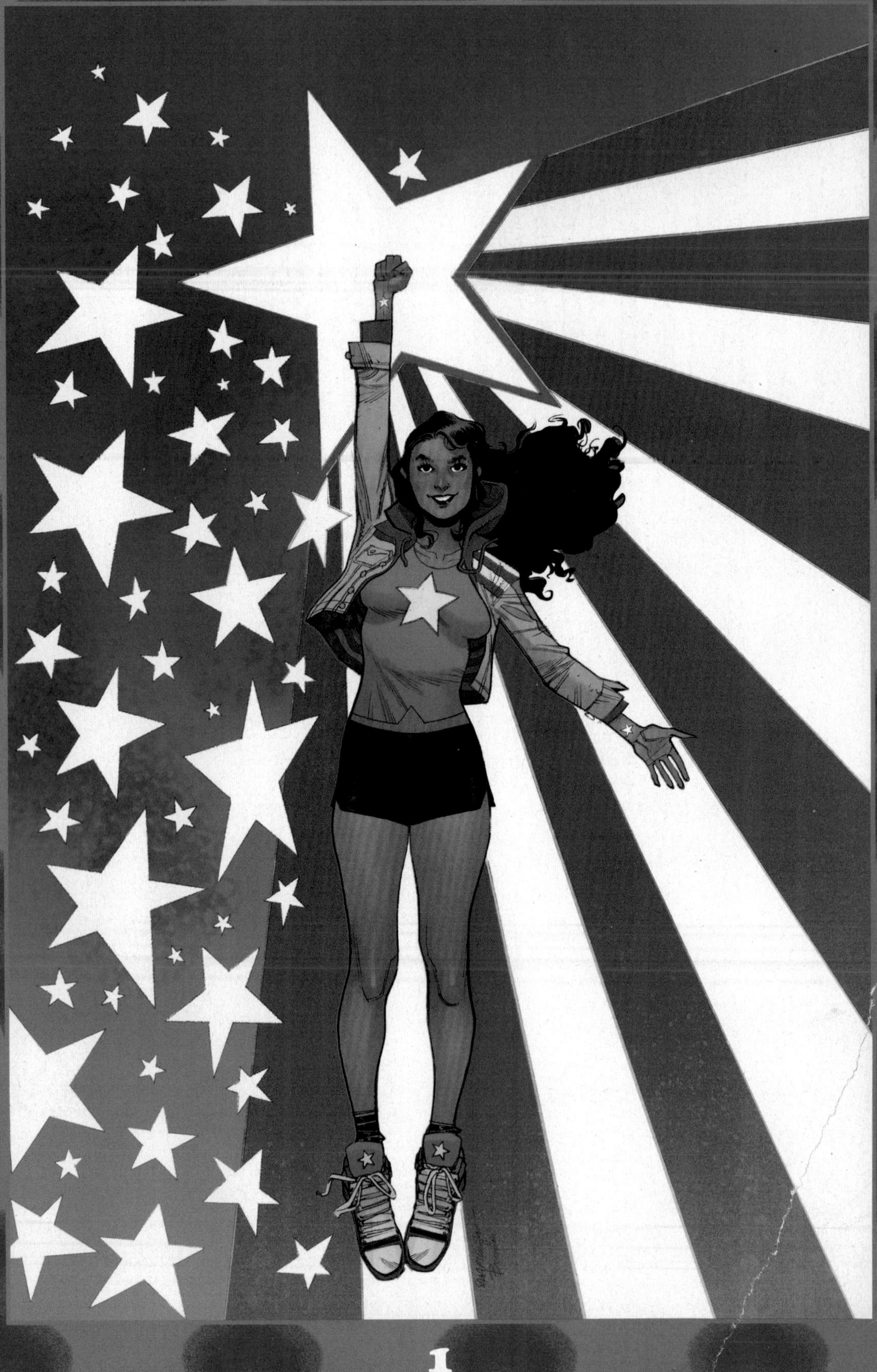

1

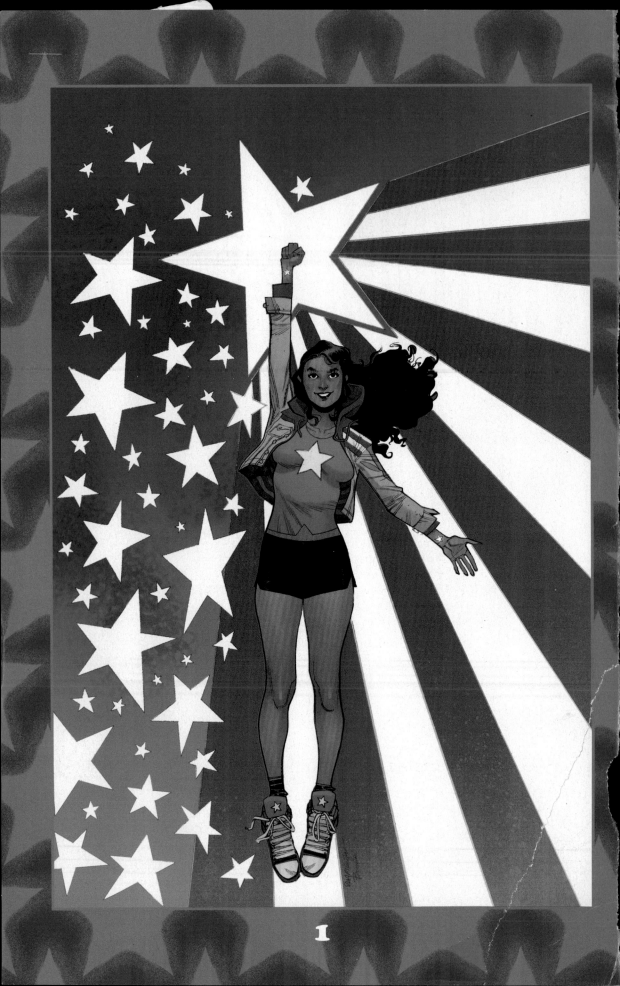

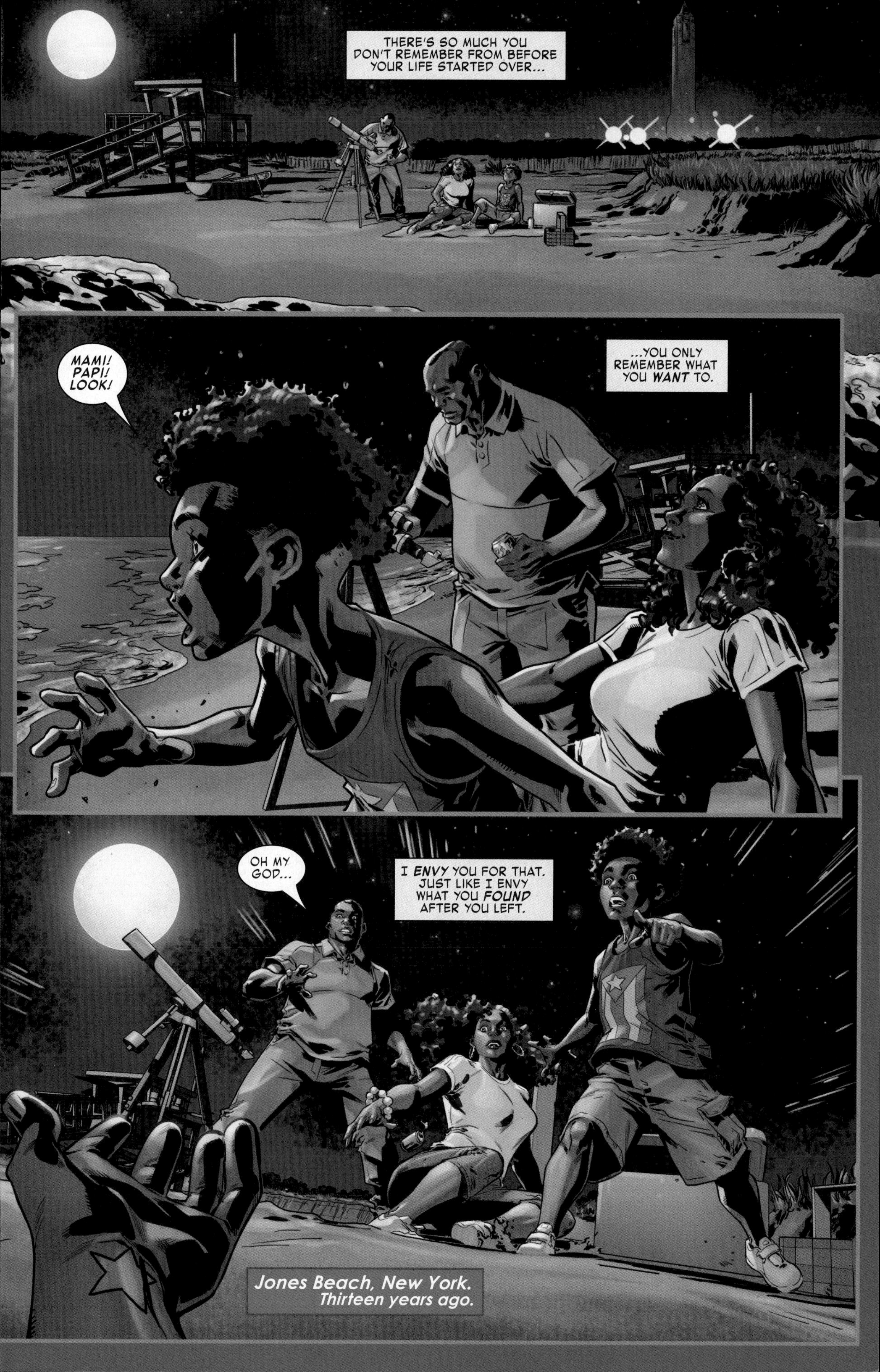
THERE'S SO MUCH YOU DON'T REMEMBER FROM BEFORE YOUR LIFE STARTED OVER...
MAMI! PAPI! LOOK!
...YOU ONLY REMEMBER WHAT YOU *WANT* TO.
OH MY GOD...
I *ENVY* YOU FOR THAT. JUST LIKE I ENVY WHAT YOU *FOUND* AFTER YOU LEFT.
Jones Beach, New York. Thirteen years ago.

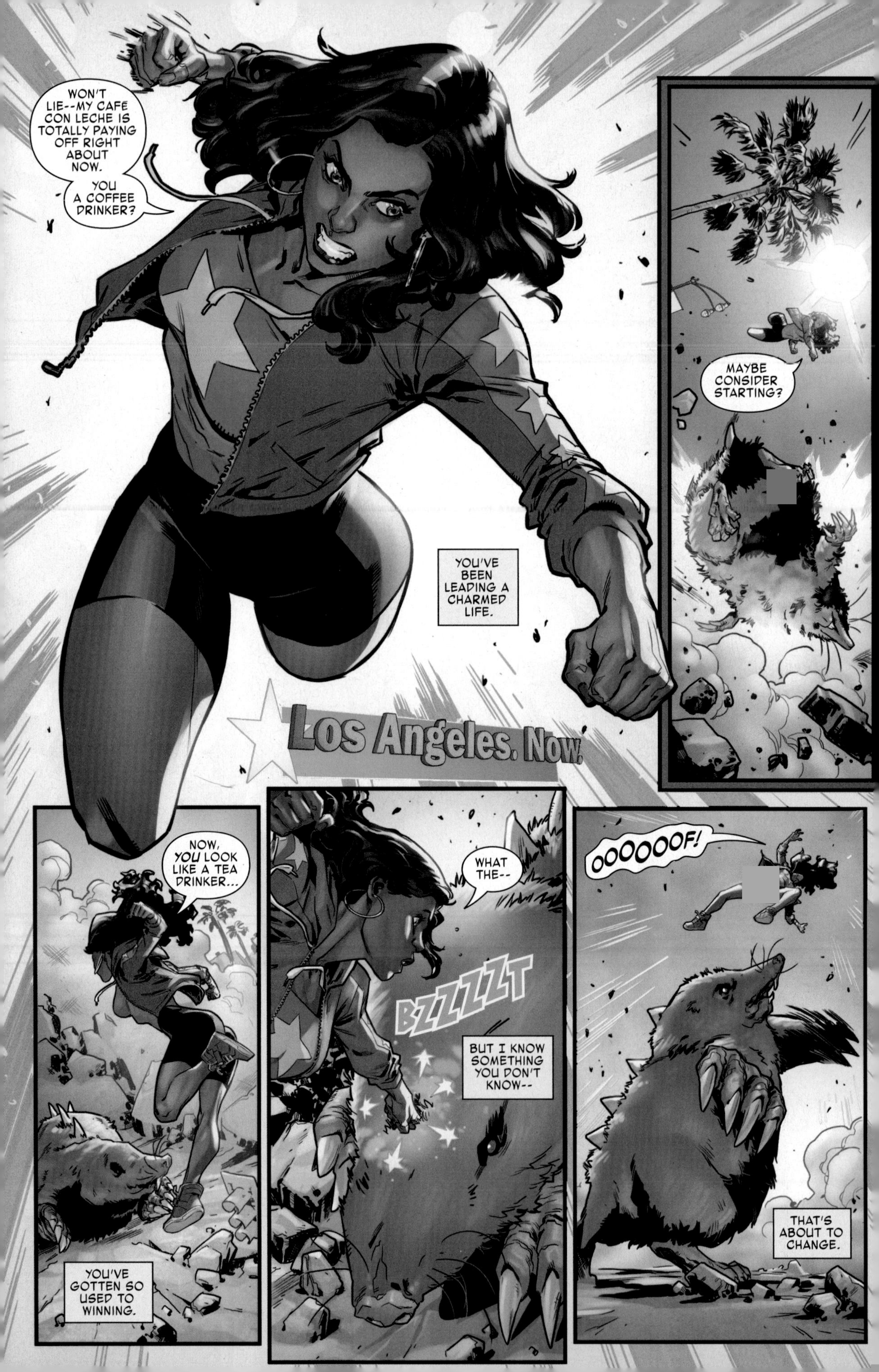

WON'T LIE--MY CAFÉ CON LECHE IS TOTALLY PAYING OFF RIGHT ABOUT NOW.
YOU A COFFEE DRINKER?
MAYBE CONSIDER STARTING?
YOU'VE BEEN LEADING A CHARMED LIFE.
Los Angeles. Now.
NOW, YOU LOOK LIKE A TEA DRINKER...
YOU'VE GOTTEN SO USED TO WINNING.
WHAT THE--
BZZZZZT
BUT I KNOW SOMETHING YOU DON'T KNOW--
OOOOOOF!
THAT'S ABOUT TO CHANGE.

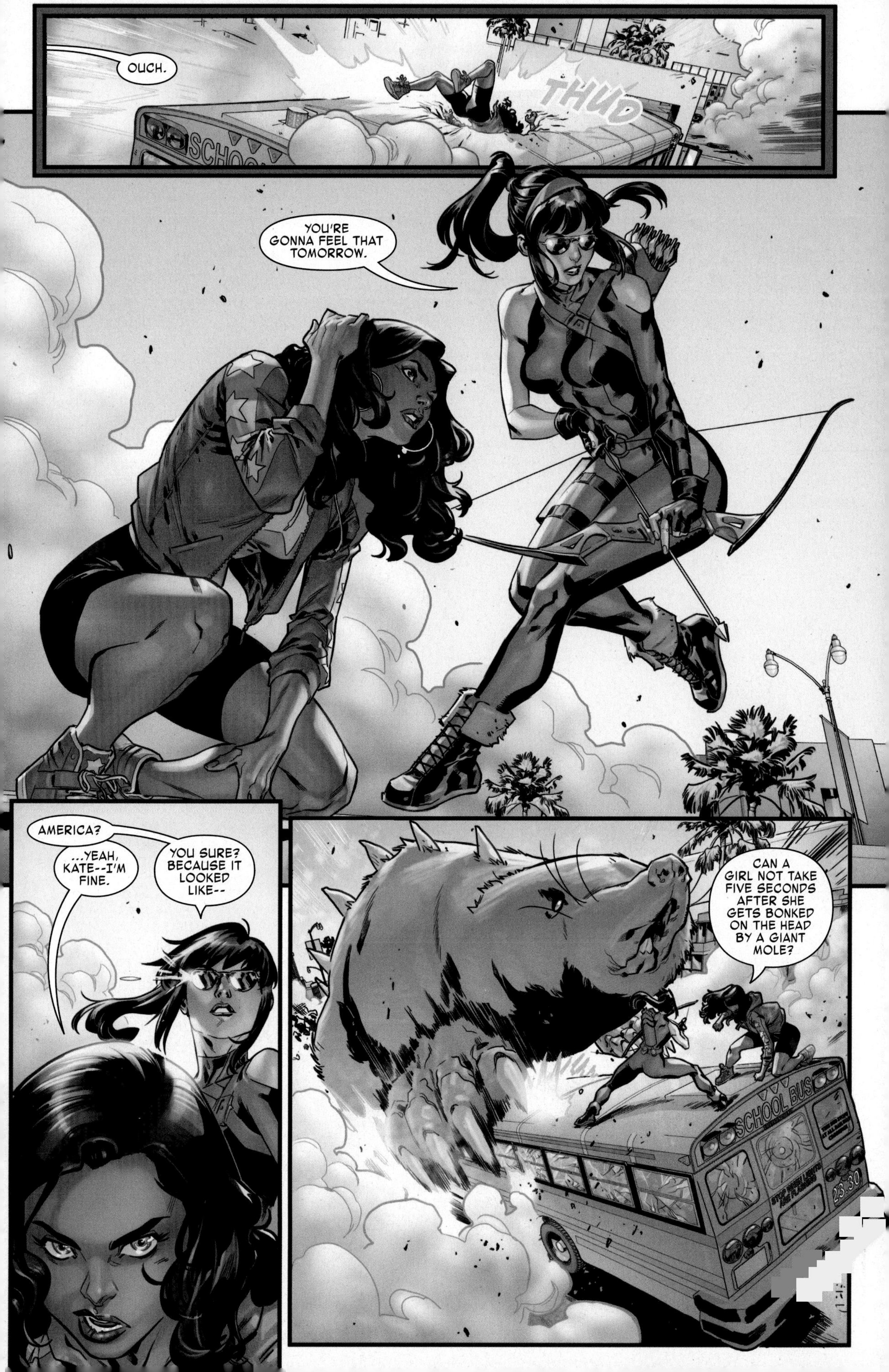
OUCH.
THUD
YOU'RE GONNA FEEL THAT TOMORROW.
AMERICA?
...YEAH, KATE--I'M FINE.
YOU SURE? BECAUSE IT LOOKED LIKE--
CAN A GIRL NOT TAKE FIVE SECONDS AFTER SHE GETS BONKED ON THE HEAD BY A GIANT MOLE?
SCHOOL BUS

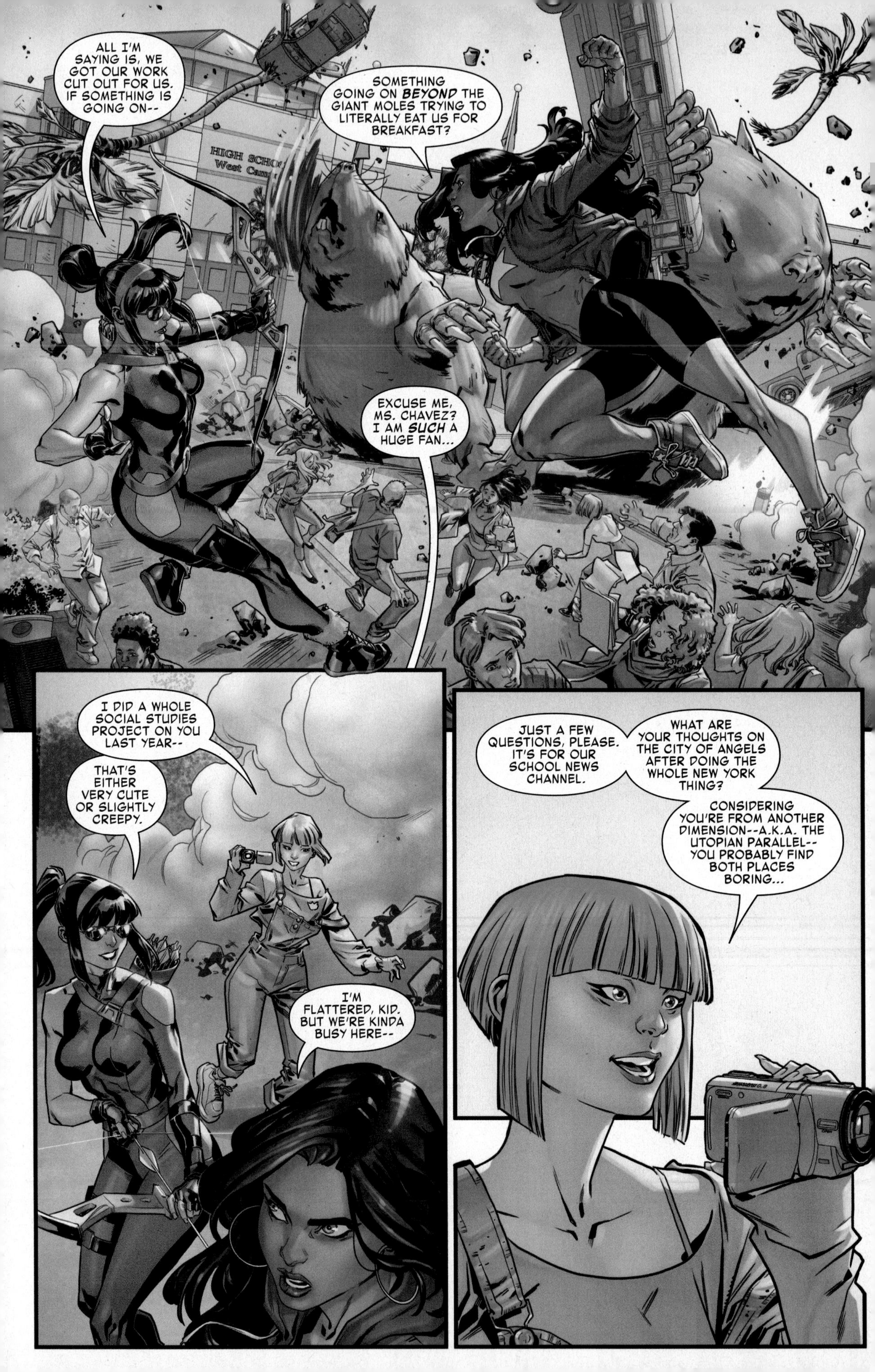
HIGH SCHO
West Camp
ALL I'M SAYING IS, WE GOT OUR WORK CUT OUT FOR US. IF SOMETHING IS GOING ON--
SOMETHING GOING ON BEYOND THE GIANT MOLES TRYING TO LITERALLY EAT US FOR BREAKFAST?
EXCUSE ME, MS. CHAVEZ? I AM SUCH A HUGE FAN...
I DID A WHOLE SOCIAL STUDIES PROJECT ON YOU LAST YEAR--
THAT'S EITHER VERY CUTE OR SLIGHTLY CREEPY.
I'M FLATTERED, KID. BUT WE'RE KINDA BUSY HERE--
JUST A FEW QUESTIONS, PLEASE. IT'S FOR OUR SCHOOL NEWS CHANNEL.
WHAT ARE YOUR THOUGHTS ON THE CITY OF ANGELS AFTER DOING THE WHOLE NEW YORK THING?
CONSIDERING YOU'RE FROM ANOTHER DIMENSION--A.K.A. THE UTOPIAN PARALLEL--YOU PROBABLY FIND BOTH PLACES BORING...

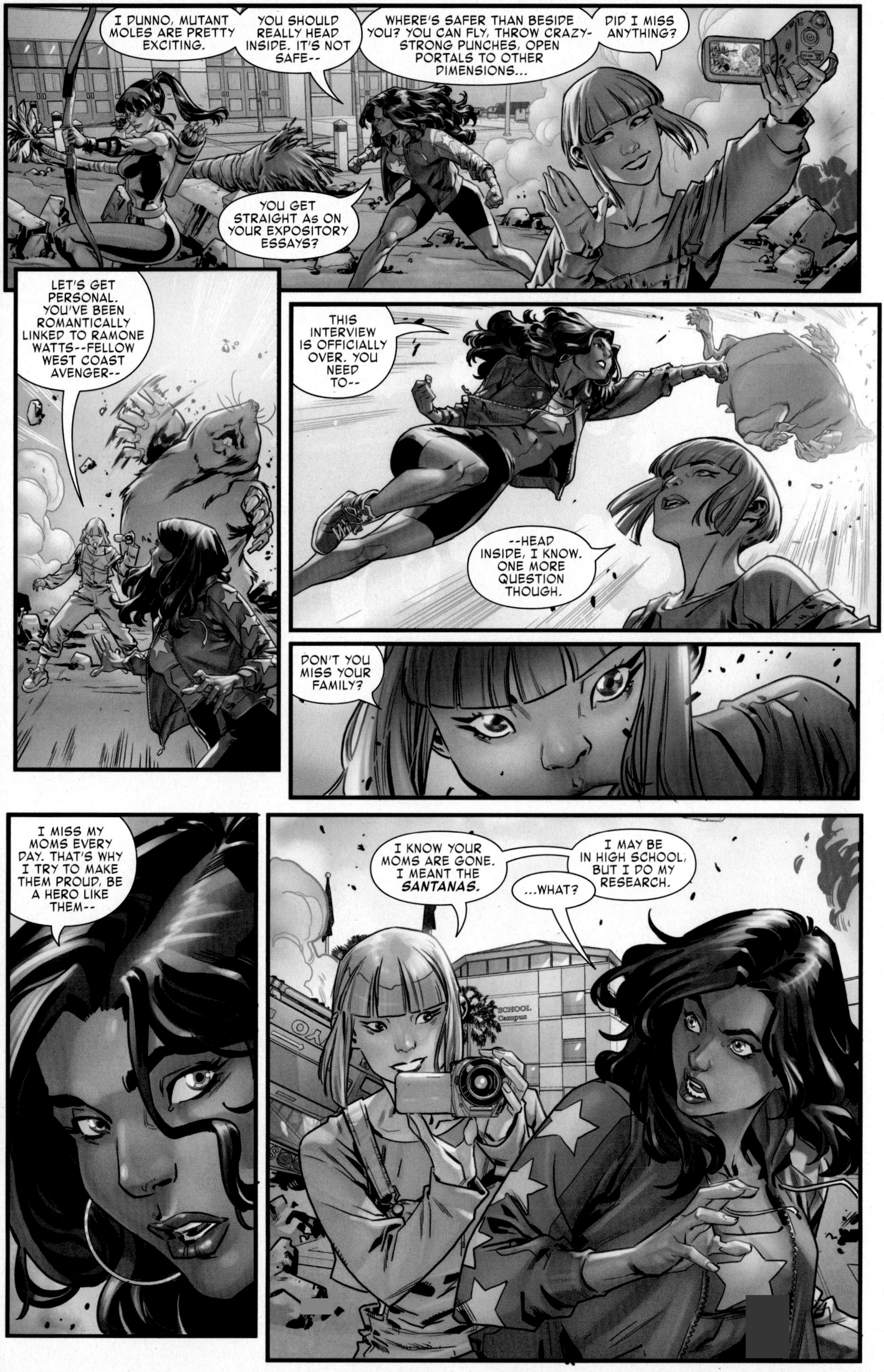
I DUNNO, MUTANT MOLES ARE PRETTY EXCITING.
YOU SHOULD REALLY HEAD INSIDE. IT'S NOT SAFE--
WHERE'S SAFER THAN BESIDE YOU? YOU CAN FLY, THROW CRAZY-STRONG PUNCHES, OPEN PORTALS TO OTHER DIMENSIONS...
DID I MISS ANYTHING?
YOU GET STRAIGHT As ON YOUR EXPOSITORY ESSAYS?
LET'S GET PERSONAL. YOU'VE BEEN ROMANTICALLY LINKED TO RAMONE WATTS--FELLOW WEST COAST AVENGER--
THIS INTERVIEW IS OFFICIALLY OVER. YOU NEED TO--
--HEAD INSIDE, I KNOW. ONE MORE QUESTION THOUGH.
DON'T YOU MISS YOUR FAMILY?
I MISS MY MOMS EVERY DAY. THAT'S WHY I TRY TO MAKE THEM PROUD, BE A HERO LIKE THEM--
I KNOW YOUR MOMS ARE GONE. I MEANT THE *SANTANAS.*
...WHAT?
I MAY BE IN HIGH SCHOOL, BUT I DO MY RESEARCH.
SCHOOL
Campus

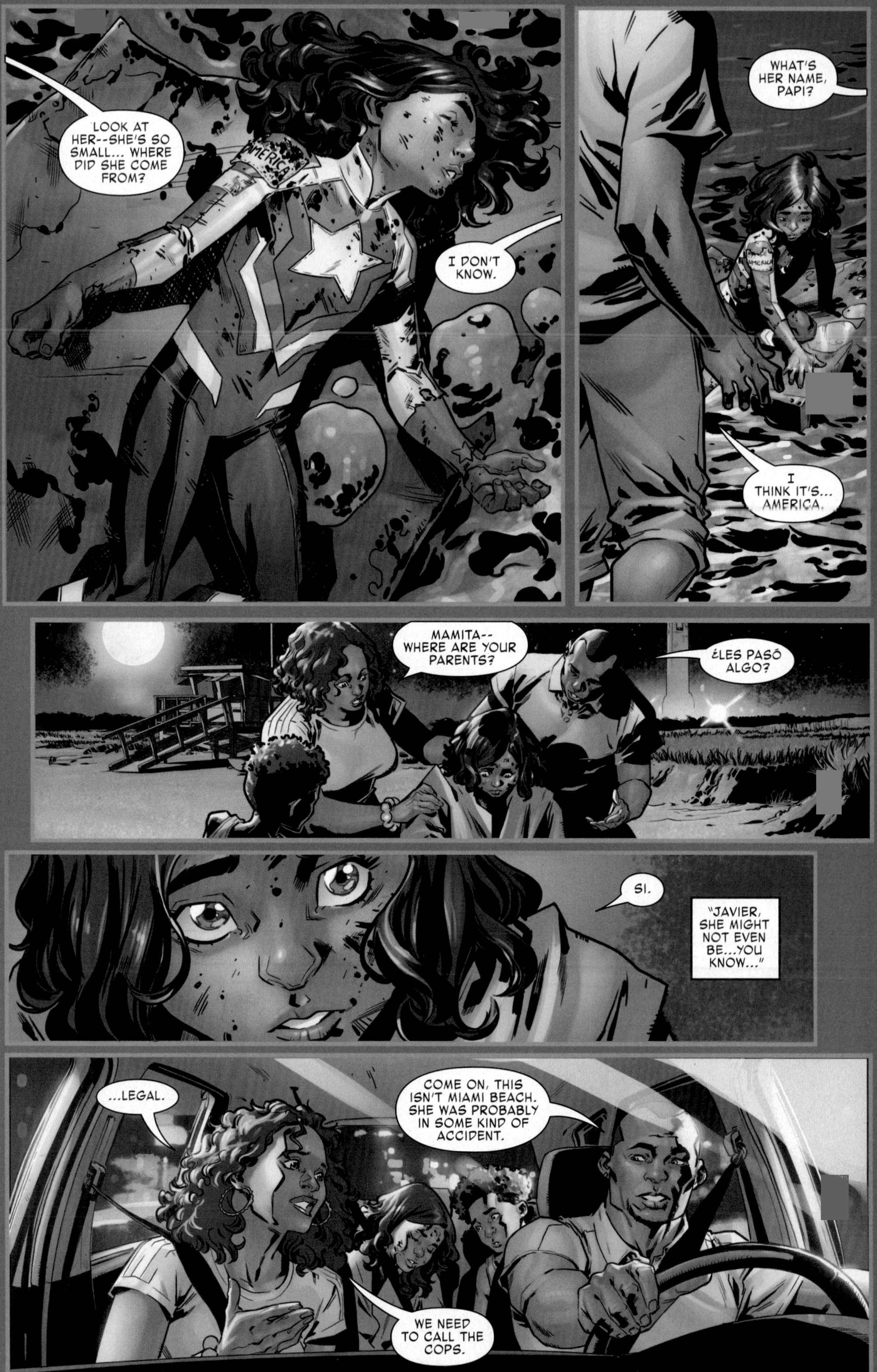
LOOK AT HER--SHE'S SO SMALL... WHERE DID SHE COME FROM?
I DON'T KNOW.
WHAT'S HER NAME, PAPI?
I THINK IT'S... AMERICA.
MAMITA-- WHERE ARE YOUR PARENTS?
¿LES PASÓ ALGO?
SI.
"JAVIER, SHE MIGHT NOT EVEN BE...YOU KNOW..."
...LEGAL.
COME ON, THIS ISN'T MIAMI BEACH. SHE WAS PROBABLY IN SOME KIND OF ACCIDENT.
WE NEED TO CALL THE COPS.

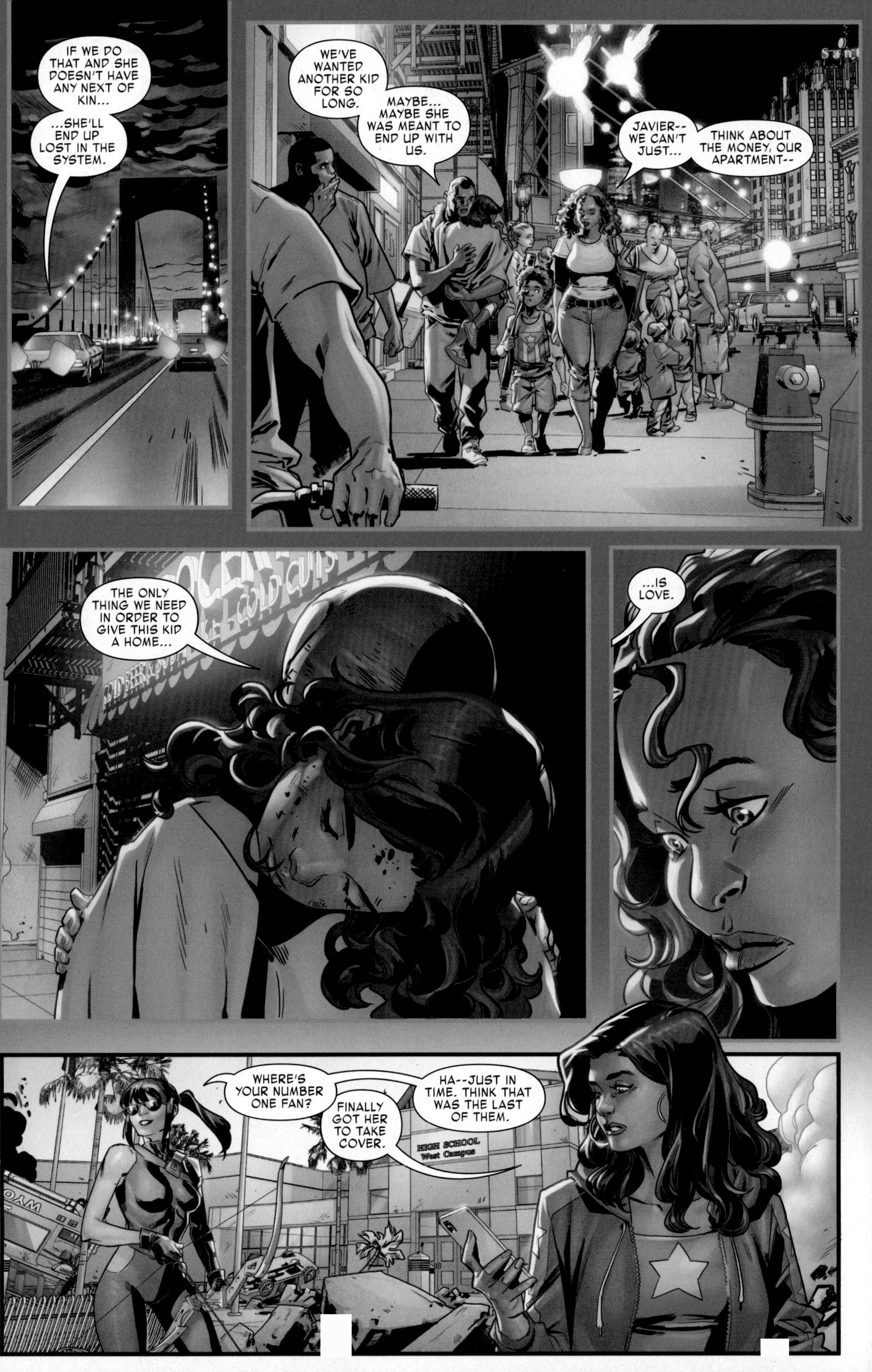
IF WE DO THAT AND SHE DOESN'T HAVE ANY NEXT OF KIN...
...SHE'LL END UP LOST IN THE SYSTEM.
WE'VE WANTED ANOTHER KID FOR SO LONG.
MAYBE... MAYBE SHE WAS MEANT TO END UP WITH US.
JAVIER-- WE CAN'T JUST...
THINK ABOUT THE MONEY, OUR APARTMENT--
THE ONLY THING WE NEED IN ORDER TO GIVE THIS KID A HOME...
...IS LOVE.
WHERE'S YOUR NUMBER ONE FAN?
HA--JUST IN TIME. THINK THAT WAS THE LAST OF THEM.
FINALLY GOT HER TO TAKE COVER.
HIGH SCHOOL
West Campus

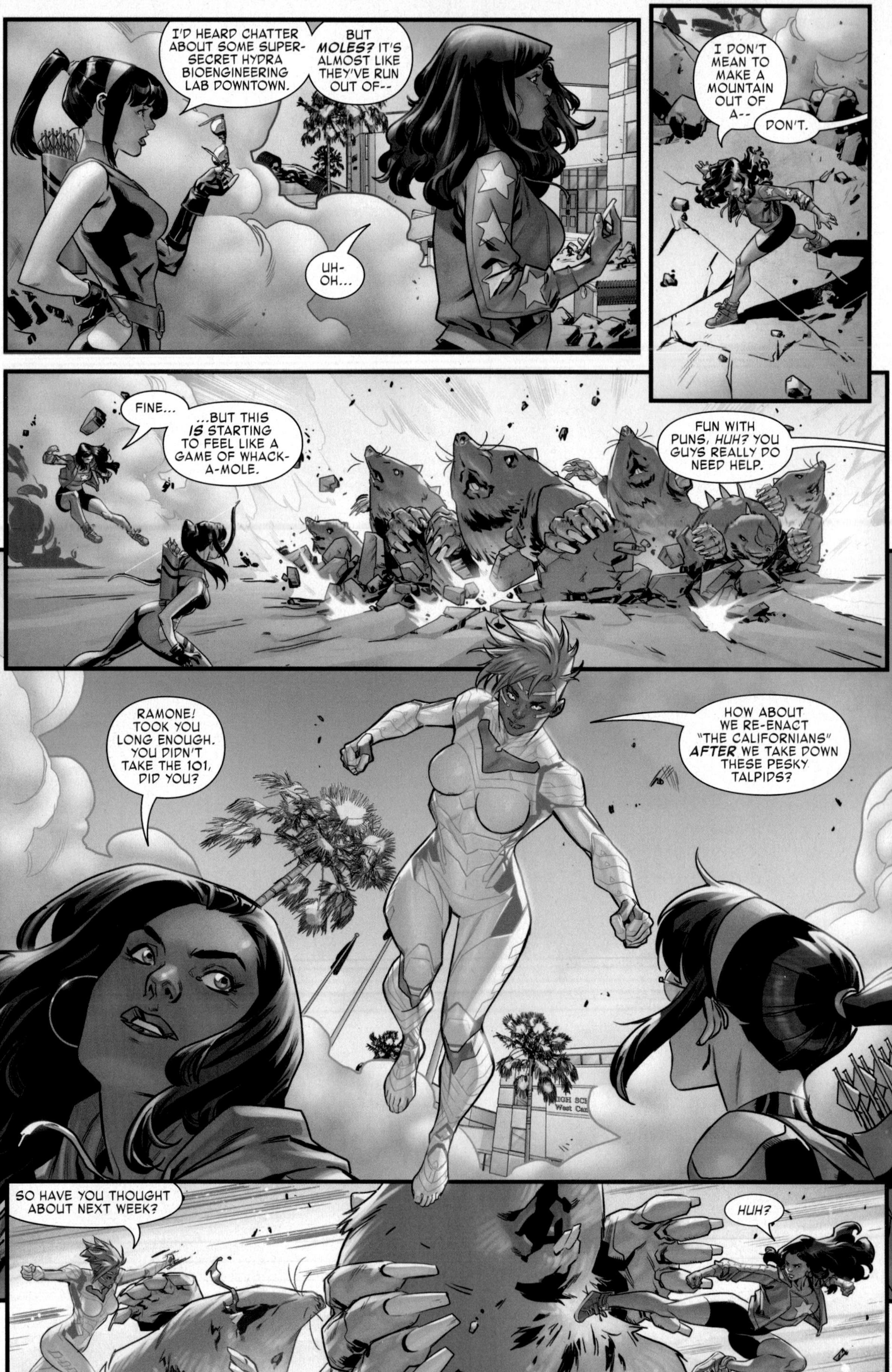
I'D HEARD CHATTER ABOUT SOME SUPER-SECRET HYDRA BIOENGINEERING LAB DOWNTOWN.
BUT MOLES? IT'S ALMOST LIKE THEY'VE RUN OUT OF--
UH-OH...
I DON'T MEAN TO MAKE A MOUNTAIN OUT OF A--
DON'T.
FINE...
...BUT THIS IS STARTING TO FEEL LIKE A GAME OF WHACK-A-MOLE.
FUN WITH PUNS, HUH? YOU GUYS REALLY DO NEED HELP.
RAMONE! TOOK YOU LONG ENOUGH. YOU DIDN'T TAKE THE 101, DID YOU?
HOW ABOUT WE RE-ENACT "THE CALIFORNIANS" AFTER WE TAKE DOWN THESE PESKY TALPIDS?
SO HAVE YOU THOUGHT ABOUT NEXT WEEK?
HUH?

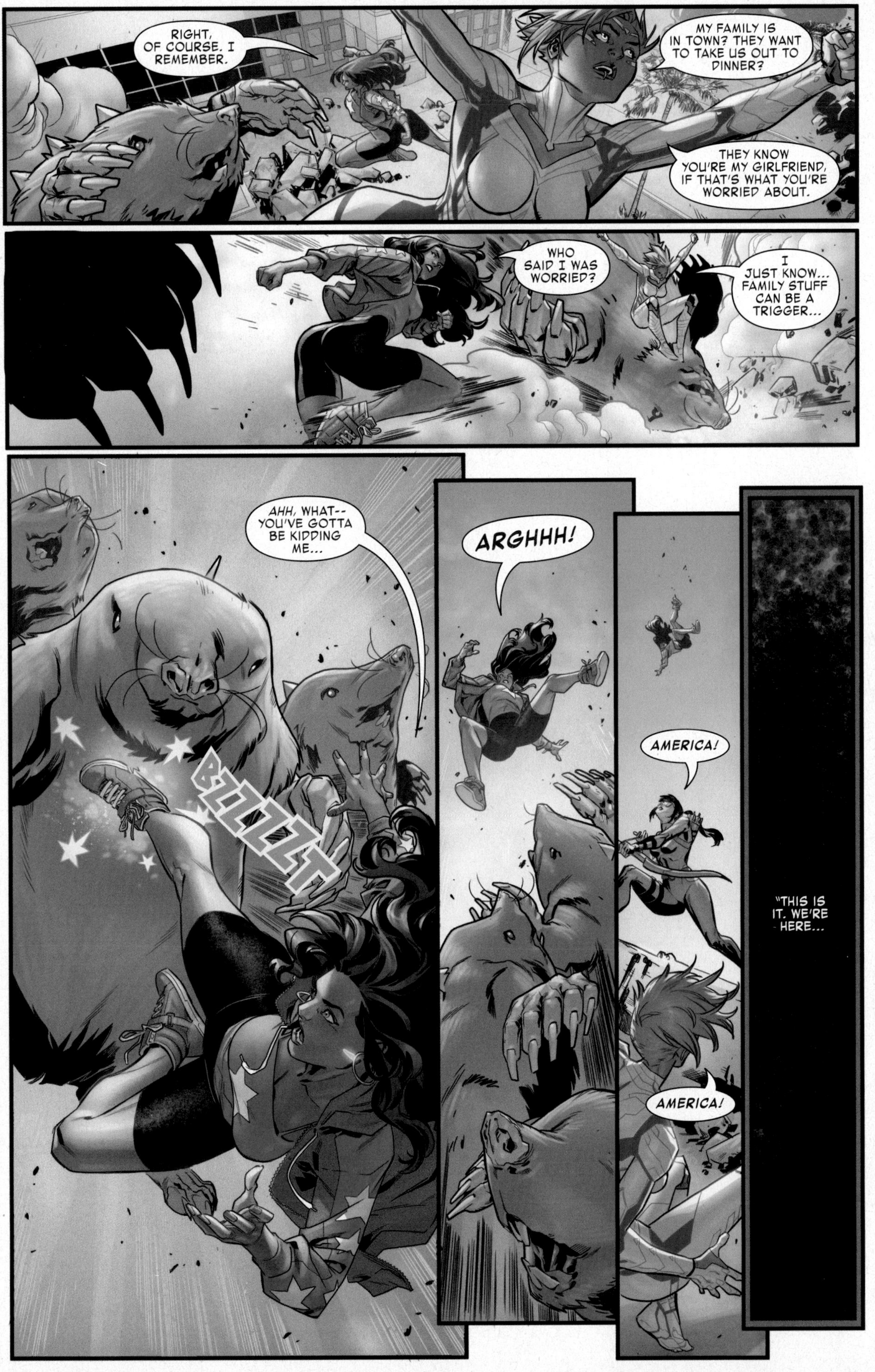
RIGHT, OF COURSE. I REMEMBER.
MY FAMILY IS IN TOWN? THEY WANT TO TAKE US OUT TO DINNER?
THEY KNOW YOU'RE MY GIRLFRIEND, IF THAT'S WHAT YOU'RE WORRIED ABOUT.
WHO SAID I WAS WORRIED?
I JUST KNOW... FAMILY STUFF CAN BE A TRIGGER...
AHH, WHAT-- YOU'VE GOTTA BE KIDDING ME...
BZZZZT
ARGHHH!
AMERICA!
AMERICA!
"THIS IS IT. WE'RE HERE...

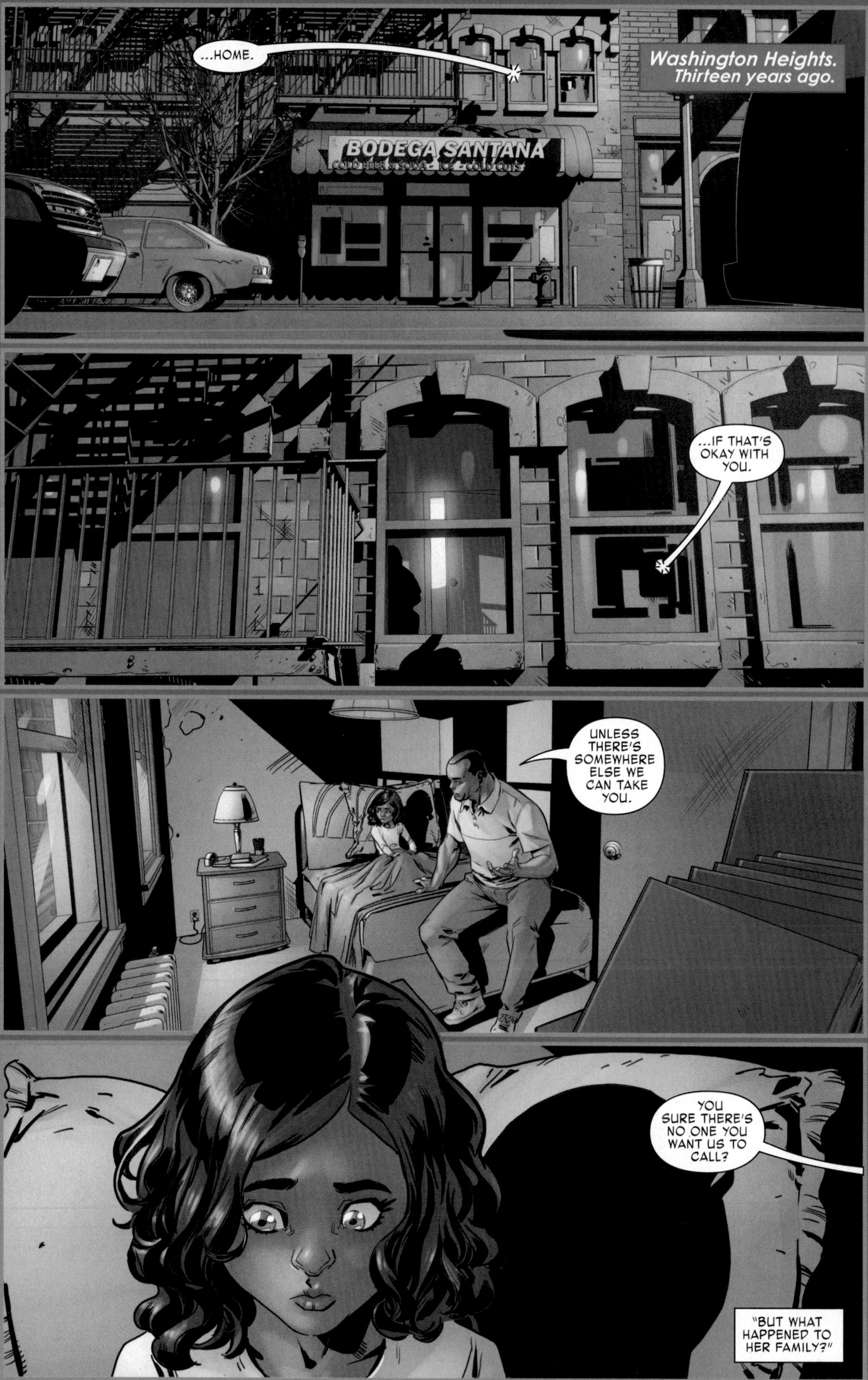
...HOME.
Washington Heights. Thirteen years ago.
BODEGA SANTANA
COLD BEER & SODA - ICE - COLD CUTS
...IF THAT'S OKAY WITH YOU.
UNLESS THERE'S SOMEWHERE ELSE WE CAN TAKE YOU.
YOU SURE THERE'S NO ONE YOU WANT US TO CALL?
"BUT WHAT HAPPENED TO HER FAMILY?"

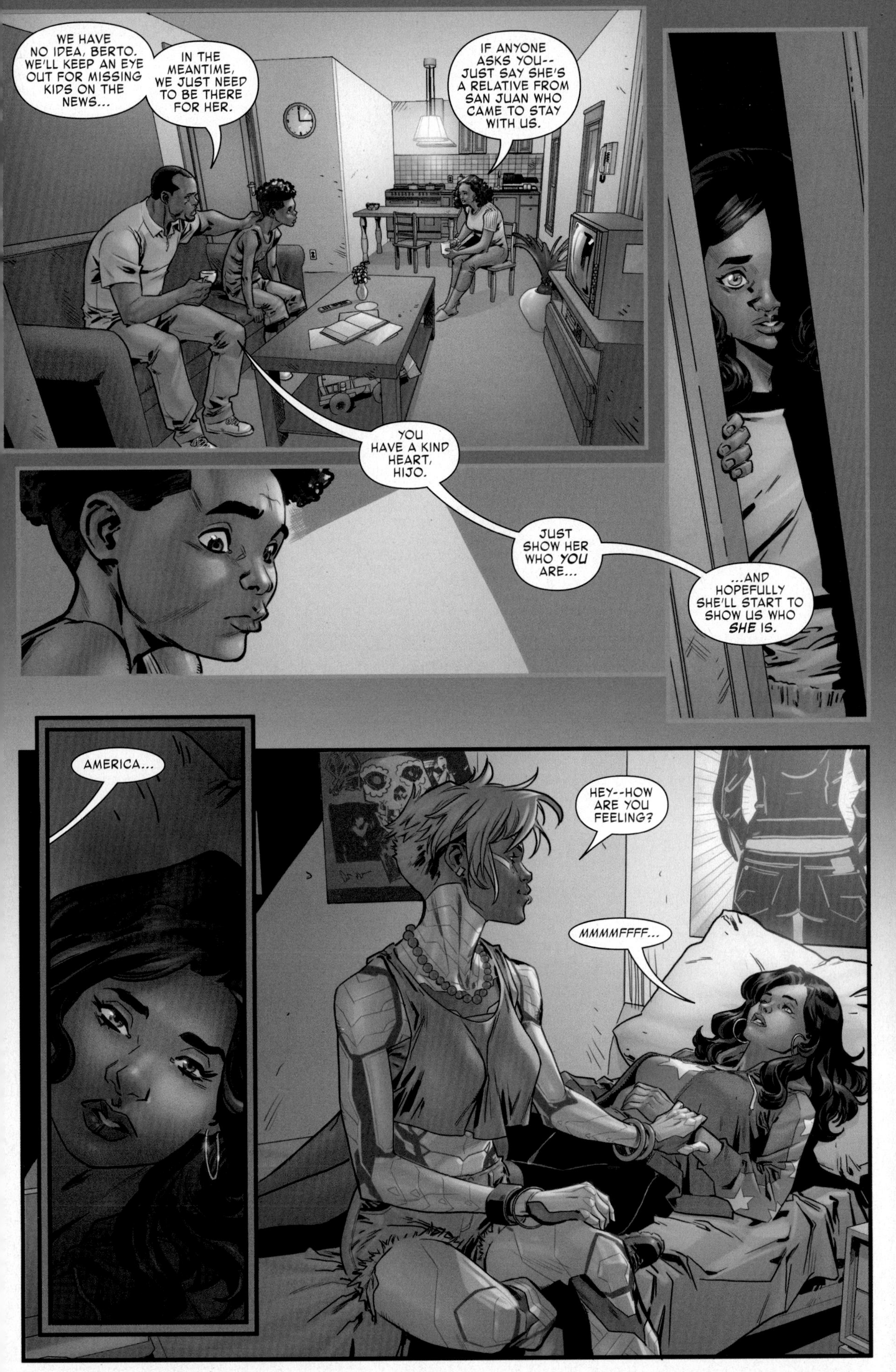
WE HAVE NO IDEA, BERTO. WE'LL KEEP AN EYE OUT FOR MISSING KIDS ON THE NEWS...
IN THE MEANTIME, WE JUST NEED TO BE THERE FOR HER.
IF ANYONE ASKS YOU--JUST SAY SHE'S A RELATIVE FROM SAN JUAN WHO CAME TO STAY WITH US.
YOU HAVE A KIND HEART, HIJO.
JUST SHOW HER WHO *YOU* ARE...
...AND HOPEFULLY SHE'LL START TO SHOW US WHO *SHE* IS.
AMERICA...
HEY--HOW ARE YOU FEELING?
MMMMFFFF...

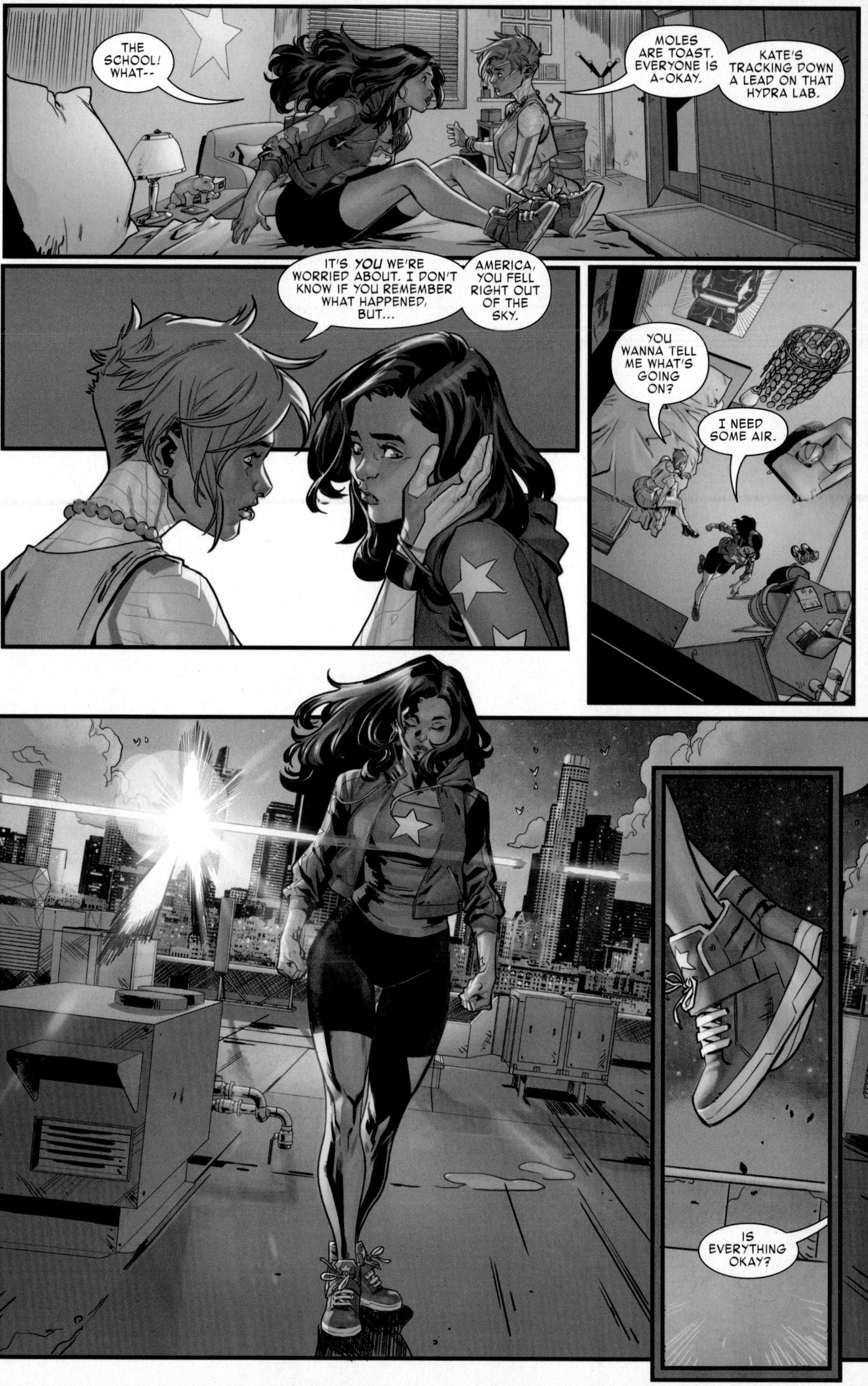
THE SCHOOL! WHAT--
MOLES ARE TOAST. EVERYONE IS A-OKAY.
KATE'S TRACKING DOWN A LEAD ON THAT HYDRA LAB.
IT'S *YOU* WE'RE WORRIED ABOUT. I DON'T KNOW IF YOU REMEMBER WHAT HAPPENED, BUT...
AMERICA, YOU FELL RIGHT OUT OF THE SKY.
YOU WANNA TELL ME WHAT'S GOING ON?
I NEED SOME AIR.
IS EVERYTHING OKAY?

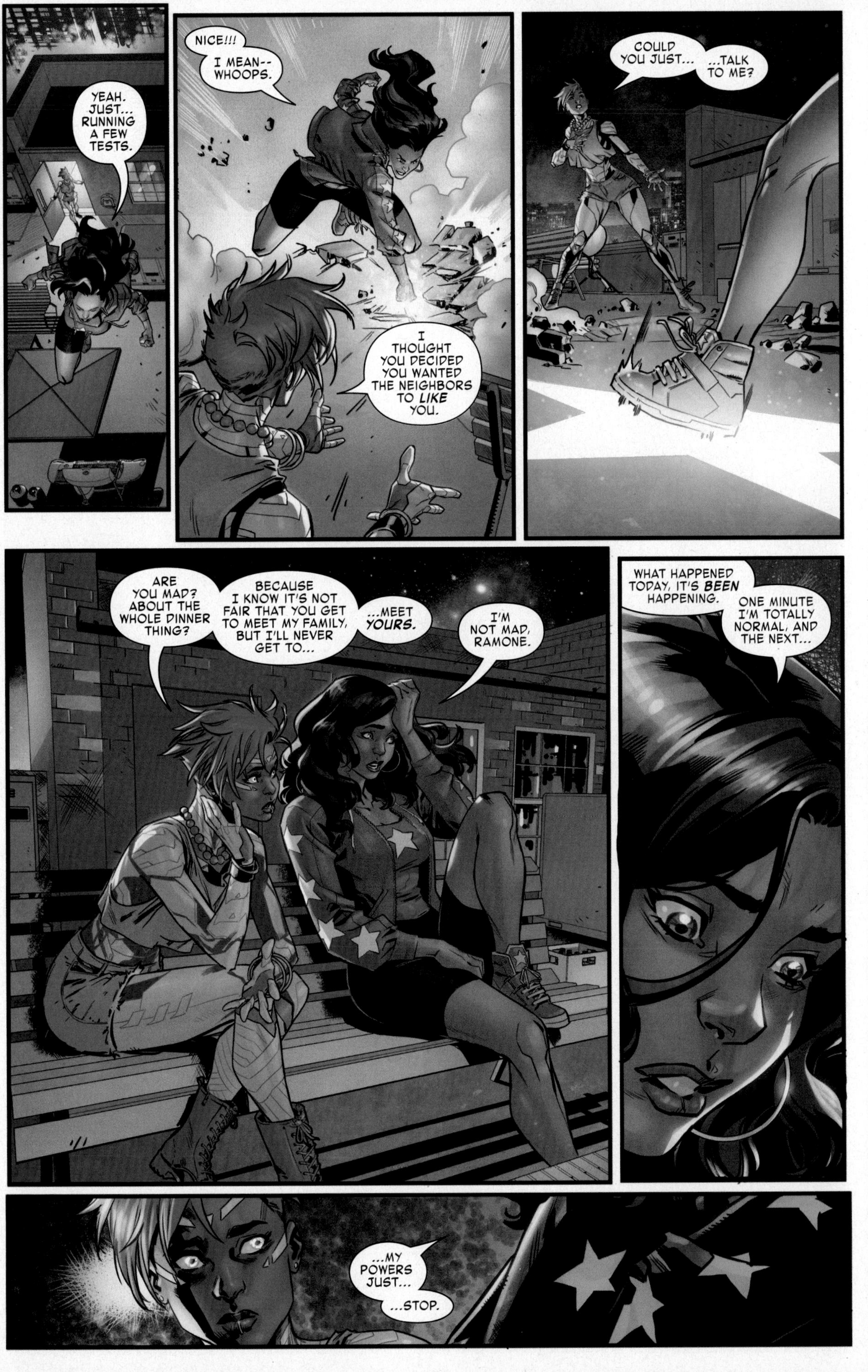
YEAH. JUST... RUNNING A FEW TESTS.
NICE!!! I MEAN-- WHOOPS.
I THOUGHT YOU DECIDED YOU WANTED THE NEIGHBORS TO LIKE YOU.
COULD YOU JUST...
...TALK TO ME?
ARE YOU MAD? ABOUT THE WHOLE DINNER THING?
BECAUSE I KNOW IT'S NOT FAIR THAT YOU GET TO MEET MY FAMILY, BUT I'LL NEVER GET TO...
...MEET YOURS.
I'M NOT MAD, RAMONE.
WHAT HAPPENED TODAY, IT'S BEEN HAPPENING.
ONE MINUTE I'M TOTALLY NORMAL, AND THE NEXT...
...MY POWERS JUST...
...STOP.

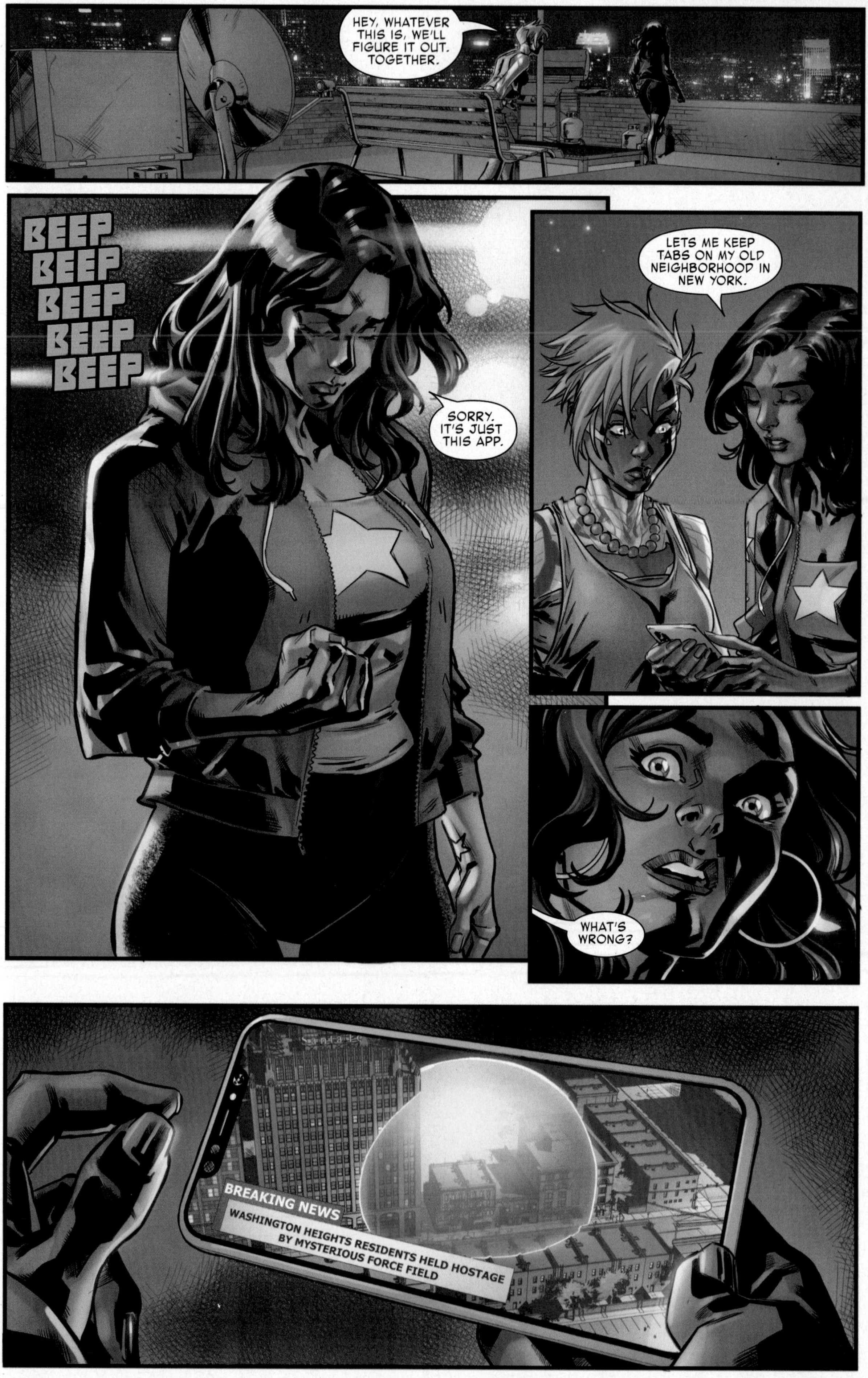
HEY, WHATEVER THIS IS, WE'LL FIGURE IT OUT. TOGETHER.
BEEP BEEP BEEP BEEP BEEP
SORRY. IT'S JUST THIS APP.
LETS ME KEEP TABS ON MY OLD NEIGHBORHOOD IN NEW YORK.
WHAT'S WRONG?
BREAKING NEWS
WASHINGTON HEIGHTS RESIDENTS HELD HOSTAGE BY MYSTERIOUS FORCE FIELD

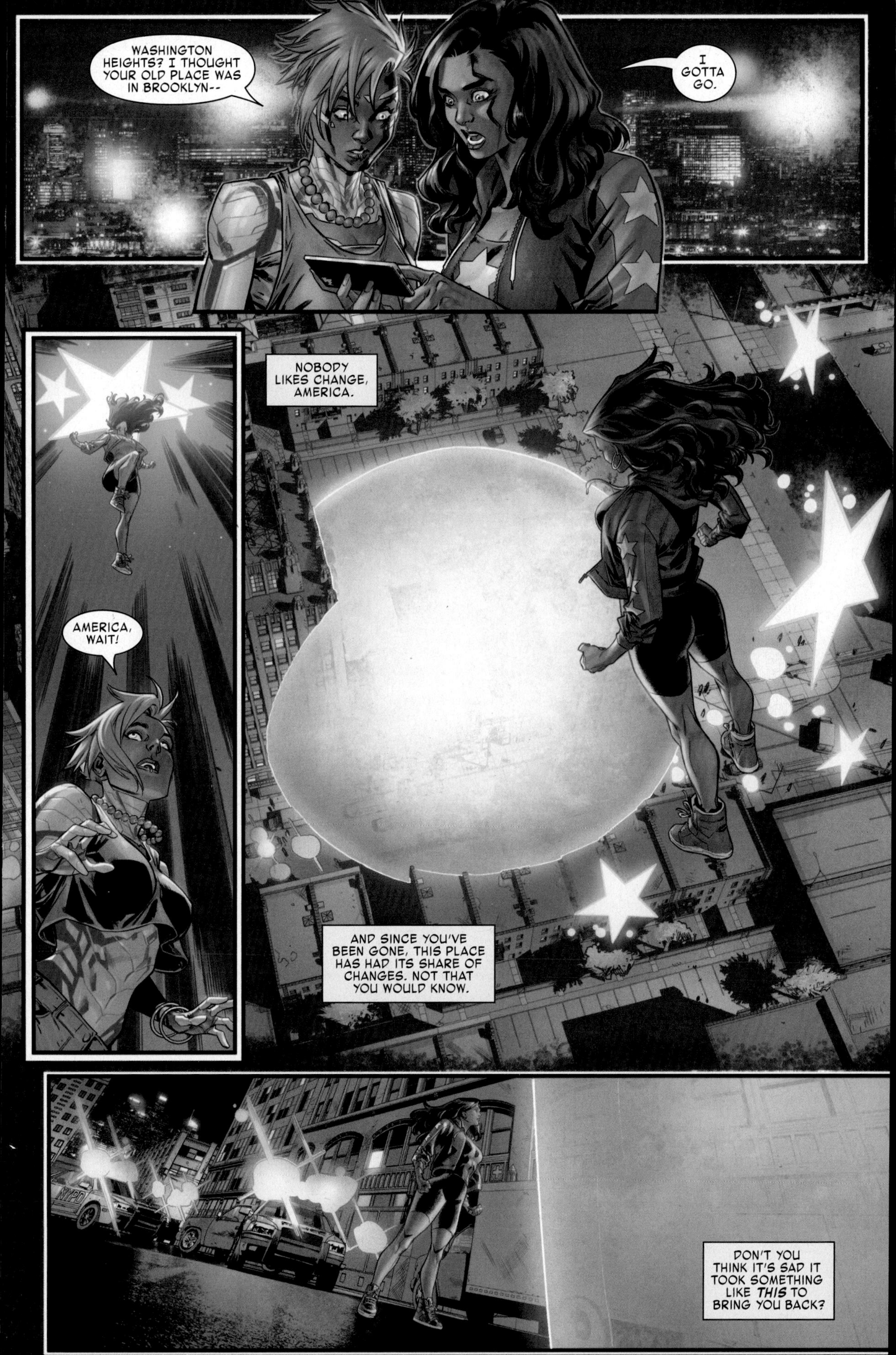

WASHINGTON HEIGHTS? I THOUGHT YOUR OLD PLACE WAS IN BROOKLYN--
I GOTTA GO.
NOBODY LIKES CHANGE, AMERICA.
AMERICA, WAIT!
AND SINCE YOU'VE BEEN GONE, THIS PLACE HAS HAD ITS SHARE OF CHANGES. NOT THAT YOU WOULD KNOW.
NYPD
DON'T YOU THINK IT'S SAD IT TOOK SOMETHING LIKE *THIS* TO BRING YOU BACK?

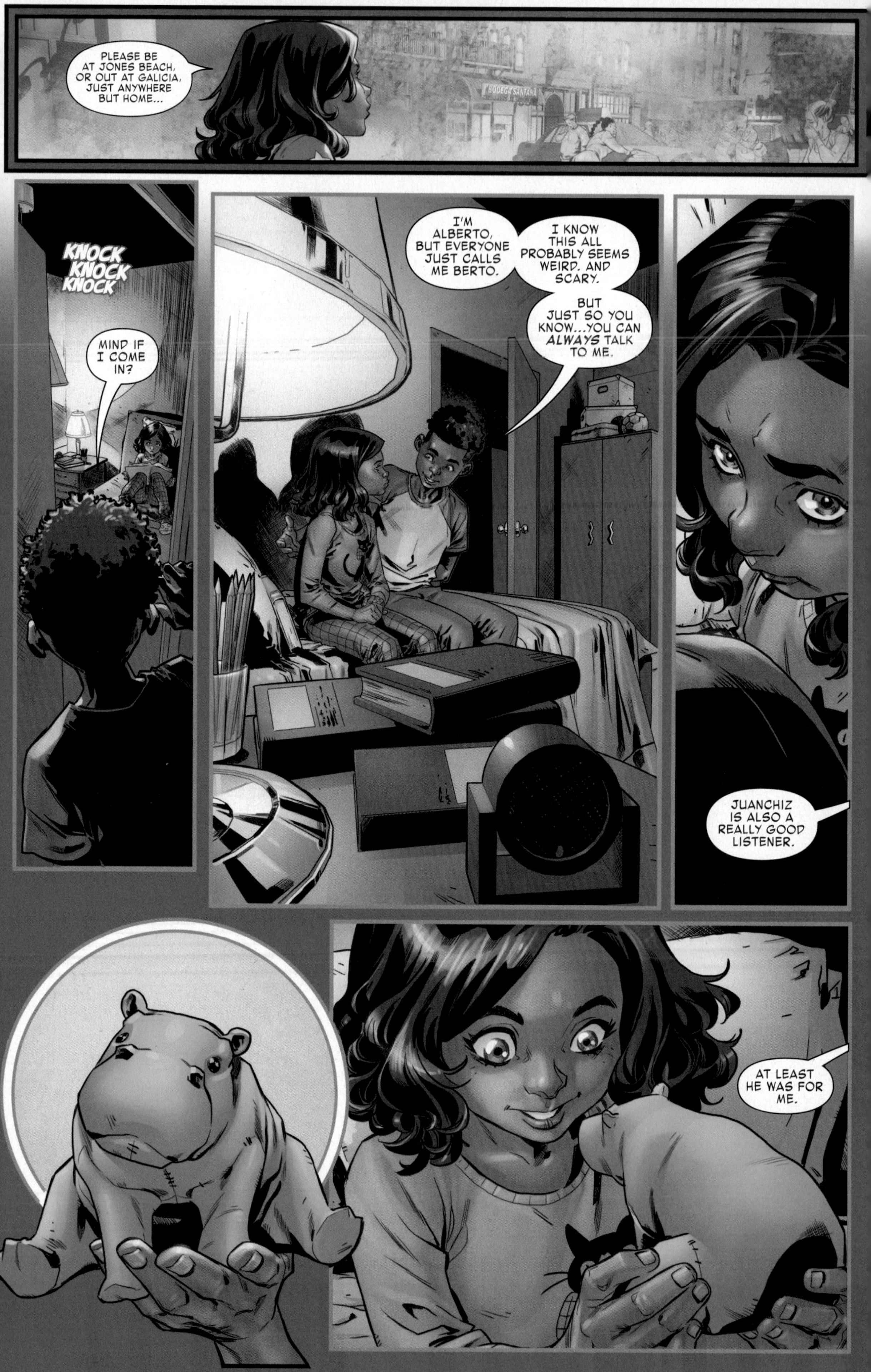

PLEASE BE AT JONES BEACH, OR OUT AT GALICIA, JUST ANYWHERE BUT HOME...
BODEGA SANTANA
KNOCK KNOCK KNOCK
MIND IF I COME IN?
I'M ALBERTO, BUT EVERYONE JUST CALLS ME BERTO.
I KNOW THIS ALL PROBABLY SEEMS WEIRD. AND SCARY.
BUT JUST SO YOU KNOW...YOU CAN ALWAYS TALK TO ME.
JUANCHIZ IS ALSO A REALLY GOOD LISTENER.
AT LEAST HE WAS FOR ME.

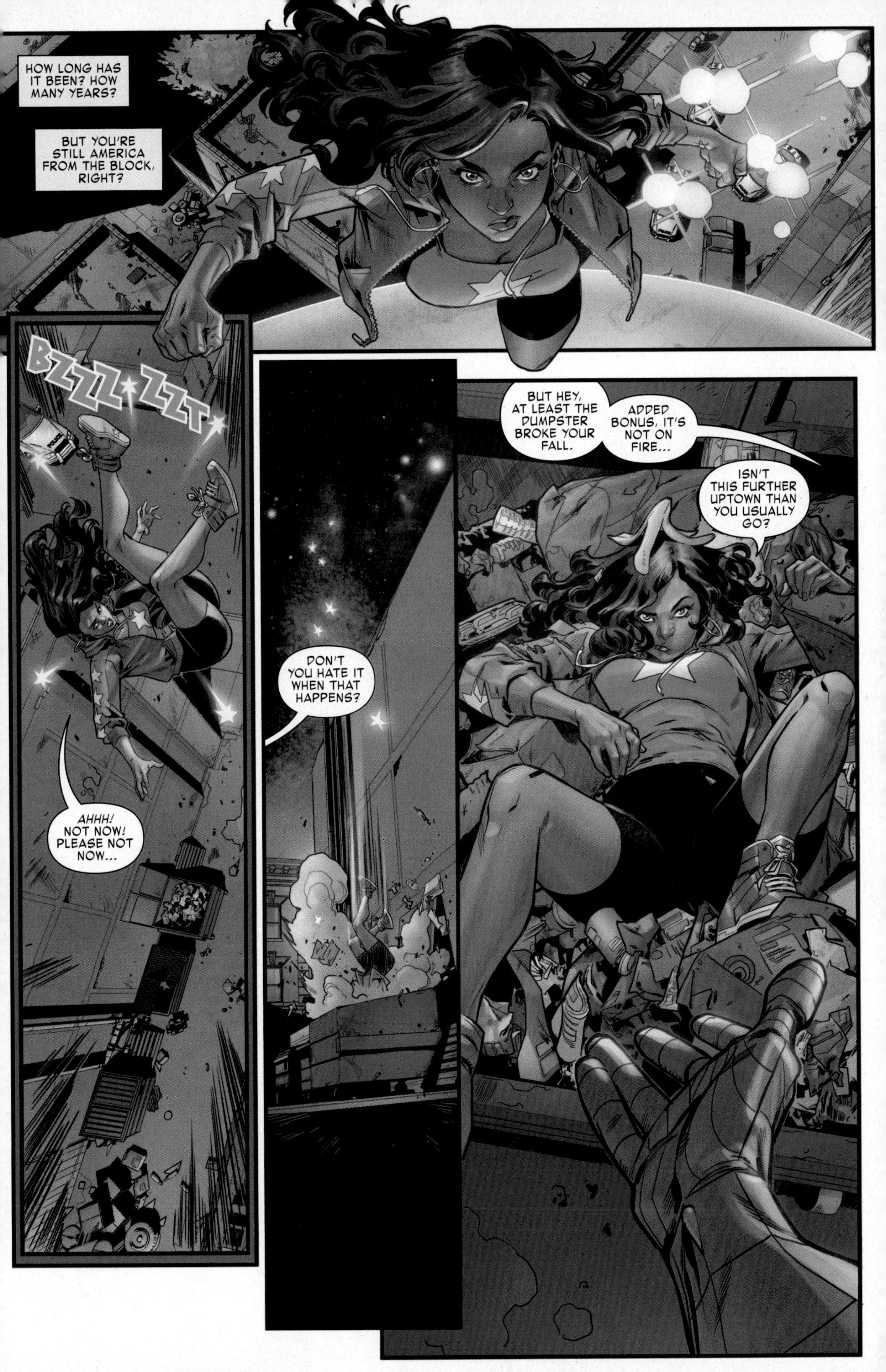

HOW LONG HAS IT BEEN? HOW MANY YEARS?
BUT YOU'RE STILL AMERICA FROM THE BLOCK, RIGHT?
BZZZ*ZZT*
AHHH! NOT NOW! PLEASE NOT NOW...
DON'T YOU HATE IT WHEN THAT HAPPENS?
BUT HEY, AT LEAST THE DUMPSTER BROKE YOUR FALL.
ADDED BONUS, IT'S NOT ON FIRE...
ISN'T THIS FURTHER UPTOWN THAN YOU USUALLY GO?

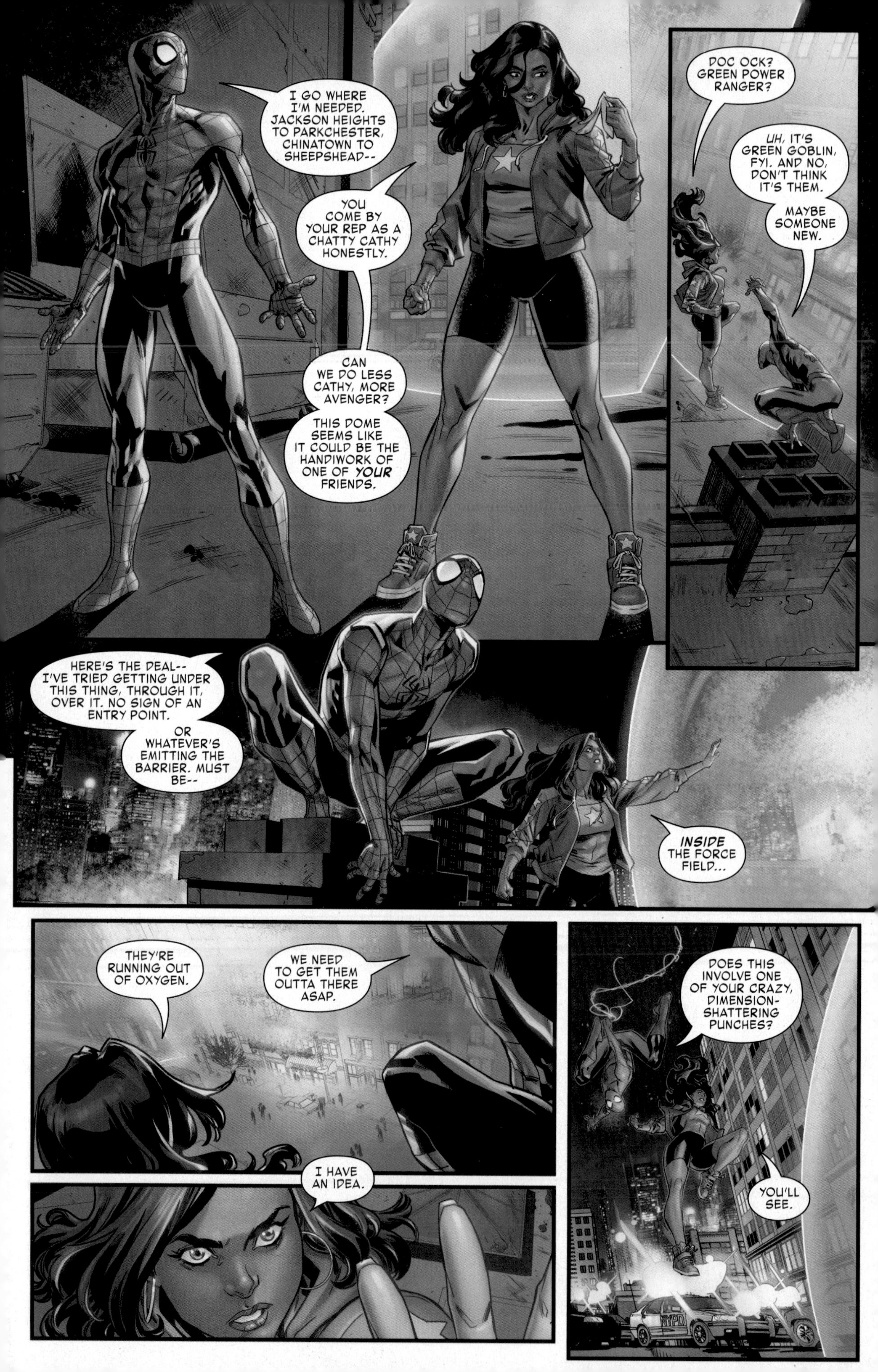
I GO WHERE I'M NEEDED. JACKSON HEIGHTS TO PARKCHESTER, CHINATOWN TO SHEEPSHEAD--
YOU COME BY YOUR REP AS A CHATTY CATHY HONESTLY.
CAN WE DO LESS CATHY, MORE AVENGER?
THIS DOME SEEMS LIKE IT COULD BE THE HANDIWORK OF ONE OF *YOUR* FRIENDS.
DOC OCK? GREEN POWER RANGER?
UH, IT'S GREEN GOBLIN, FYI. AND NO, DON'T THINK IT'S THEM.
MAYBE SOMEONE NEW.
HERE'S THE DEAL-- I'VE TRIED GETTING UNDER THIS THING, THROUGH IT, OVER IT. NO SIGN OF AN ENTRY POINT.
OR WHATEVER'S EMITTING THE BARRIER. MUST BE--
INSIDE THE FORCE FIELD...
THEY'RE RUNNING OUT OF OXYGEN.
WE NEED TO GET THEM OUTTA THERE ASAP.
I HAVE AN IDEA.
DOES THIS INVOLVE ONE OF YOUR CRAZY, DIMENSION-SHATTERING PUNCHES?
YOU'LL SEE.
NYPD

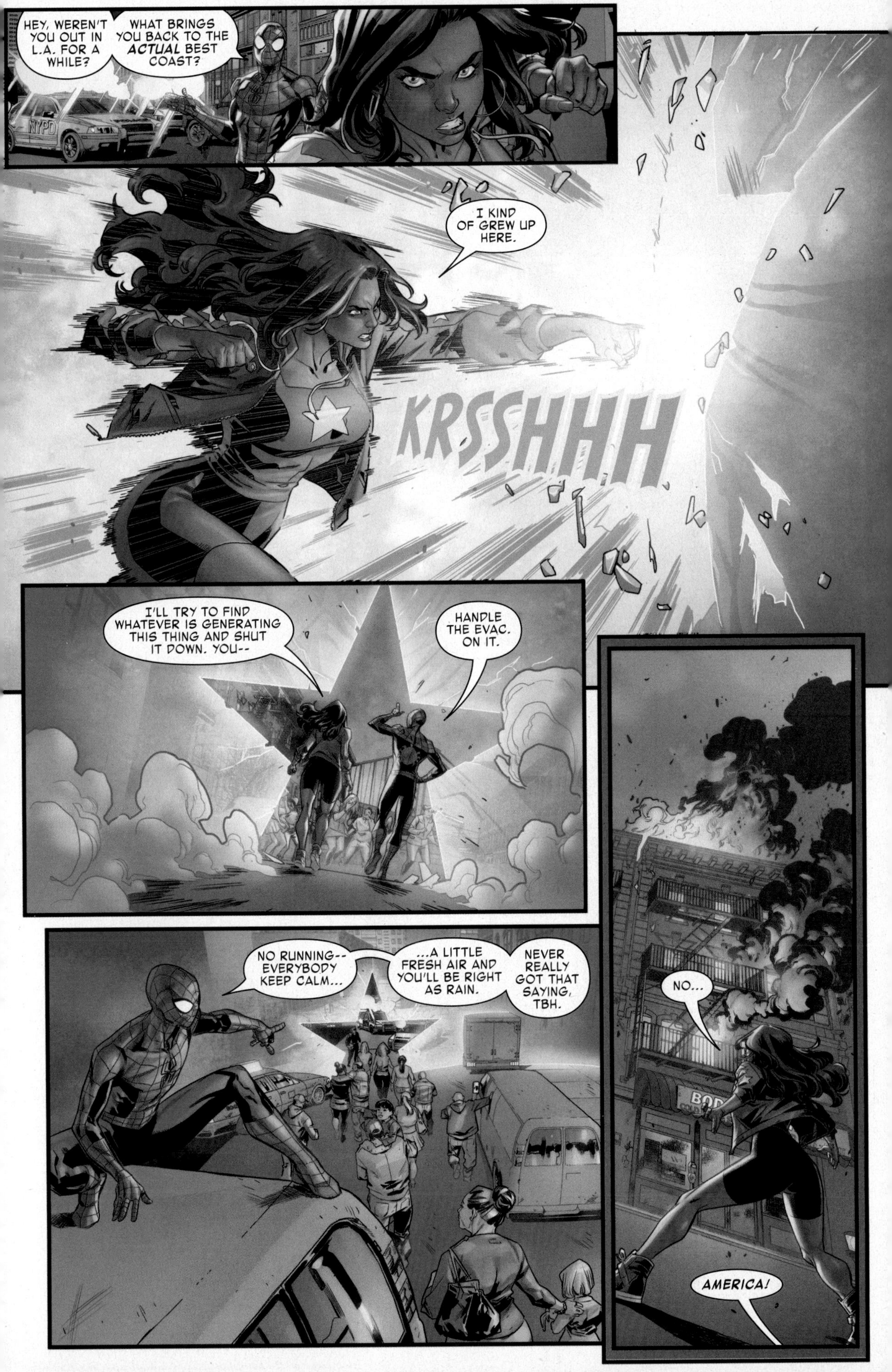
HEY, WEREN'T YOU OUT IN L.A. FOR A WHILE?
WHAT BRINGS YOU BACK TO THE ACTUAL BEST COAST?
NYPD
I KIND OF GREW UP HERE.
KRSSHHH
I'LL TRY TO FIND WHATEVER IS GENERATING THIS THING AND SHUT IT DOWN. YOU--
HANDLE THE EVAC. ON IT.
NO RUNNING--EVERYBODY KEEP CALM...
...A LITTLE FRESH AIR AND YOU'LL BE RIGHT AS RAIN.
NEVER REALLY GOT THAT SAYING, TBH.
NO...
AMERICA!

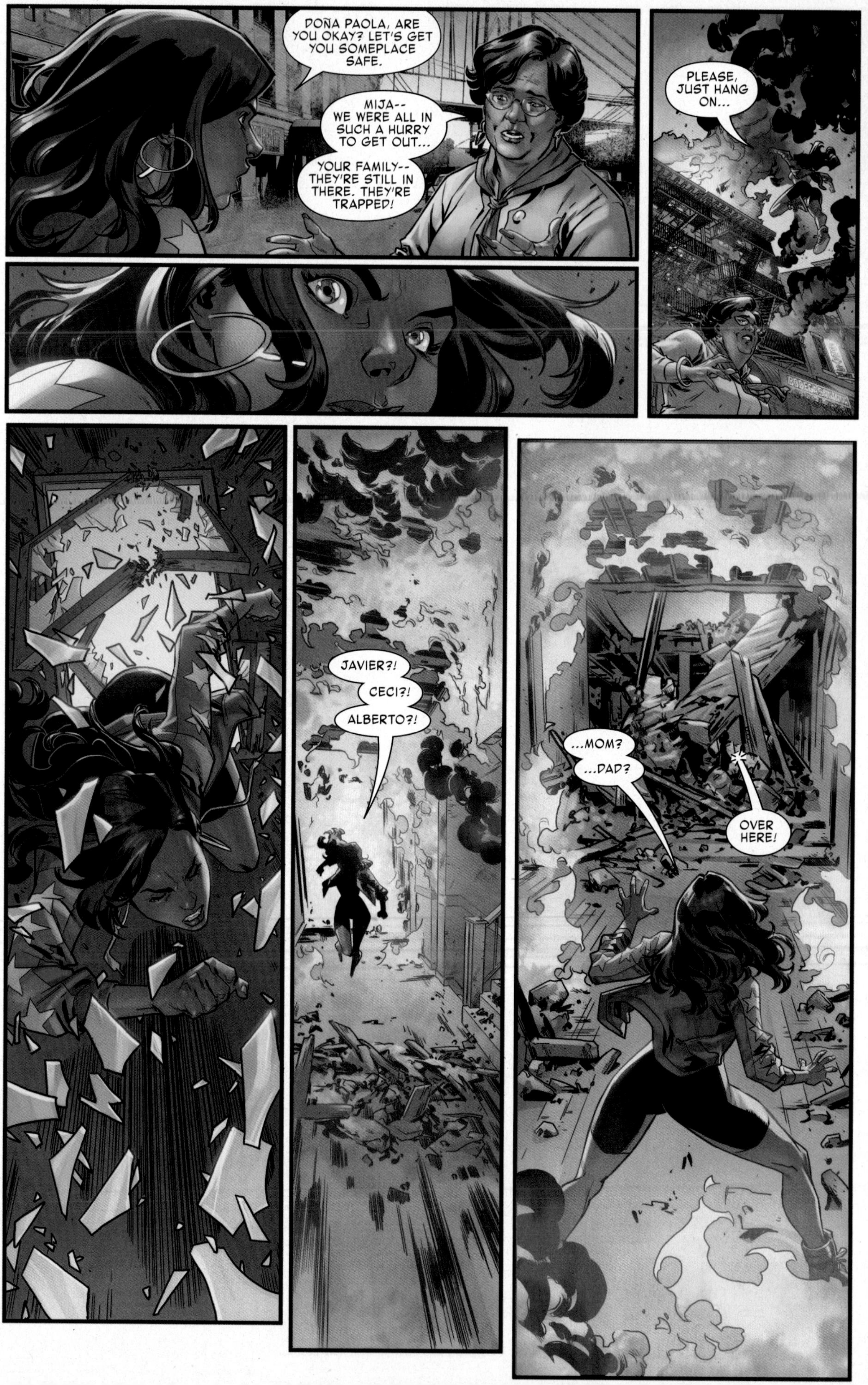
DOÑA PAOLA, ARE YOU OKAY? LET'S GET YOU SOMEPLACE SAFE.
MIJA-- WE WERE ALL IN SUCH A HURRY TO GET OUT...
YOUR FAMILY-- THEY'RE STILL IN THERE. THEY'RE TRAPPED!
PLEASE, JUST HANG ON...
JAVIER?!
CECI?!
ALBERTO?!
...MOM?
...DAD?
OVER HERE!

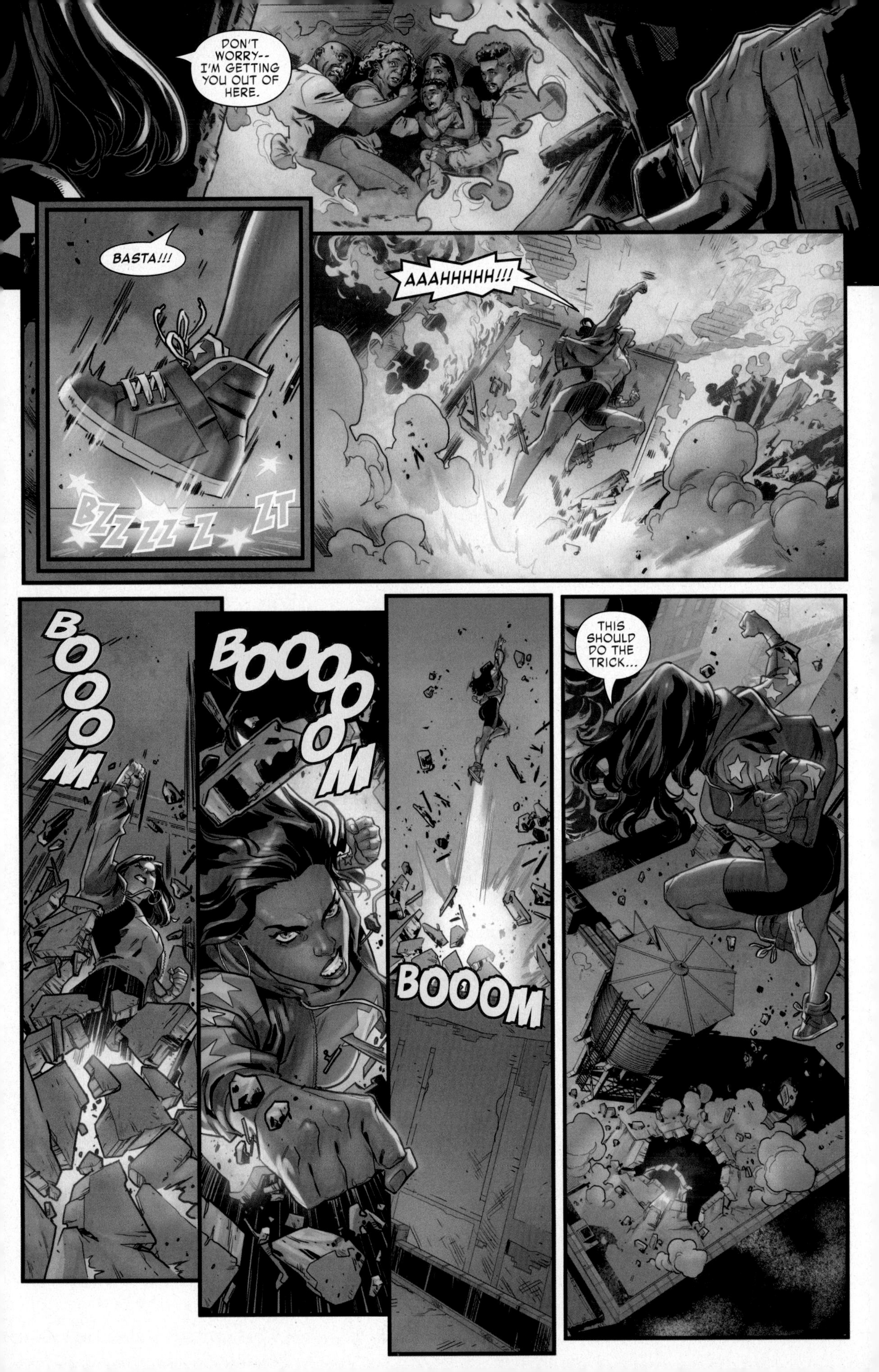
DON'T WORRY-- I'M GETTING YOU OUT OF HERE.
BASTA!!!
BZZZZZ Z ZT
AAAHHHHH!!!
BOOOM
BOOOOOOM
BOOOM
THIS SHOULD DO THE TRICK...

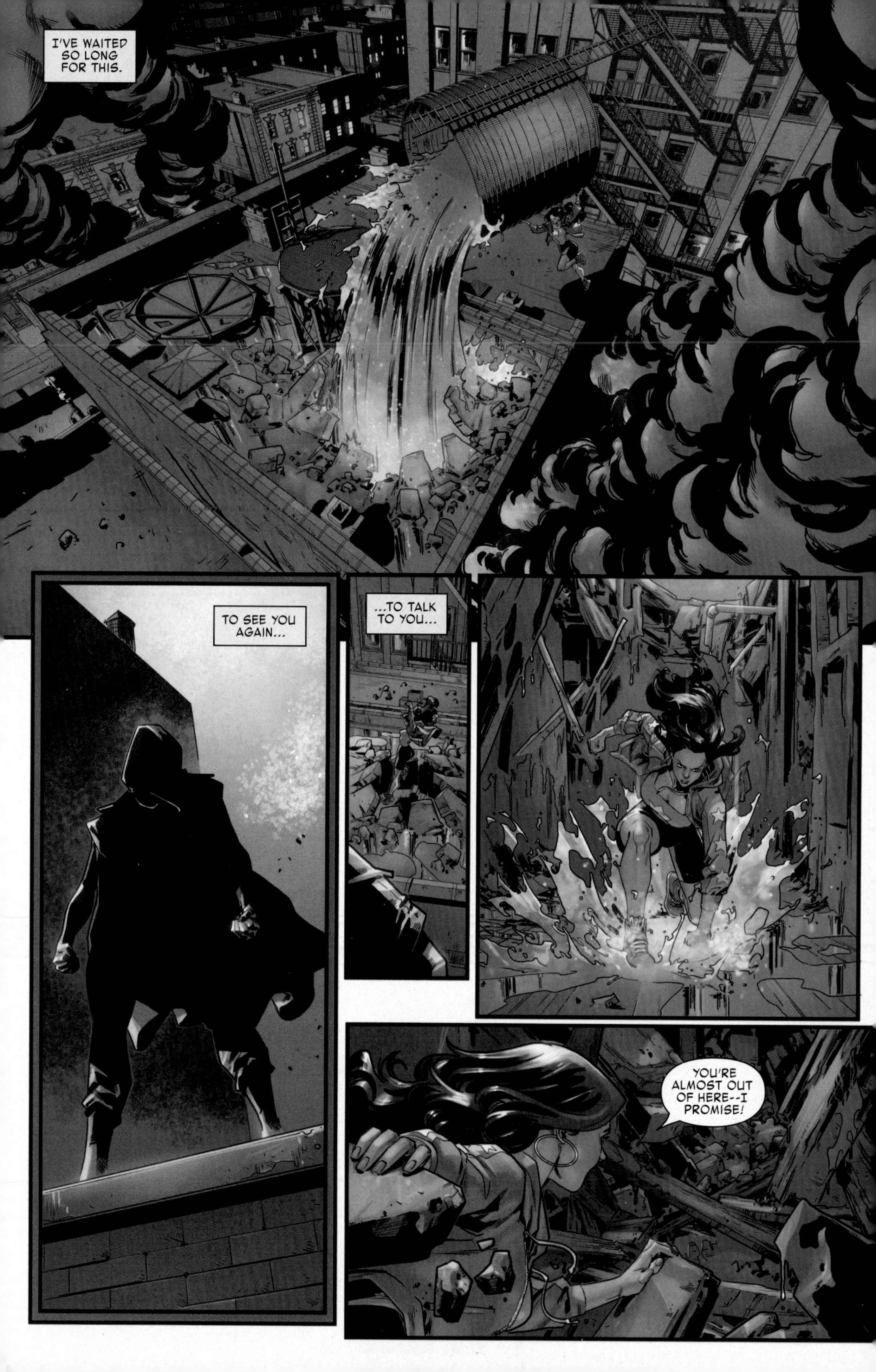
I'VE WAITED SO LONG FOR THIS.
TO SEE YOU AGAIN...
...TO TALK TO YOU...
YOU'RE ALMOST OUT OF HERE--I PROMISE!

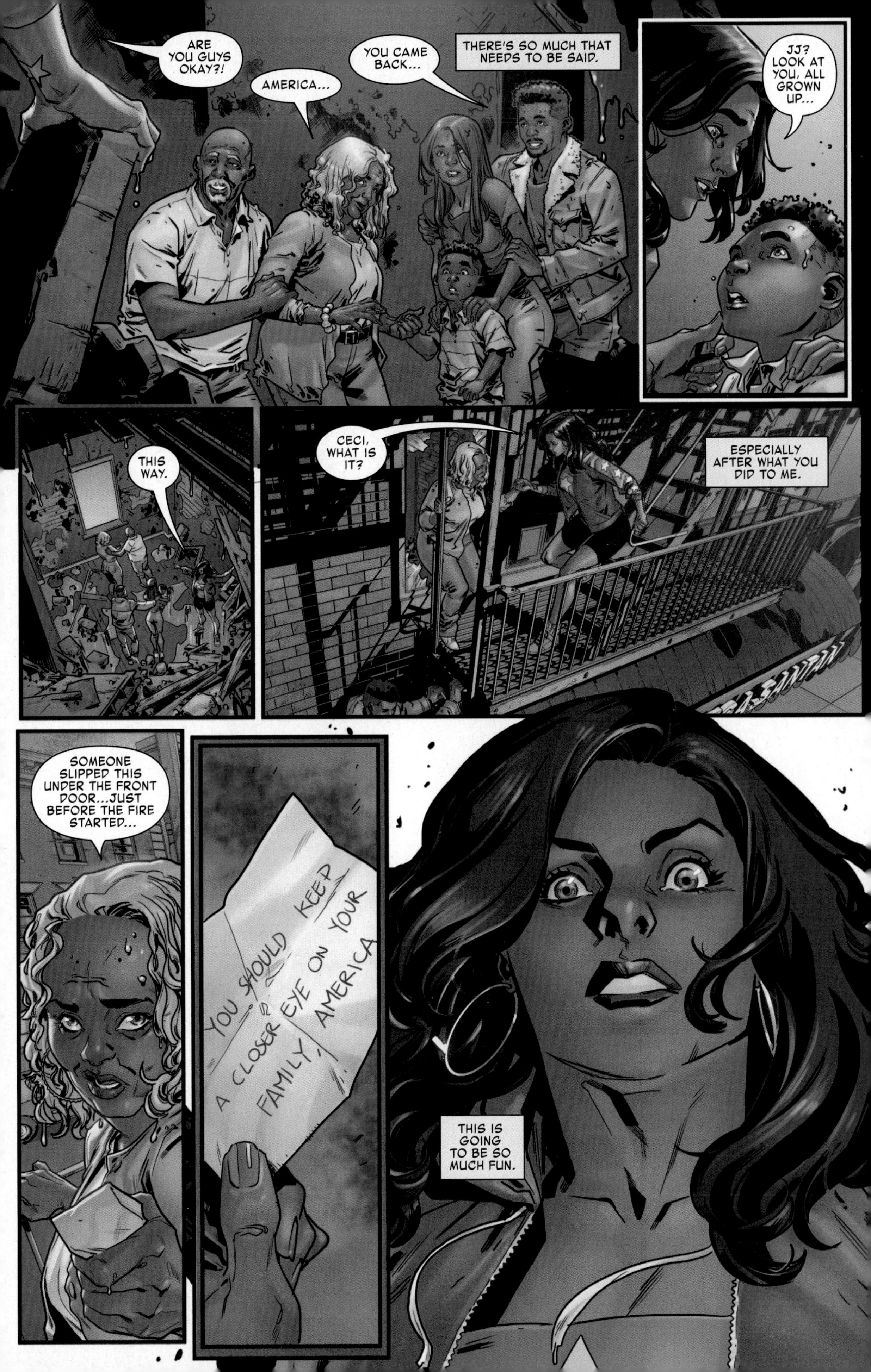

ARE YOU GUYS OKAY?!
AMERICA...
YOU CAME BACK...
THERE'S SO MUCH THAT NEEDS TO BE SAID.
JJ? LOOK AT YOU, ALL GROWN UP...
THIS WAY.
CECI, WHAT IS IT?
ESPECIALLY AFTER WHAT YOU DID TO ME.
SOMEONE SLIPPED THIS UNDER THE FRONT DOOR...JUST BEFORE THE FIRE STARTED...
YOU SHOULD KEEP A CLOSER EYE ON YOUR FAMILY, AMERICA
THIS IS GOING TO BE SO MUCH FUN.

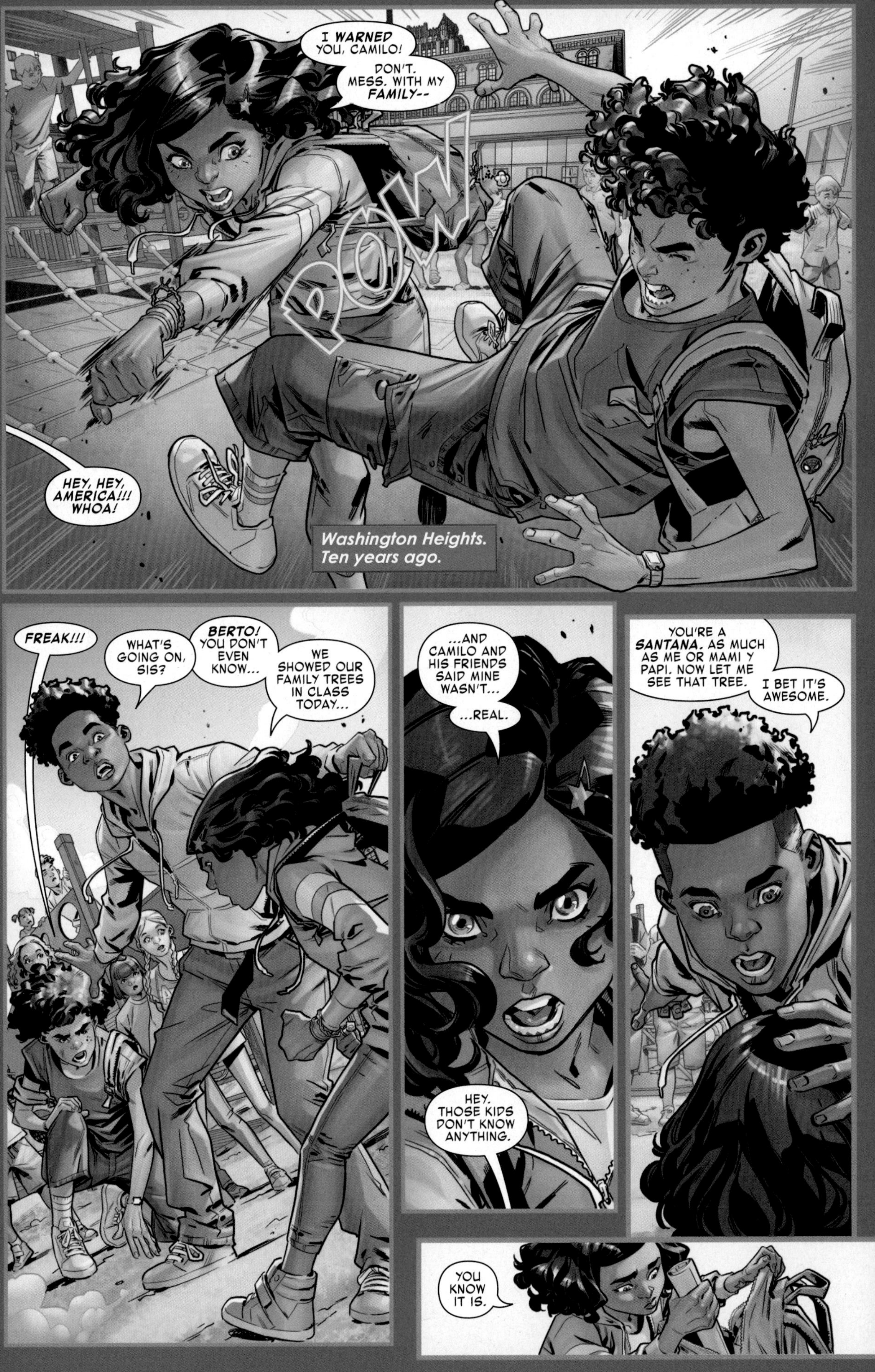

I WARNED YOU, CAMILO!
DON'T. MESS. WITH MY FAMILY--
POW
HEY, HEY, AMERICA!!! WHOA!
Washington Heights. Ten years ago.
FREAK!!!
WHAT'S GOING ON, SIS?
BERTO! YOU DON'T EVEN KNOW...
WE SHOWED OUR FAMILY TREES IN CLASS TODAY...
...AND CAMILO AND HIS FRIENDS SAID MINE WASN'T...
...REAL.
HEY. THOSE KIDS DON'T KNOW ANYTHING.
YOU'RE A SANTANA. AS MUCH AS ME OR MAMI Y PAPI. NOW LET ME SEE THAT TREE.
I BET IT'S AWESOME.
YOU KNOW IT IS.

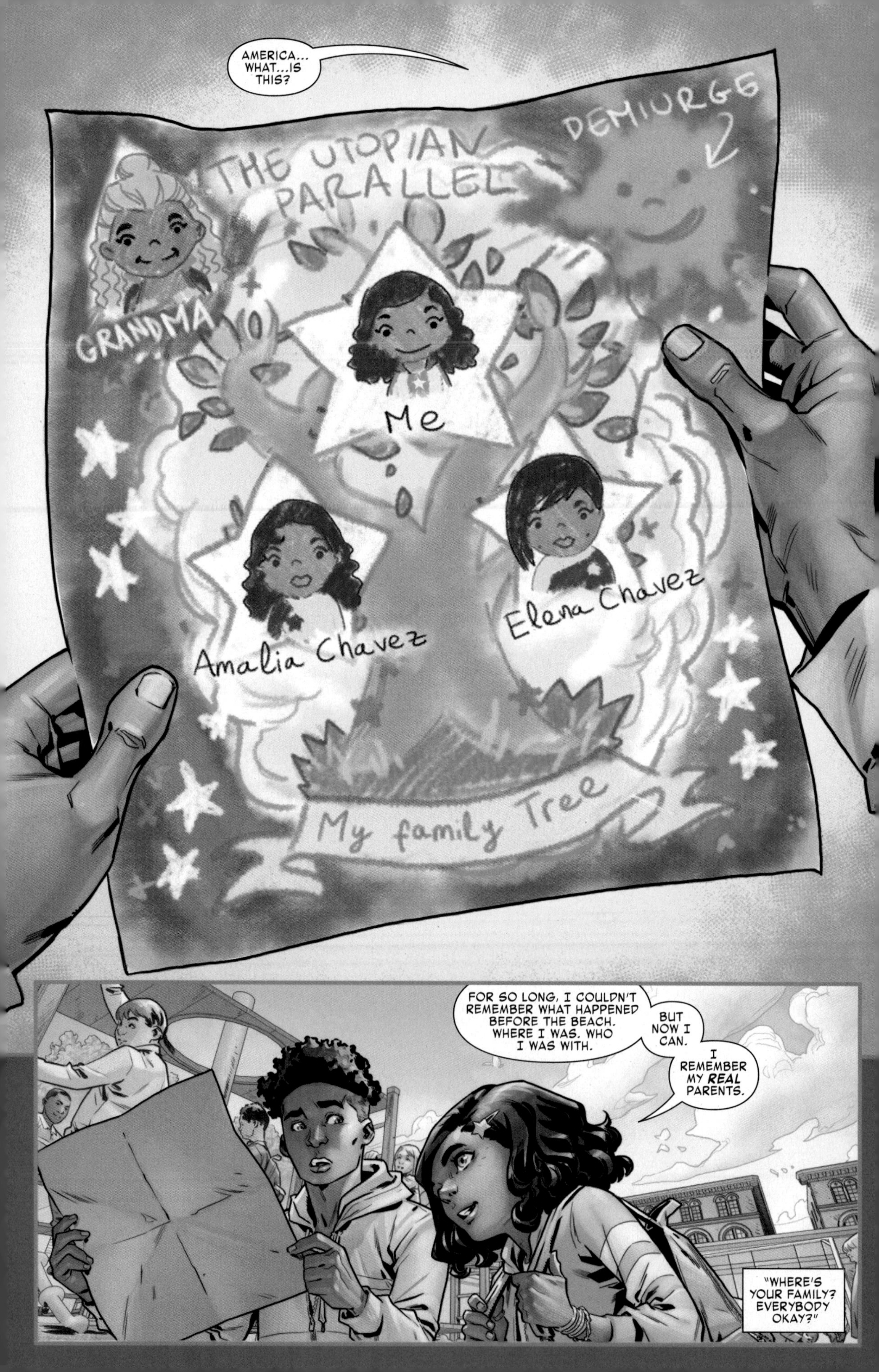
AMERICA... WHAT...IS THIS?
DEMIURGE
THE UTOPIAN PARALLEL
GRANDMA
Me
Amalia Chavez
Elena Chavez
My family Tree
FOR SO LONG, I COULDN'T REMEMBER WHAT HAPPENED BEFORE THE BEACH. WHERE I WAS. WHO I WAS WITH.
BUT NOW I CAN.
I REMEMBER MY *REAL* PARENTS.
"WHERE'S YOUR FAMILY? EVERYBODY OKAY?"

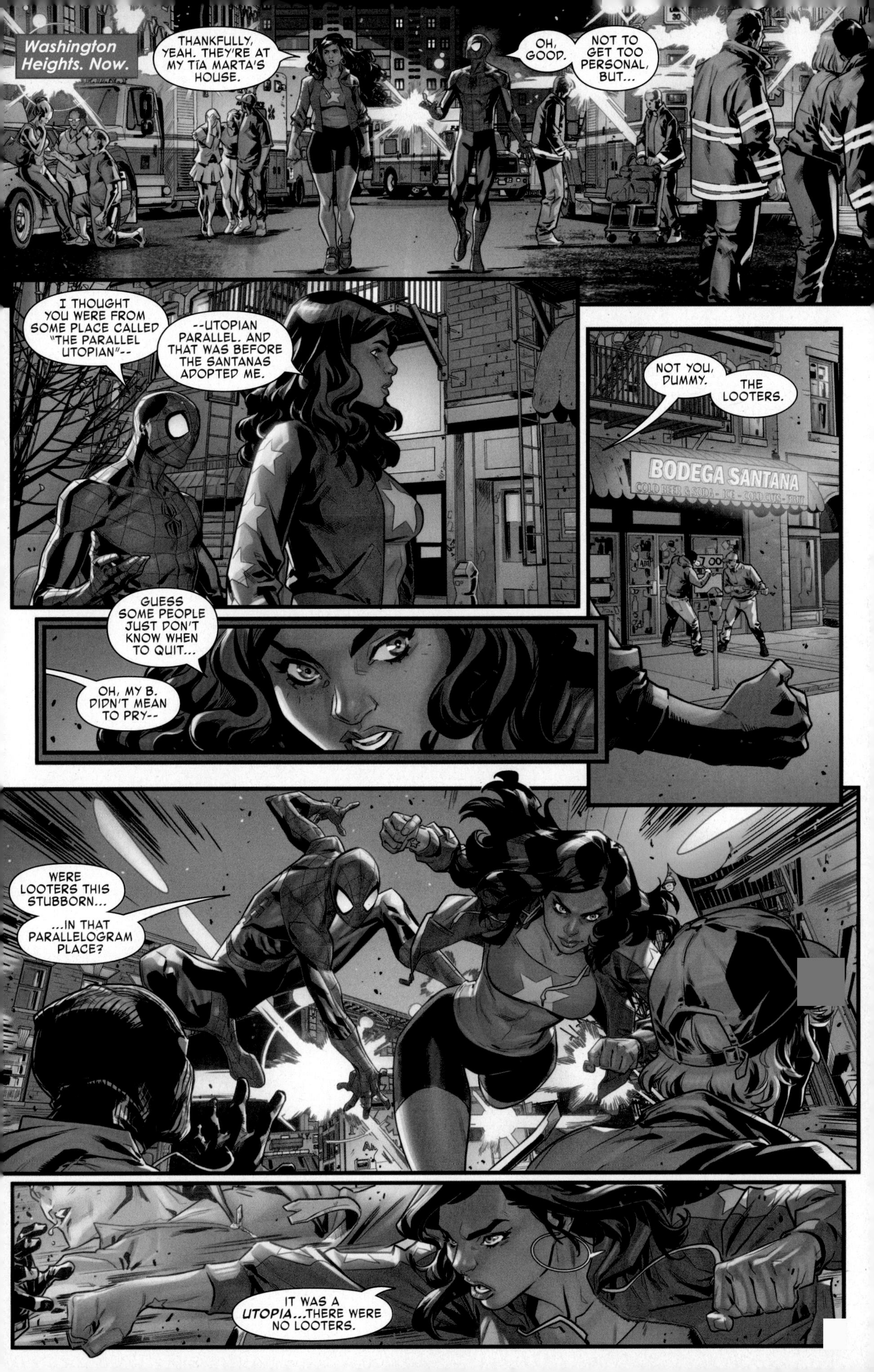
Washington Heights. Now.
THANKFULLY, YEAH. THEY'RE AT MY TÍA MARTA'S HOUSE.
OH, GOOD.
NOT TO GET TOO PERSONAL, BUT...
I THOUGHT YOU WERE FROM SOME PLACE CALLED "THE PARALLEL UTOPIAN"--
--UTOPIAN PARALLEL. AND THAT WAS BEFORE THE SANTANAS ADOPTED ME.
NOT YOU, DUMMY.
THE LOOTERS.
BODEGA SANTANA
GUESS SOME PEOPLE JUST DON'T KNOW WHEN TO QUIT...
OH, MY B. DIDN'T MEAN TO PRY--
WERE LOOTERS THIS STUBBORN...
...IN THAT PARALLELOGRAM PLACE?
IT WAS A UTOPIA...THERE WERE NO LOOTERS.

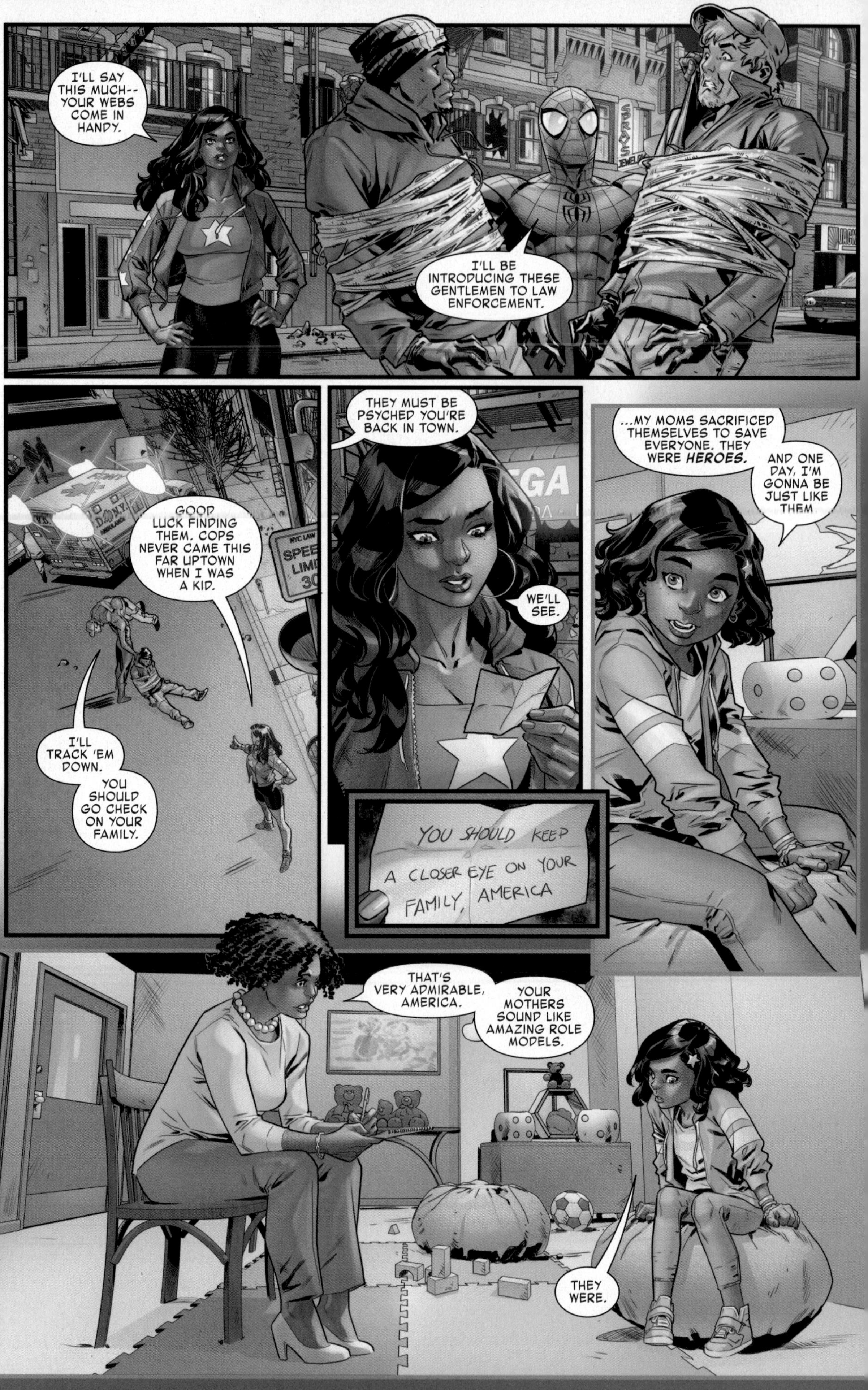
I'LL SAY THIS MUCH-- YOUR WEBS COME IN HANDY.
I'LL BE INTRODUCING THESE GENTLEMEN TO LAW ENFORCEMENT.
GOOD LUCK FINDING THEM. COPS NEVER CAME THIS FAR UPTOWN WHEN I WAS A KID.
I'LL TRACK 'EM DOWN.
YOU SHOULD GO CHECK ON YOUR FAMILY.
THEY MUST BE PSYCHED YOU'RE BACK IN TOWN.
WE'LL SEE.
YOU SHOULD KEEP A CLOSER EYE ON YOUR FAMILY, AMERICA
...MY MOMS SACRIFICED THEMSELVES TO SAVE EVERYONE. THEY WERE HEROES.
AND ONE DAY, I'M GONNA BE JUST LIKE THEM
THAT'S VERY ADMIRABLE, AMERICA.
YOUR MOTHERS SOUND LIKE AMAZING ROLE MODELS.
THEY WERE.

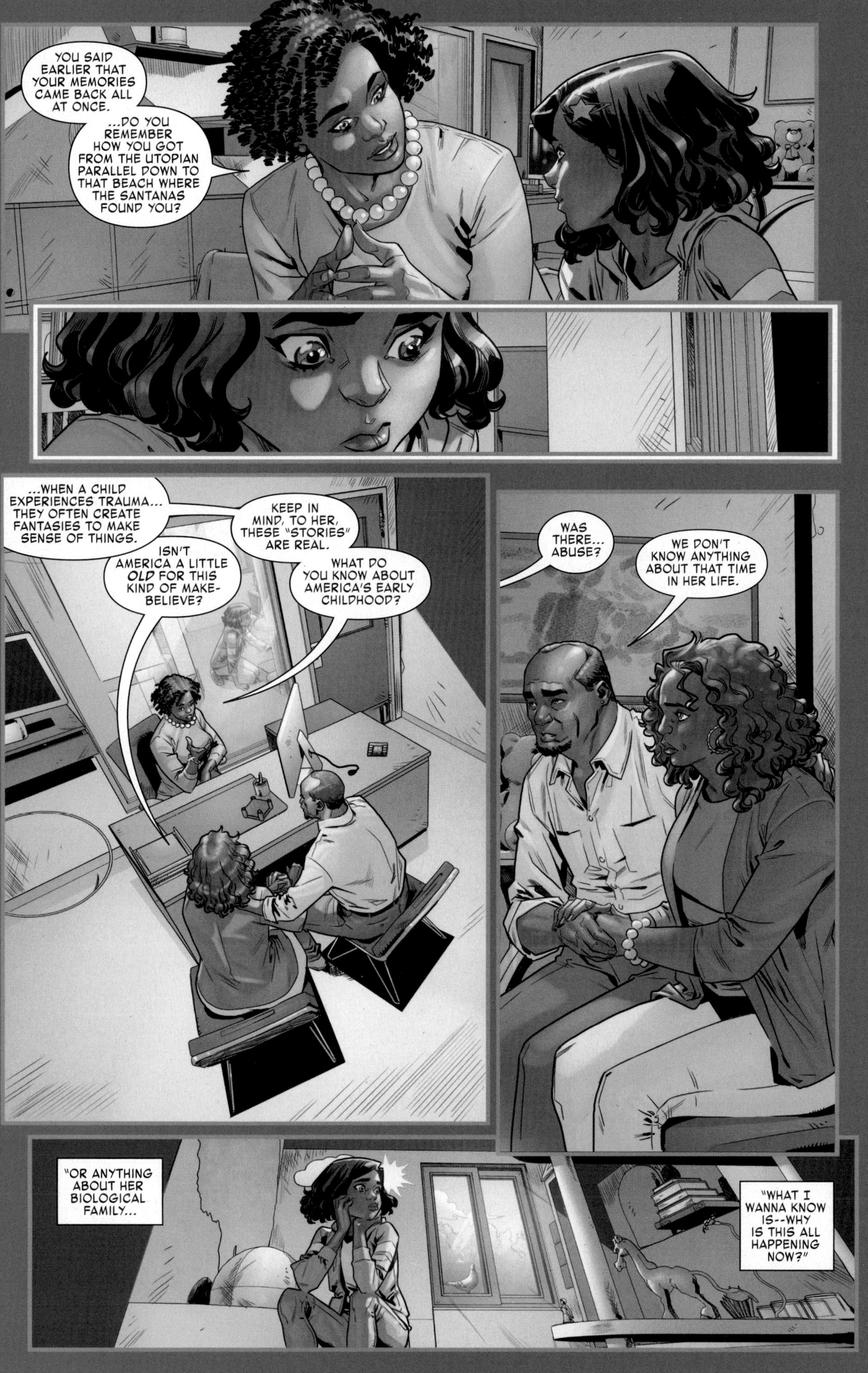

YOU SAID EARLIER THAT YOUR MEMORIES CAME BACK ALL AT ONCE.
...DO YOU REMEMBER HOW YOU GOT FROM THE UTOPIAN PARALLEL DOWN TO THAT BEACH WHERE THE SANTANAS FOUND YOU?
...WHEN A CHILD EXPERIENCES TRAUMA... THEY OFTEN CREATE FANTASIES TO MAKE SENSE OF THINGS.
KEEP IN MIND, TO HER, THESE "STORIES" ARE REAL.
ISN'T AMERICA A LITTLE OLD FOR THIS KIND OF MAKE-BELIEVE?
WHAT DO YOU KNOW ABOUT AMERICA'S EARLY CHILDHOOD?
WAS THERE... ABUSE?
WE DON'T KNOW ANYTHING ABOUT THAT TIME IN HER LIFE.
"OR ANYTHING ABOUT HER BIOLOGICAL FAMILY...
"WHAT I WANNA KNOW IS--WHY IS THIS ALL HAPPENING NOW?"

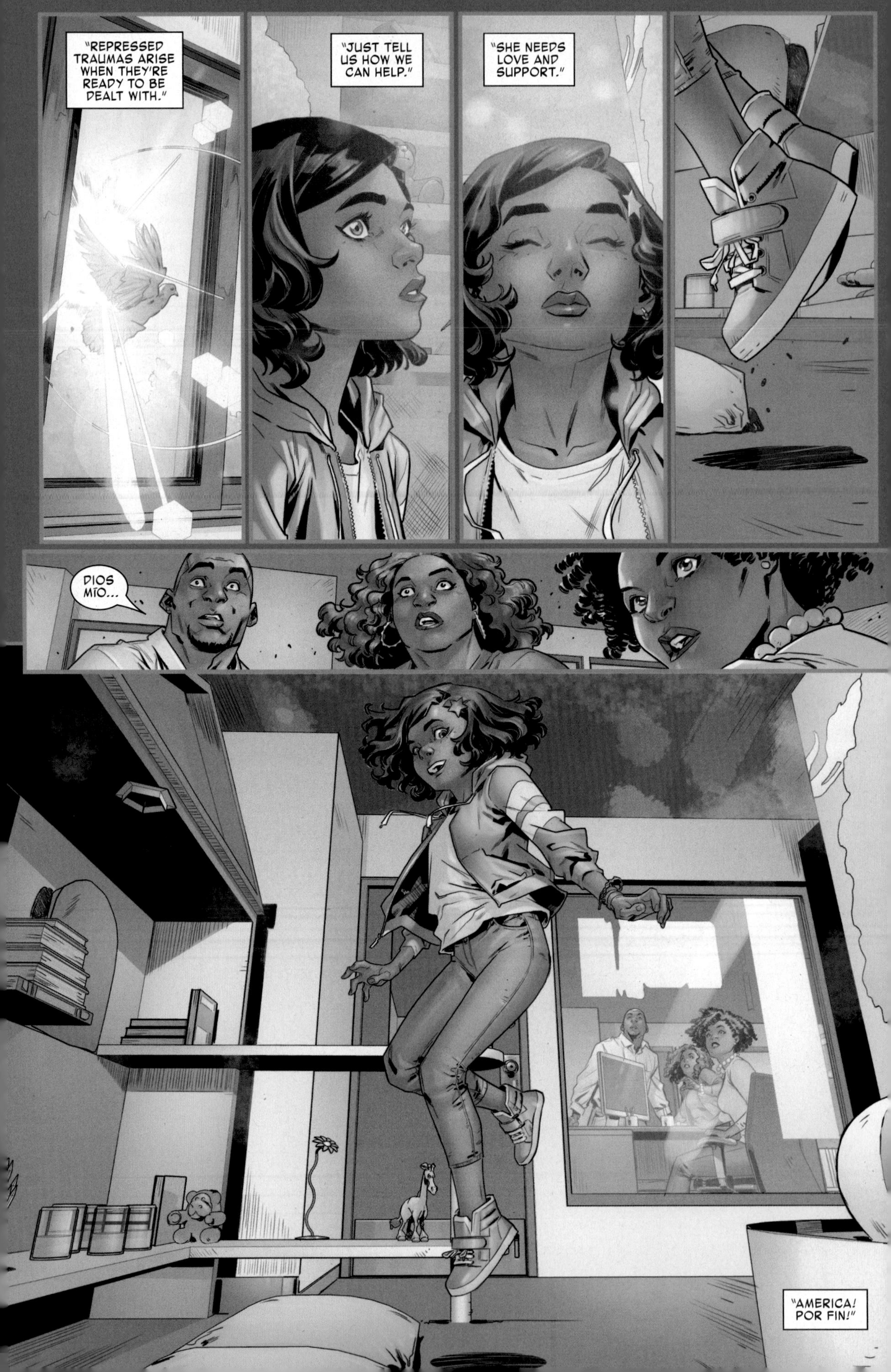
"REPRESSED TRAUMAS ARISE WHEN THEY'RE READY TO BE DEALT WITH."
"JUST TELL US HOW WE CAN HELP."
"SHE NEEDS LOVE AND SUPPORT."
DIOS MÍO...
"AMERICA! POR FIN!"

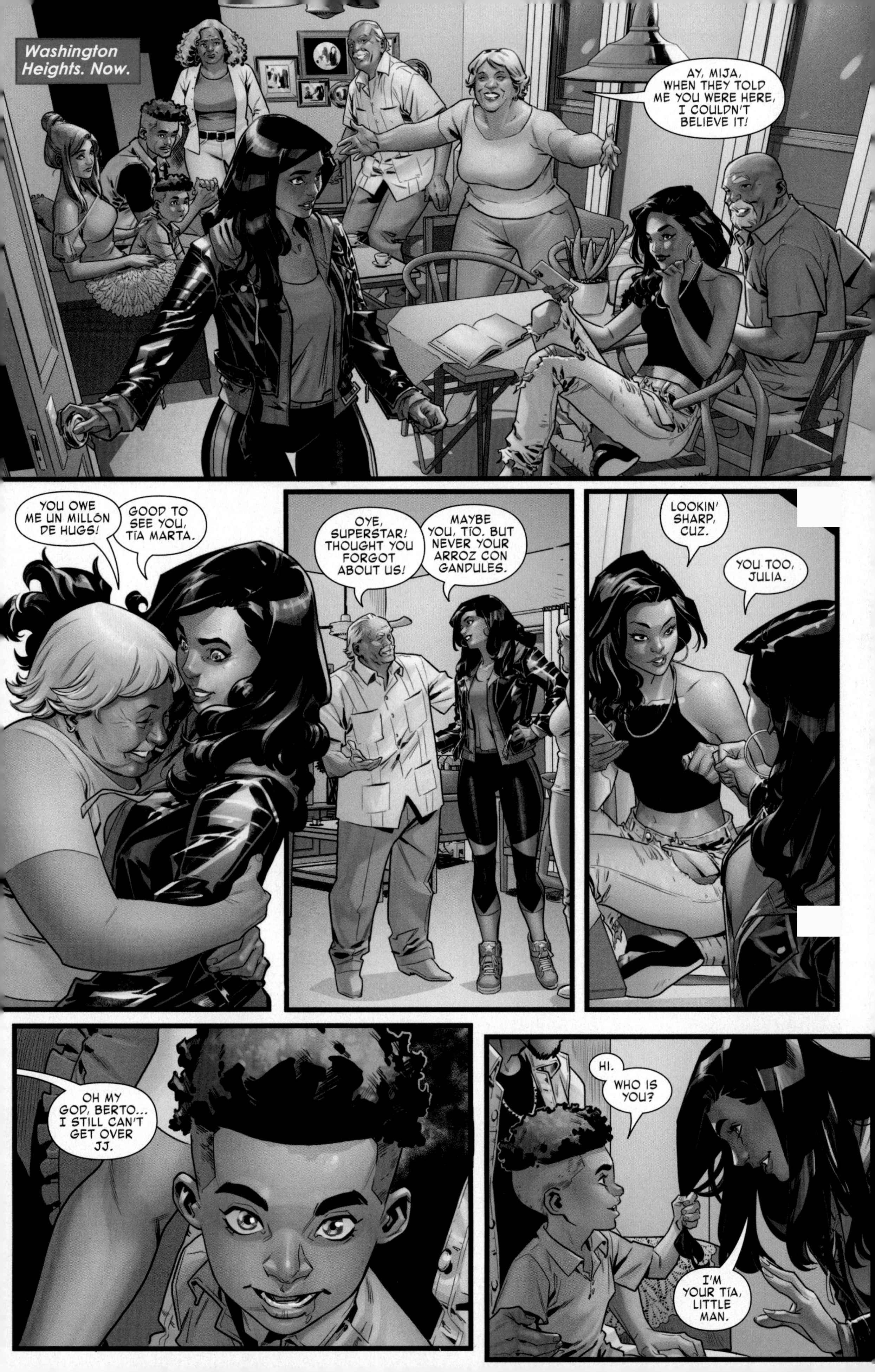
Washington Heights. Now.
AY, MIJA, WHEN THEY TOLD ME YOU WERE HERE, I COULDN'T BELIEVE IT!
YOU OWE ME UN MILLÓN DE HUGS!
GOOD TO SEE YOU, TÍA MARTA.
OYE, SUPERSTAR! THOUGHT YOU FORGOT ABOUT US!
MAYBE YOU, TÍO. BUT NEVER YOUR ARROZ CON GANDULES.
LOOKIN' SHARP, CUZ.
YOU TOO, JULIA.
OH MY GOD, BERTO... I STILL CAN'T GET OVER JJ.
HI.
WHO IS YOU?
I'M YOUR TÍA, LITTLE MAN.

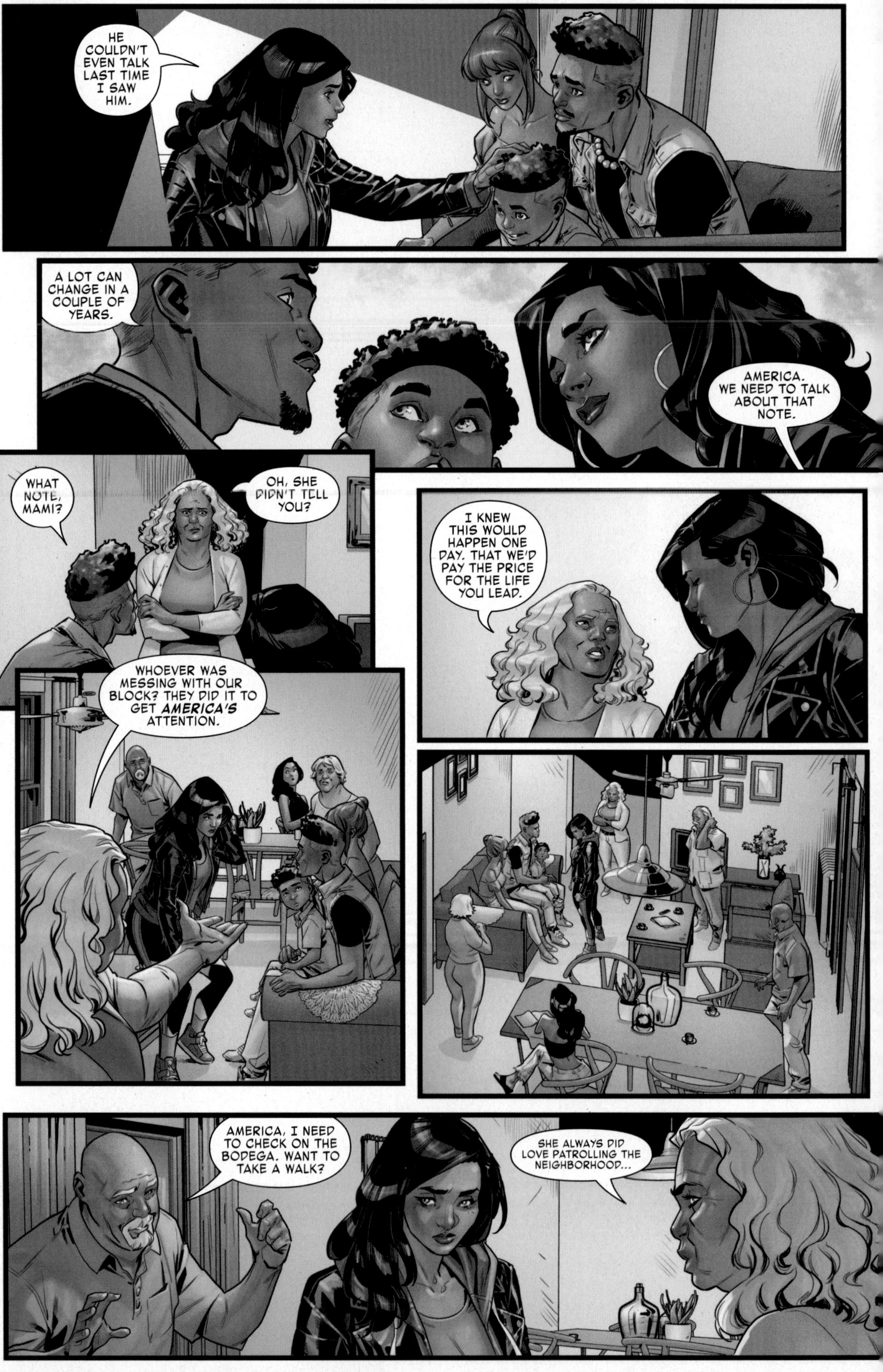
HE COULDN'T EVEN TALK LAST TIME I SAW HIM.
A LOT CAN CHANGE IN A COUPLE OF YEARS.
AMERICA. WE NEED TO TALK ABOUT THAT NOTE.
WHAT NOTE, MAMI?
OH, SHE DIDN'T TELL YOU?
WHOEVER WAS MESSING WITH OUR BLOCK? THEY DID IT TO GET AMERICA'S ATTENTION.
I KNEW THIS WOULD HAPPEN ONE DAY. THAT WE'D PAY THE PRICE FOR THE LIFE YOU LEAD.
AMERICA, I NEED TO CHECK ON THE BODEGA. WANT TO TAKE A WALK?
SHE ALWAYS DID LOVE PATROLLING THE NEIGHBORHOOD...

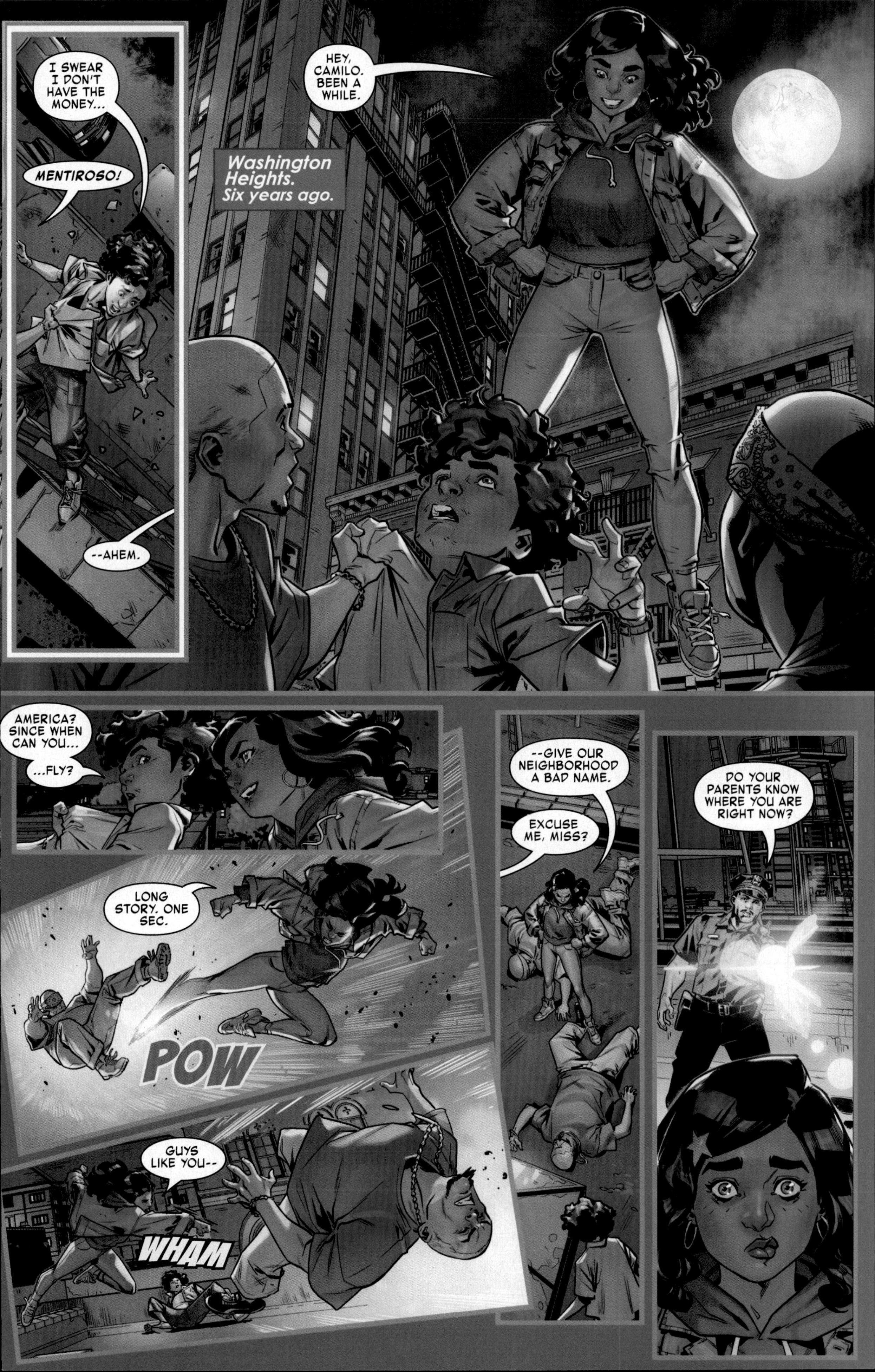

I SWEAR I DON'T HAVE THE MONEY...
MENTIROSO!
--AHEM.
HEY, CAMILO. BEEN A WHILE.
Washington Heights. Six years ago.
AMERICA? SINCE WHEN CAN YOU...
...FLY?
LONG STORY. ONE SEC.
POW
GUYS LIKE YOU--
WHAM
--GIVE OUR NEIGHBORHOOD A BAD NAME.
EXCUSE ME, MISS?
DO YOUR PARENTS KNOW WHERE YOU ARE RIGHT NOW?

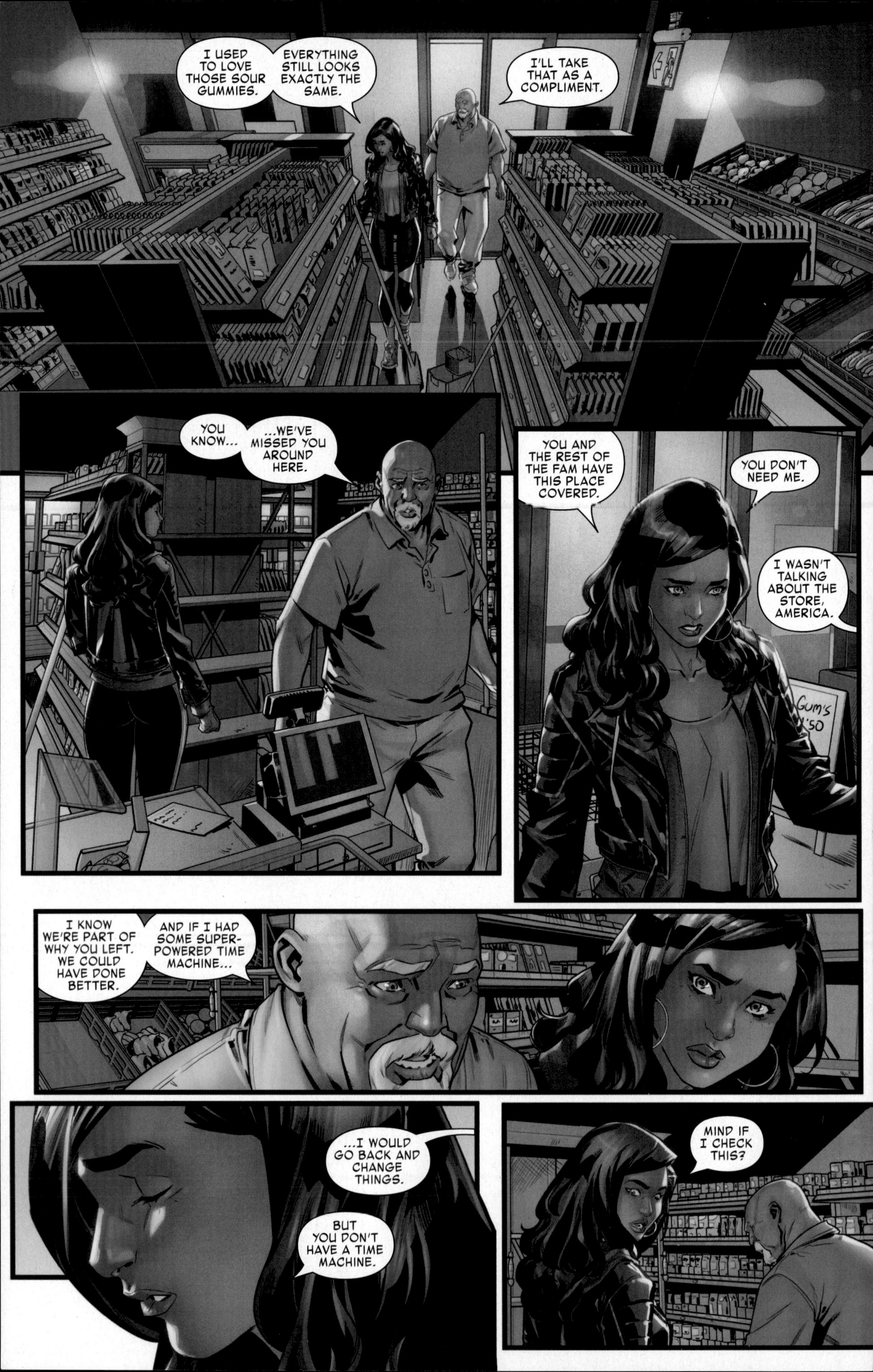
I USED TO LOVE THOSE SOUR GUMMIES.
EVERYTHING STILL LOOKS EXACTLY THE SAME.
I'LL TAKE THAT AS A COMPLIMENT.
YOU KNOW...
...WE'VE MISSED YOU AROUND HERE.
YOU AND THE REST OF THE FAM HAVE THIS PLACE COVERED.
YOU DON'T NEED ME.
I WASN'T TALKING ABOUT THE STORE, AMERICA.
GUM'S
I KNOW WE'RE PART OF WHY YOU LEFT. WE COULD HAVE DONE BETTER.
AND IF I HAD SOME SUPER-POWERED TIME MACHINE...
...I WOULD GO BACK AND CHANGE THINGS.
BUT YOU DON'T HAVE A TIME MACHINE.
MIND IF I CHECK THIS?

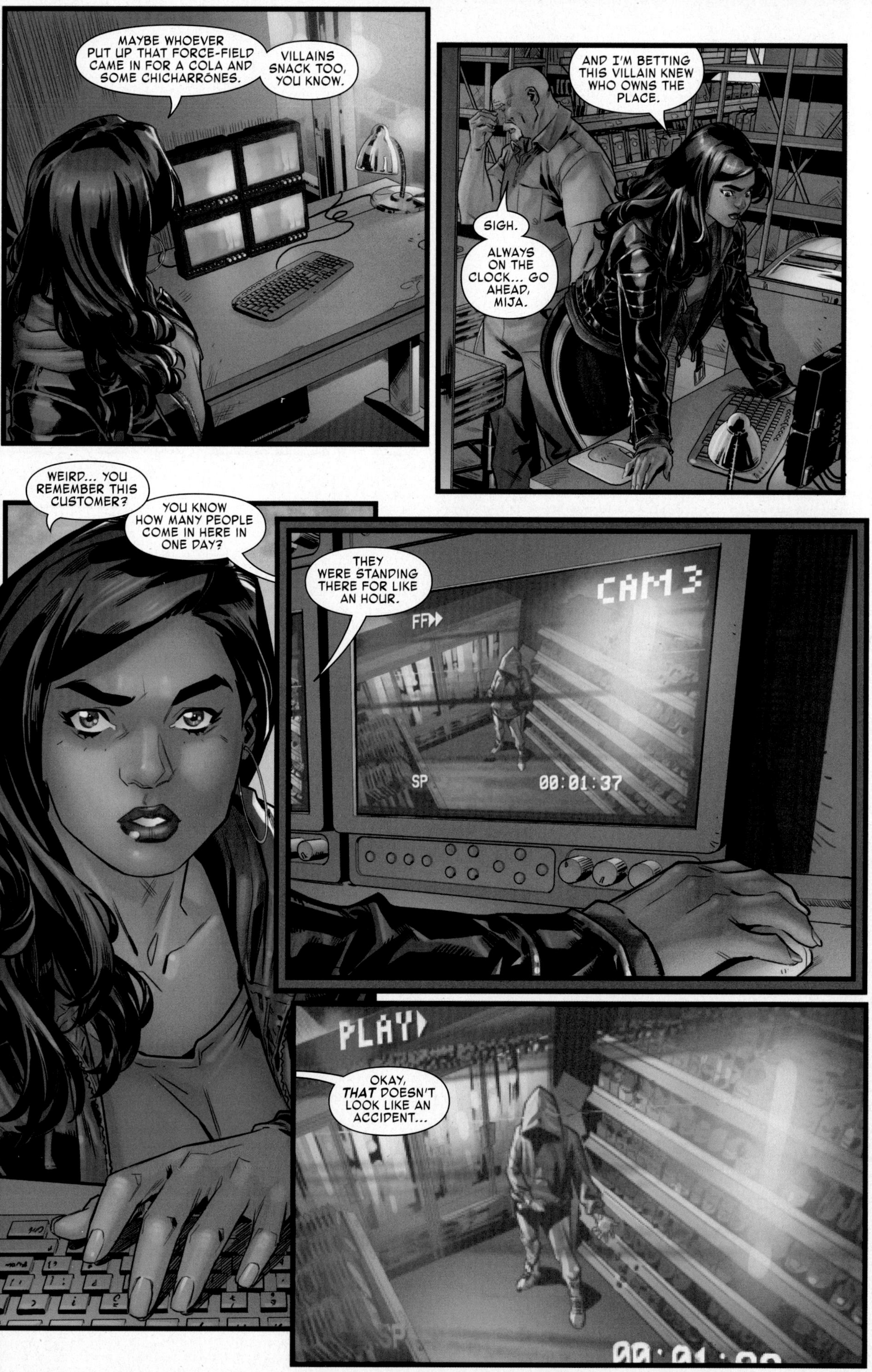
MAYBE WHOEVER PUT UP THAT FORCE-FIELD CAME IN FOR A COLA AND SOME CHICHARRONES.
VILLAINS SNACK TOO, YOU KNOW.
AND I'M BETTING THIS VILLAIN KNEW WHO OWNS THE PLACE.
SIGH.
ALWAYS ON THE CLOCK... GO AHEAD, MIJA.
WEIRD... YOU REMEMBER THIS CUSTOMER?
YOU KNOW HOW MANY PEOPLE COME IN HERE IN ONE DAY?
THEY WERE STANDING THERE FOR LIKE AN HOUR.
CAM 3
FF
SP
00:01:37
PLAY
OKAY, *THAT* DOESN'T LOOK LIKE AN ACCIDENT...

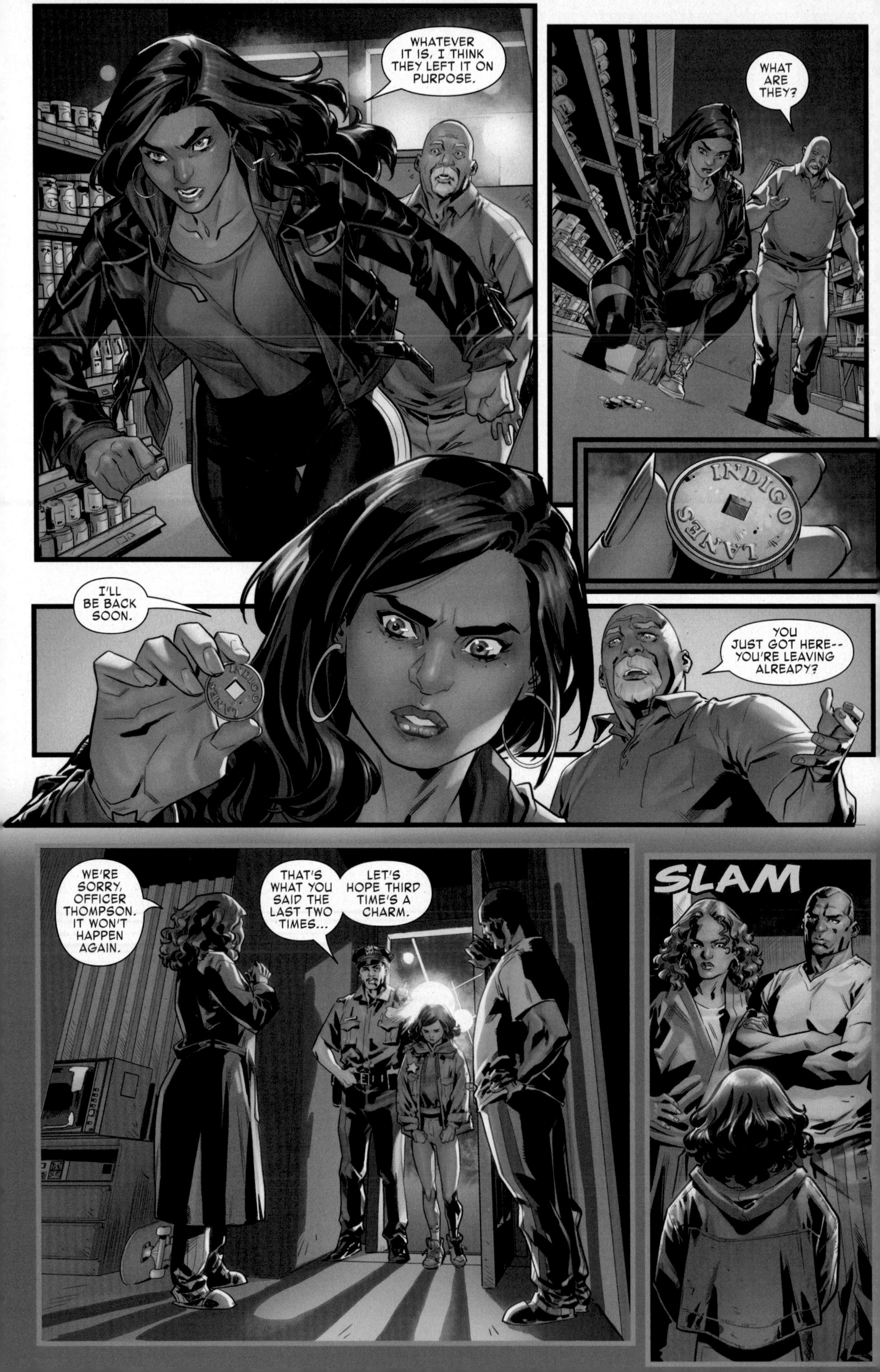
WHATEVER IT IS, I THINK THEY LEFT IT ON PURPOSE.
WHAT ARE THEY?
INDIGO LANES
I'LL BE BACK SOON.
YOU JUST GOT HERE-- YOU'RE LEAVING ALREADY?
WE'RE SORRY, OFFICER THOMPSON. IT WON'T HAPPEN AGAIN.
THAT'S WHAT YOU SAID THE LAST TWO TIMES...
LET'S HOPE THIRD TIME'S A CHARM.
SLAM

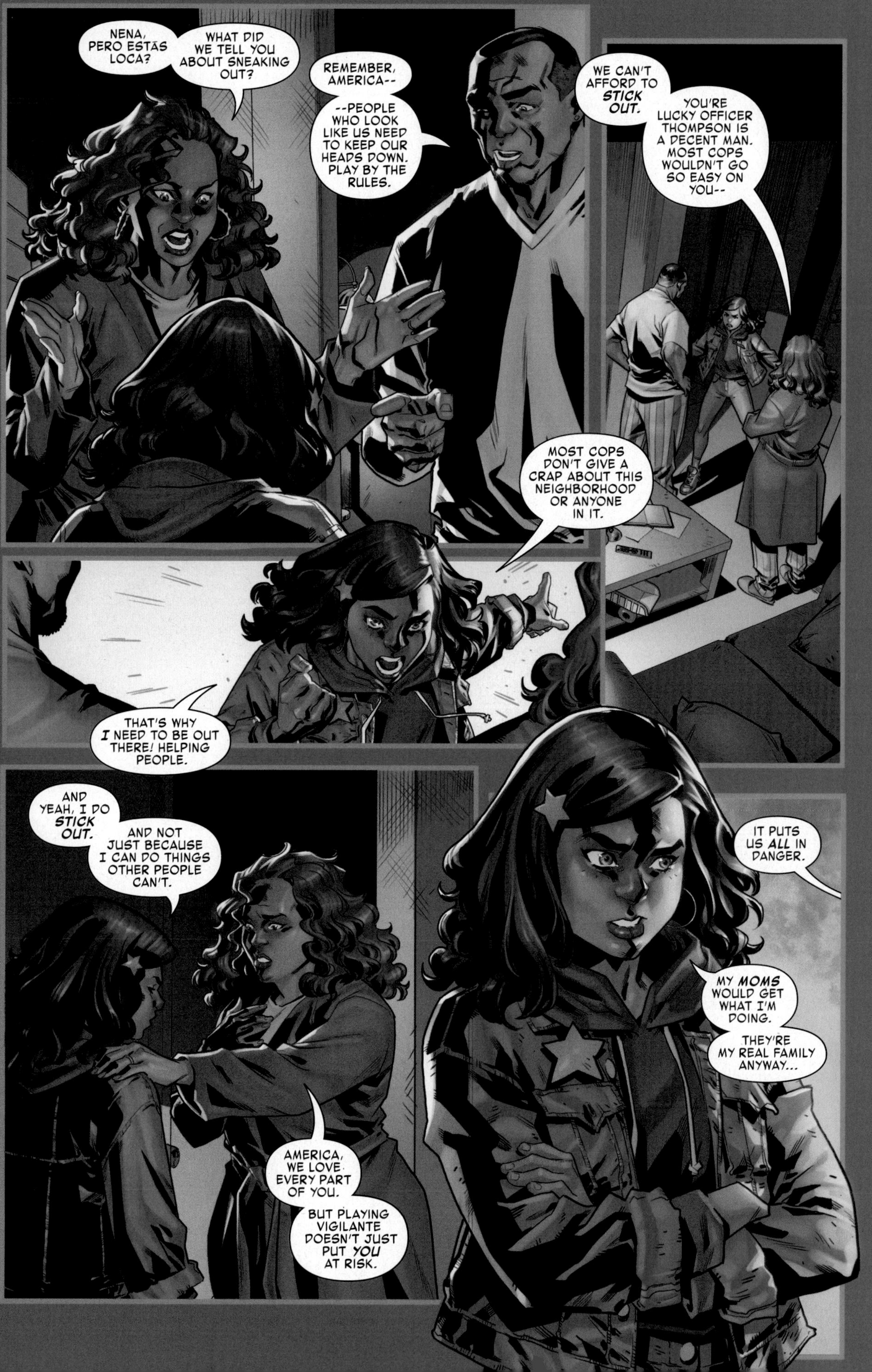
NENA, PERO ESTÁS LOCA?
WHAT DID WE TELL YOU ABOUT SNEAKING OUT?
REMEMBER, AMERICA--
--PEOPLE WHO LOOK LIKE US NEED TO KEEP OUR HEADS DOWN. PLAY BY THE RULES.
WE CAN'T AFFORD TO STICK OUT.
YOU'RE LUCKY OFFICER THOMPSON IS A DECENT MAN. MOST COPS WOULDN'T GO SO EASY ON YOU--
MOST COPS DON'T GIVE A CRAP ABOUT THIS NEIGHBORHOOD OR ANYONE IN IT.
THAT'S WHY I NEED TO BE OUT THERE! HELPING PEOPLE.
AND YEAH, I DO STICK OUT.
AND NOT JUST BECAUSE I CAN DO THINGS OTHER PEOPLE CAN'T.
AMERICA, WE LOVE EVERY PART OF YOU.
BUT PLAYING VIGILANTE DOESN'T JUST PUT YOU AT RISK.
IT PUTS US ALL IN DANGER.
MY MOMS WOULD GET WHAT I'M DOING.
THEY'RE MY REAL FAMILY ANYWAY...

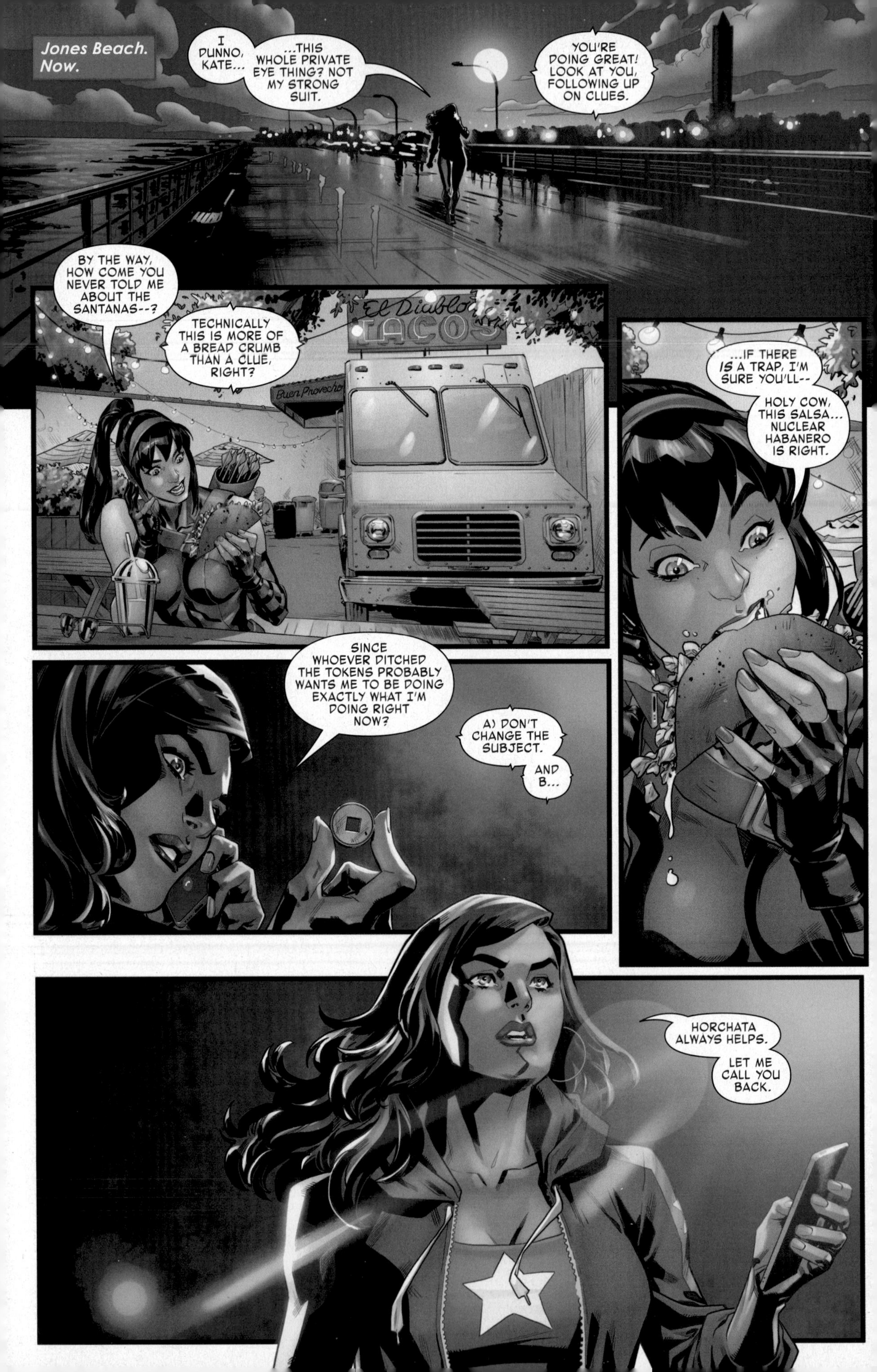
Jones Beach. Now.
I DUNNO, KATE...
...THIS WHOLE PRIVATE EYE THING? NOT MY STRONG SUIT.
YOU'RE DOING GREAT! LOOK AT YOU, FOLLOWING UP ON CLUES.
BY THE WAY, HOW COME YOU NEVER TOLD ME ABOUT THE SANTANAS--?
TECHNICALLY THIS IS MORE OF A BREAD CRUMB THAN A CLUE, RIGHT?
El Diablo TACOS
Buen Provecho
...IF THERE IS A TRAP, I'M SURE YOU'LL--
HOLY COW, THIS SALSA... NUCLEAR HABANERO IS RIGHT.
SINCE WHOEVER DITCHED THE TOKENS PROBABLY WANTS ME TO BE DOING EXACTLY WHAT I'M DOING RIGHT NOW?
A) DON'T CHANGE THE SUBJECT.
AND B...
HORCHATA ALWAYS HELPS.
LET ME CALL YOU BACK.

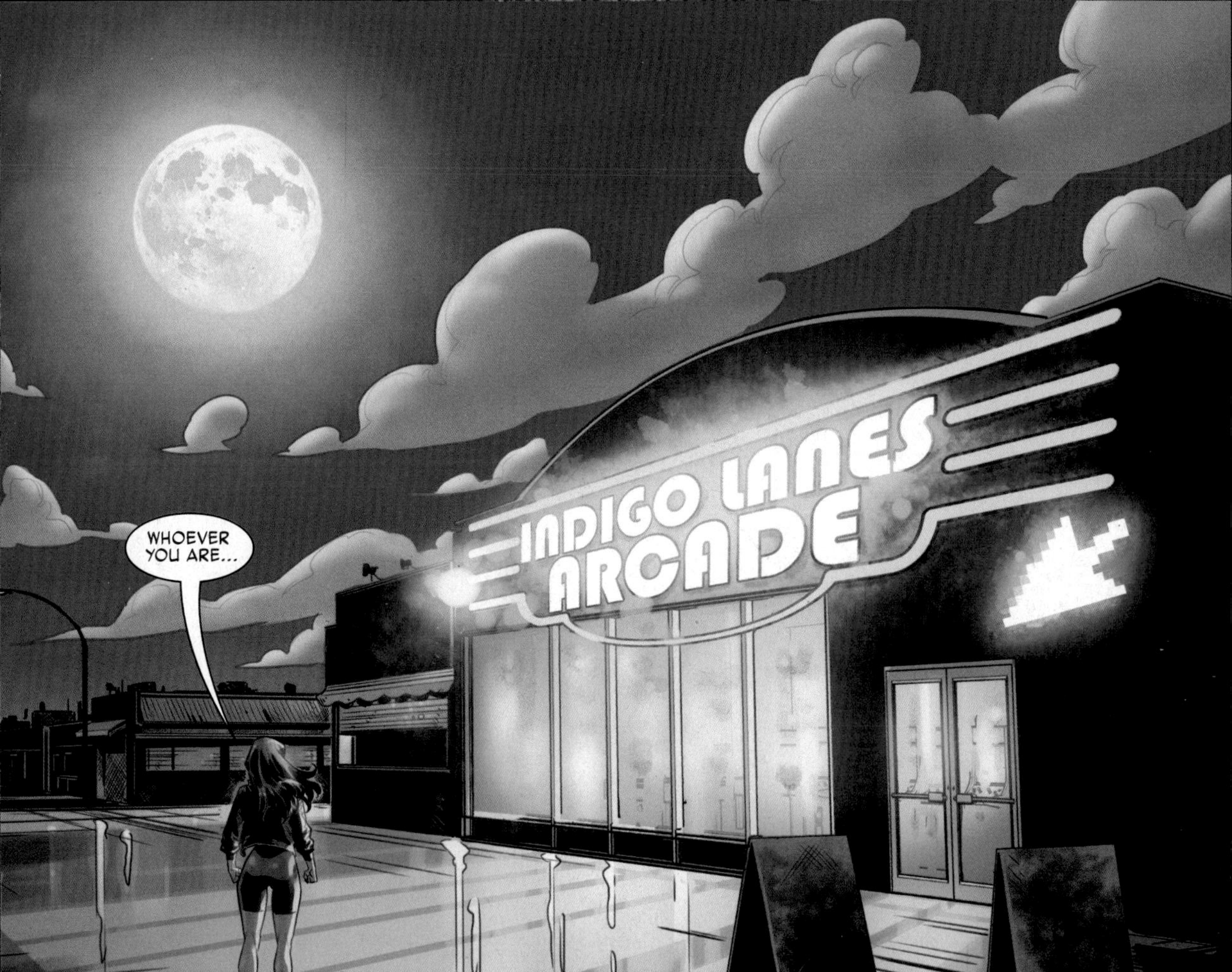
INDIGO LANES
ARCADE
WHOEVER YOU ARE...

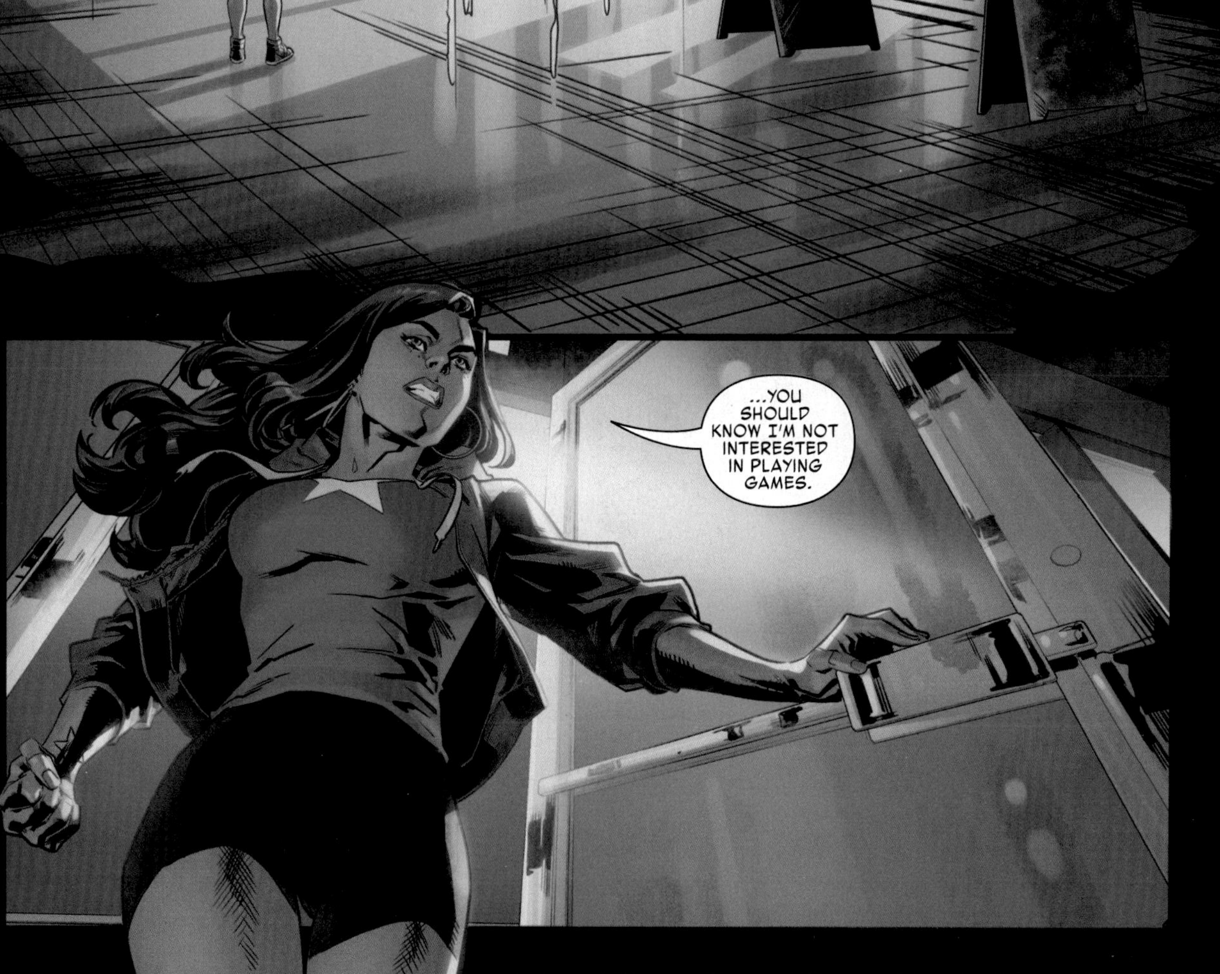
...YOU SHOULD KNOW I'M NOT INTERESTED IN PLAYING GAMES.

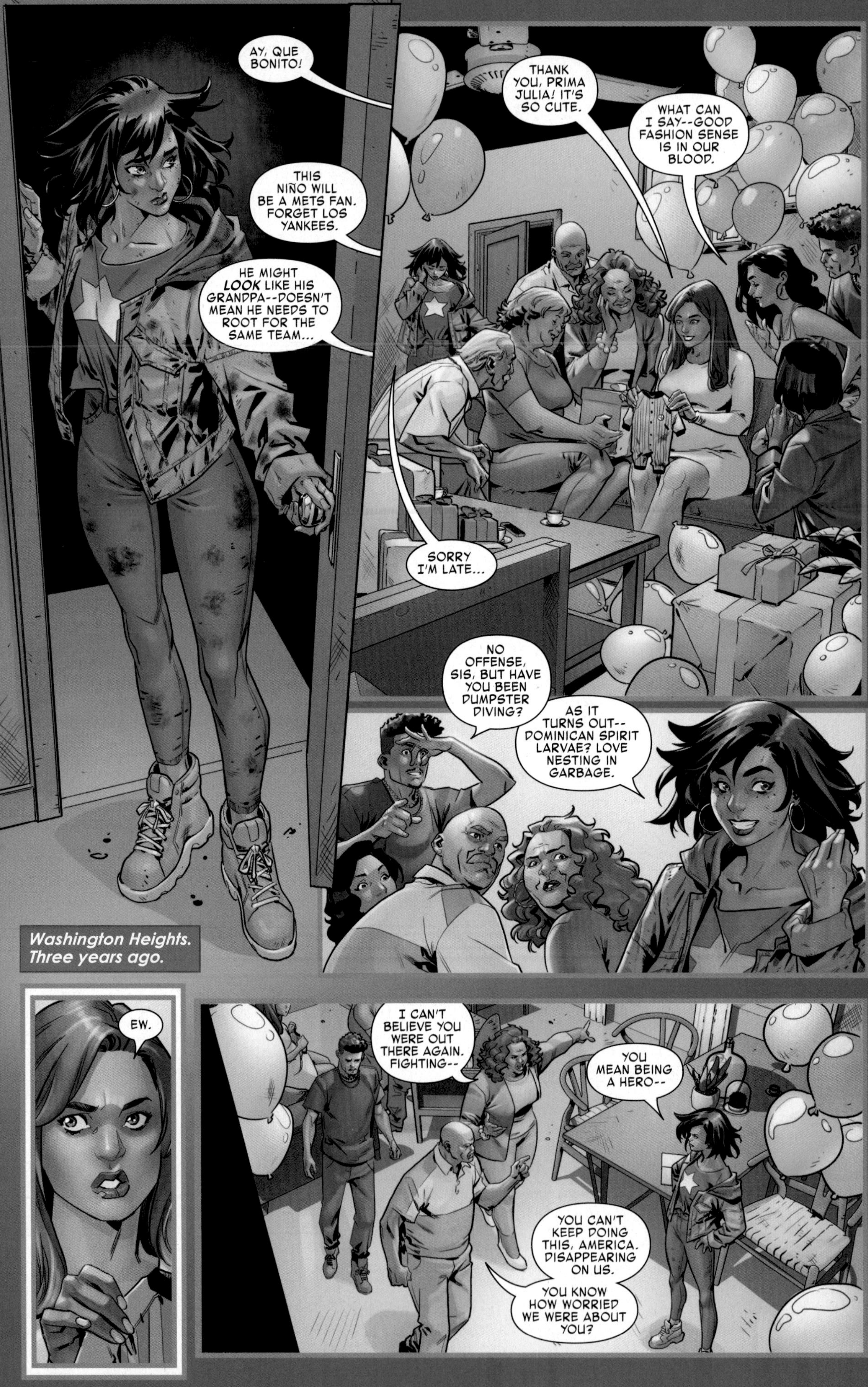

AY, QUE BONITO!
THIS NIÑO WILL BE A METS FAN. FORGET LOS YANKEES.
HE MIGHT LOOK LIKE HIS GRANDPA--DOESN'T MEAN HE NEEDS TO ROOT FOR THE SAME TEAM...
THANK YOU, PRIMA JULIA! IT'S SO CUTE.
WHAT CAN I SAY--GOOD FASHION SENSE IS IN OUR BLOOD.
SORRY I'M LATE...
Washington Heights. Three years ago.
NO OFFENSE, SIS, BUT HAVE YOU BEEN DUMPSTER DIVING?
AS IT TURNS OUT--DOMINICAN SPIRIT LARVAE? LOVE NESTING IN GARBAGE.
EW.
I CAN'T BELIEVE YOU WERE OUT THERE AGAIN. FIGHTING--
YOU MEAN BEING A HERO--
YOU CAN'T KEEP DOING THIS, AMERICA. DISAPPEARING ON US.
YOU KNOW HOW WORRIED WE WERE ABOUT YOU?

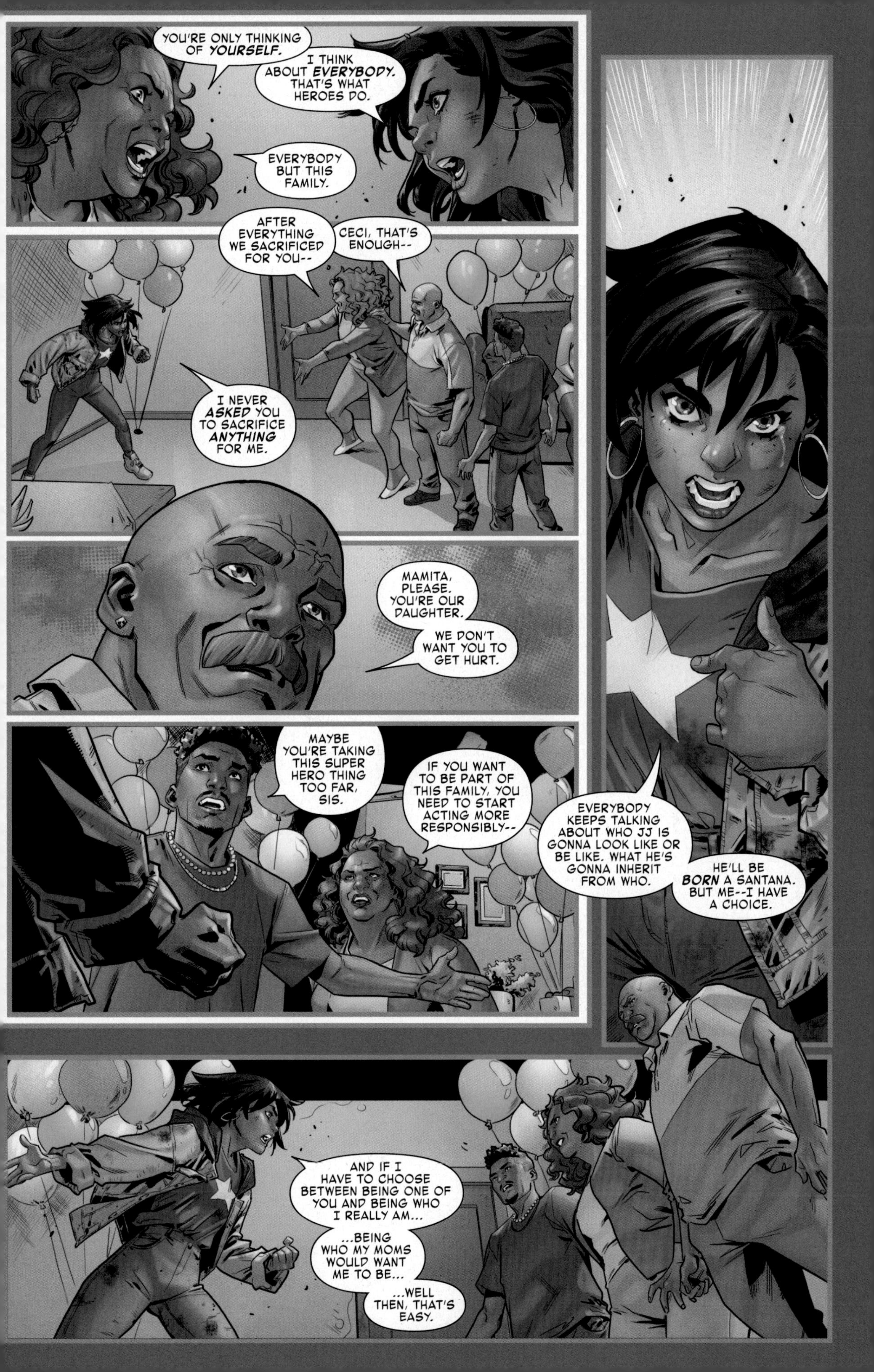

YOU'RE ONLY THINKING OF *YOURSELF.*
I THINK ABOUT *EVERYBODY.* THAT'S WHAT HEROES DO.
EVERYBODY BUT THIS FAMILY.
AFTER EVERYTHING WE SACRIFICED FOR YOU--
CECI, THAT'S ENOUGH--
I NEVER *ASKED* YOU TO SACRIFICE *ANYTHING* FOR ME.
MAMITA, PLEASE. YOU'RE OUR DAUGHTER.
WE DON'T WANT YOU TO GET HURT.
MAYBE YOU'RE TAKING THIS SUPER HERO THING TOO FAR, SIS.
IF YOU WANT TO BE PART OF THIS FAMILY, YOU NEED TO START ACTING MORE RESPONSIBLY--
EVERYBODY KEEPS TALKING ABOUT WHO JJ IS GONNA LOOK LIKE OR BE LIKE. WHAT HE'S GONNA INHERIT FROM WHO.
HE'LL BE *BORN* A SANTANA. BUT ME--I HAVE A CHOICE.
AND IF I HAVE TO CHOOSE BETWEEN BEING ONE OF YOU AND BEING WHO I REALLY AM...
...BEING WHO MY MOMS WOULD WANT ME TO BE...
...WELL THEN, THAT'S EASY.

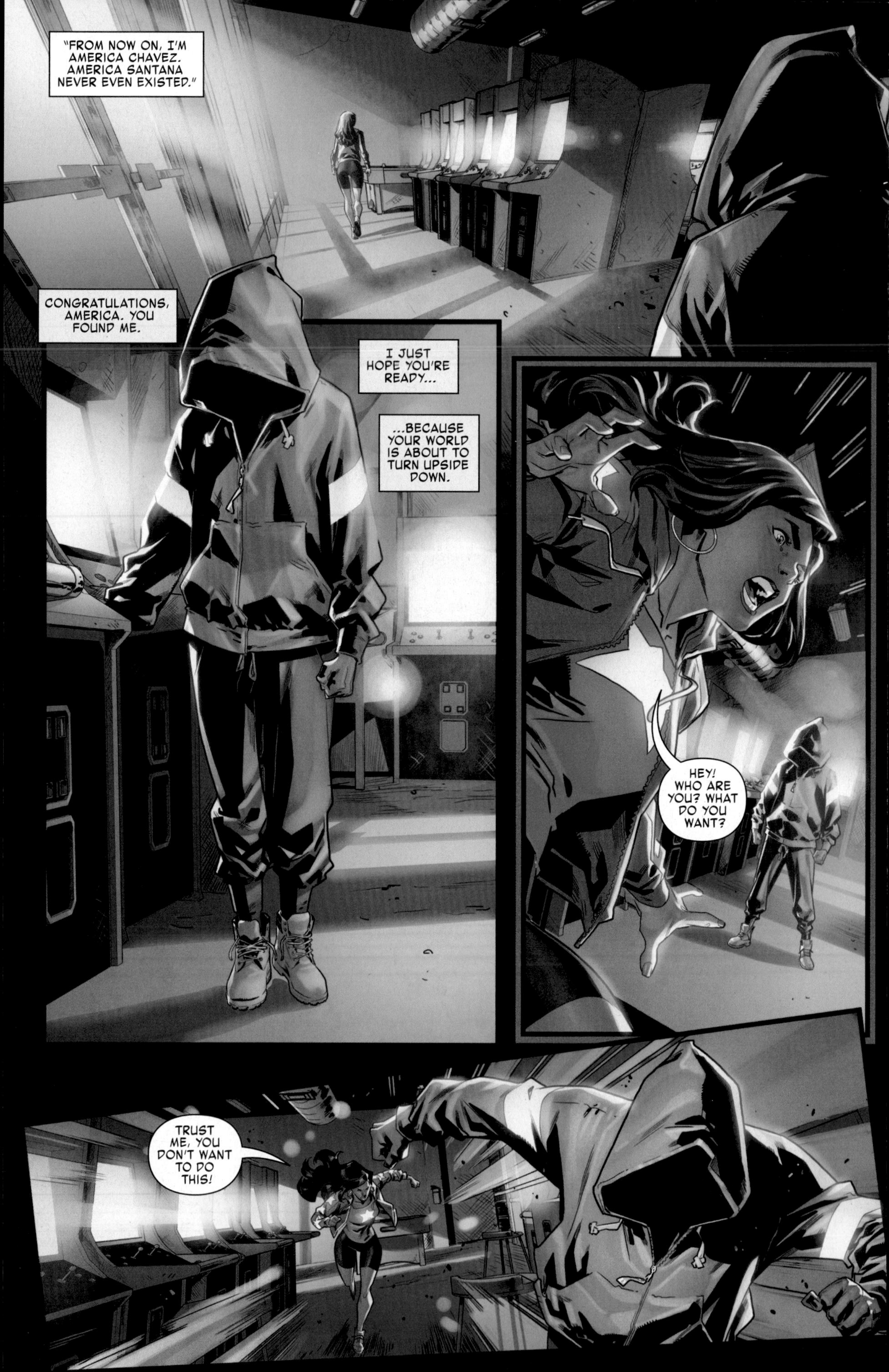
"FROM NOW ON, I'M AMERICA CHAVEZ. AMERICA SANTANA NEVER EVEN EXISTED."
CONGRATULATIONS, AMERICA. YOU FOUND ME.
I JUST HOPE YOU'RE READY...
...BECAUSE YOUR WORLD IS ABOUT TO TURN UPSIDE DOWN.
HEY! WHO ARE YOU? WHAT DO YOU WANT?
TRUST ME, YOU DON'T WANT TO DO THIS!

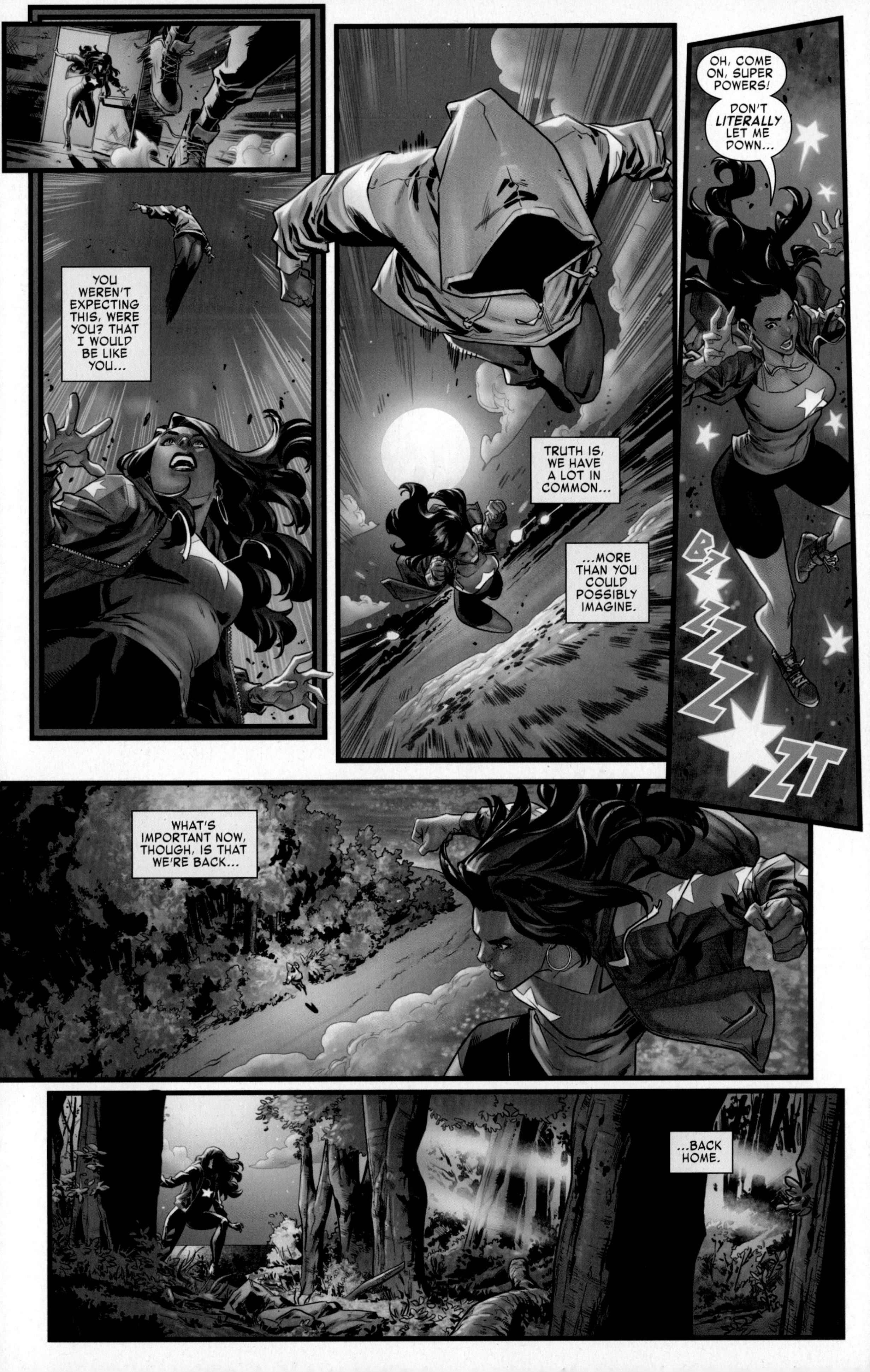

YOU WEREN'T EXPECTING THIS, WERE YOU? THAT I WOULD BE LIKE YOU...
TRUTH IS, WE HAVE A LOT IN COMMON...
...MORE THAN YOU COULD POSSIBLY IMAGINE.
OH, COME ON, SUPER POWERS!
DON'T LITERALLY LET ME DOWN...
BZZZZT
WHAT'S IMPORTANT NOW, THOUGH, IS THAT WE'RE BACK...
...BACK HOME.

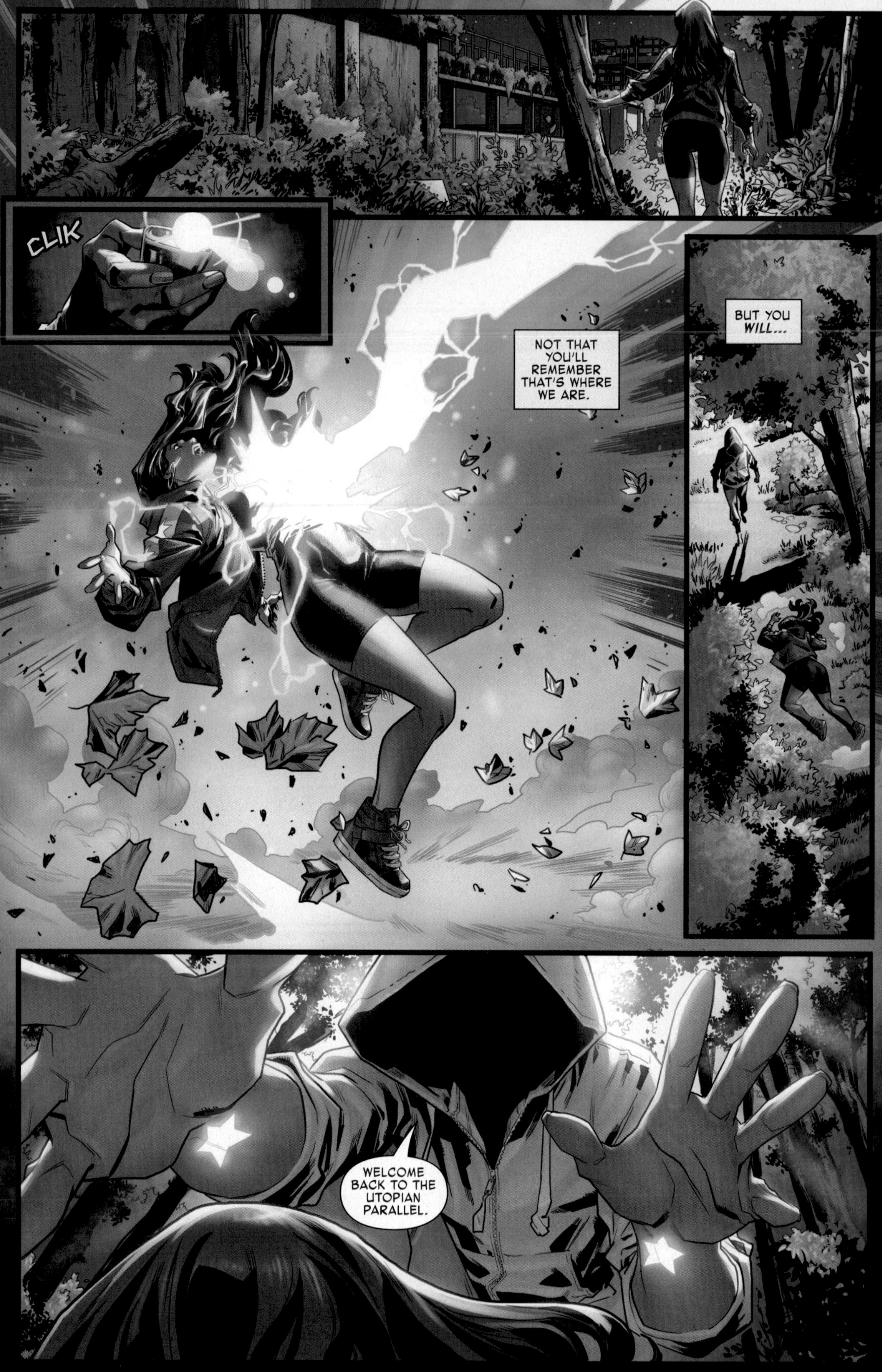
CLIK
NOT THAT YOU'LL REMEMBER THAT'S WHERE WE ARE.
BUT YOU *WILL*...
WELCOME BACK TO THE UTOPIAN PARALLEL.

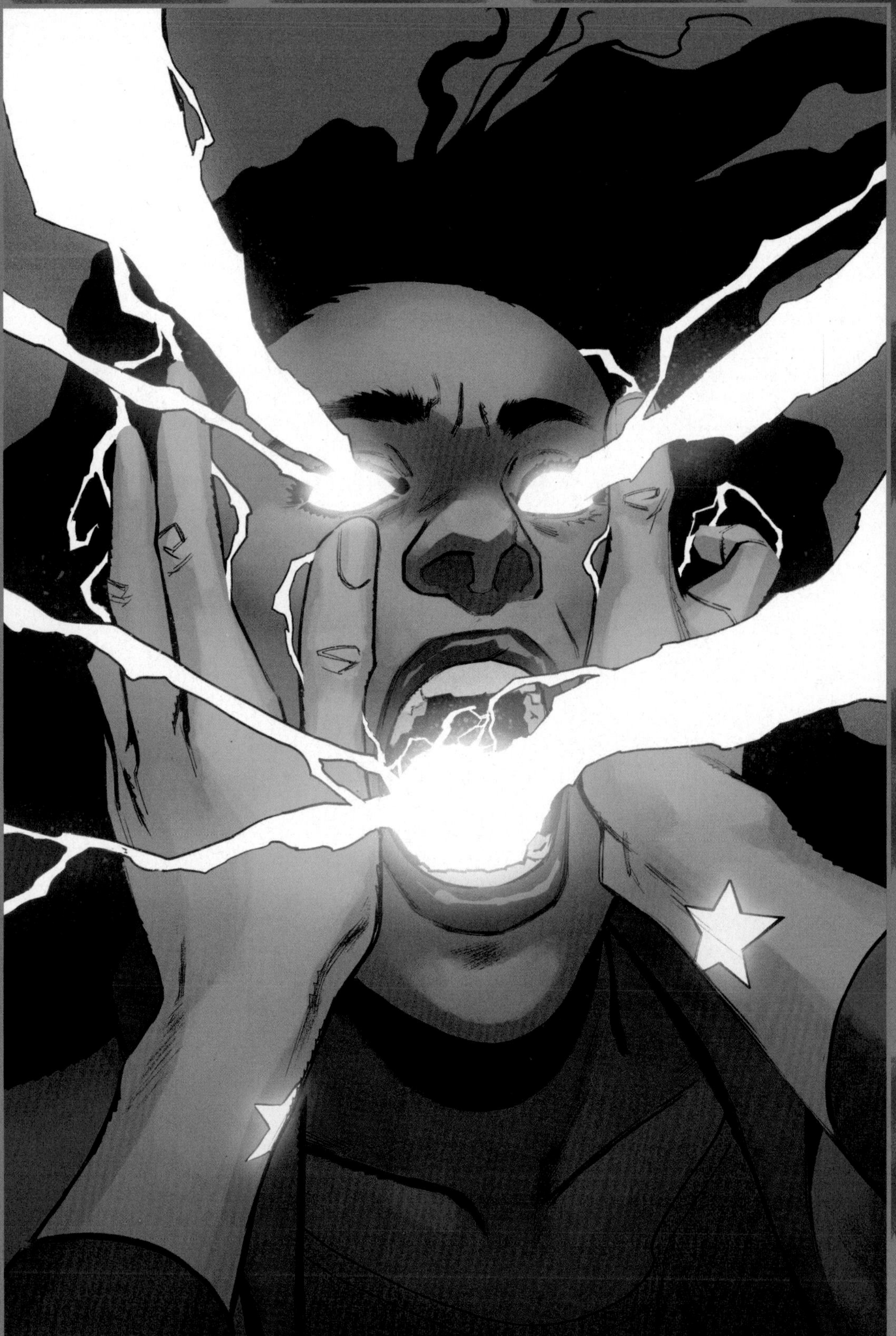

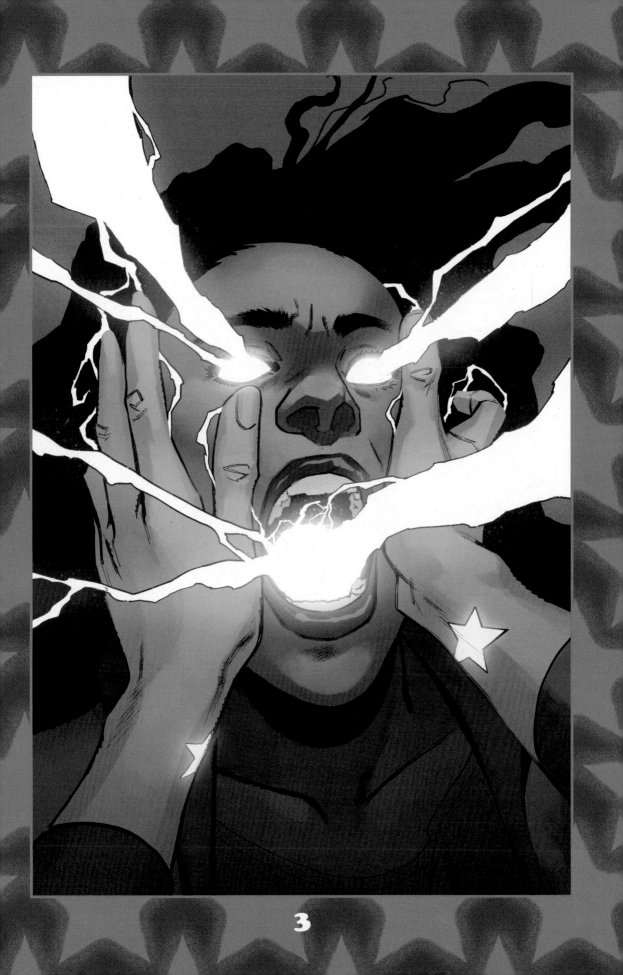

3

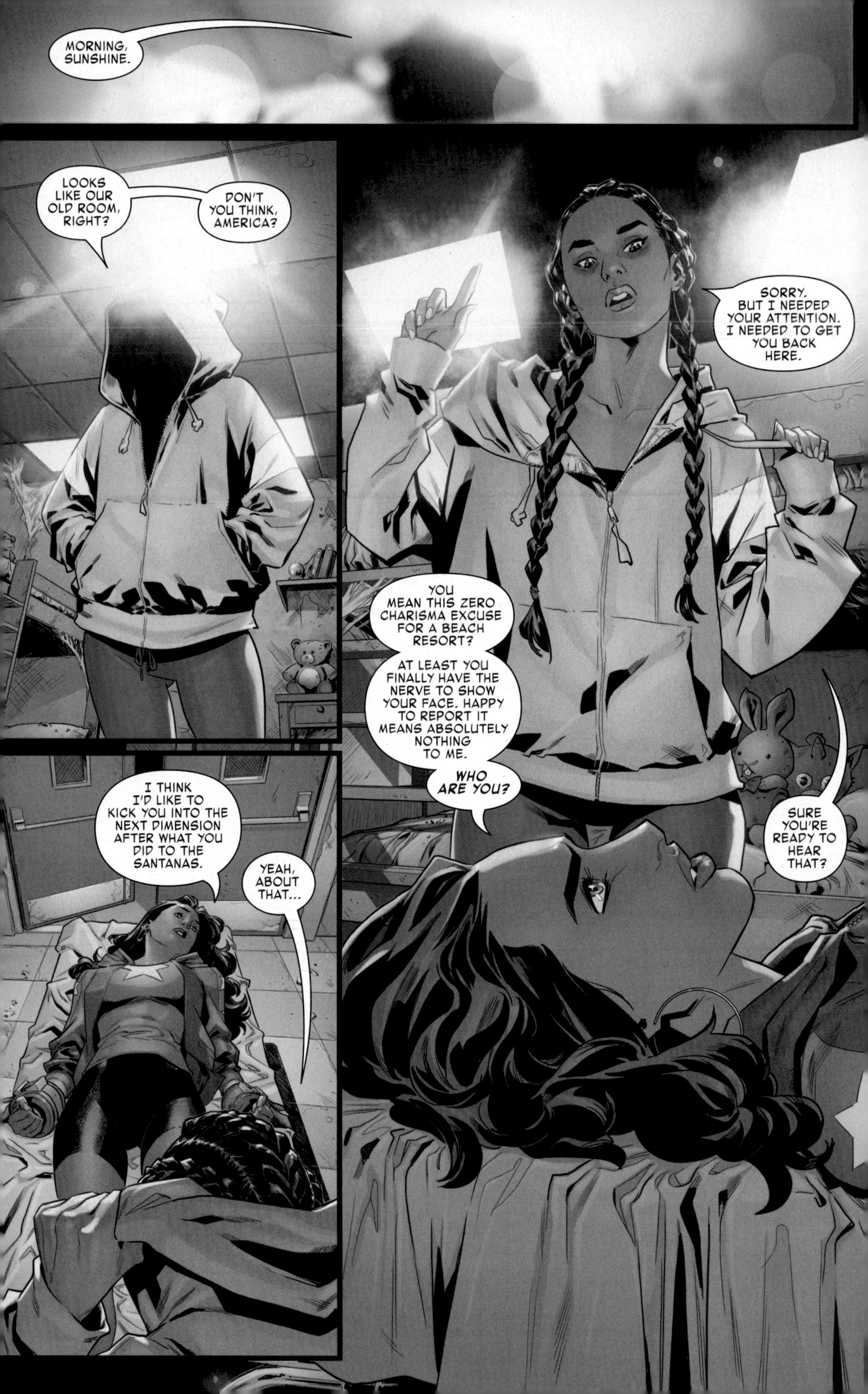
MORNING, SUNSHINE.
LOOKS LIKE OUR OLD ROOM, RIGHT?
DON'T YOU THINK, AMERICA?
SORRY. BUT I NEEDED YOUR ATTENTION. I NEEDED TO GET YOU BACK HERE.
YOU MEAN THIS ZERO CHARISMA EXCUSE FOR A BEACH RESORT?
AT LEAST YOU FINALLY HAVE THE NERVE TO SHOW YOUR FACE. HAPPY TO REPORT IT MEANS ABSOLUTELY NOTHING TO ME.
WHO ARE YOU?
SURE YOU'RE READY TO HEAR THAT?
I THINK I'D LIKE TO KICK YOU INTO THE NEXT DIMENSION AFTER WHAT YOU DID TO THE SANTANAS.
YEAH, ABOUT THAT...

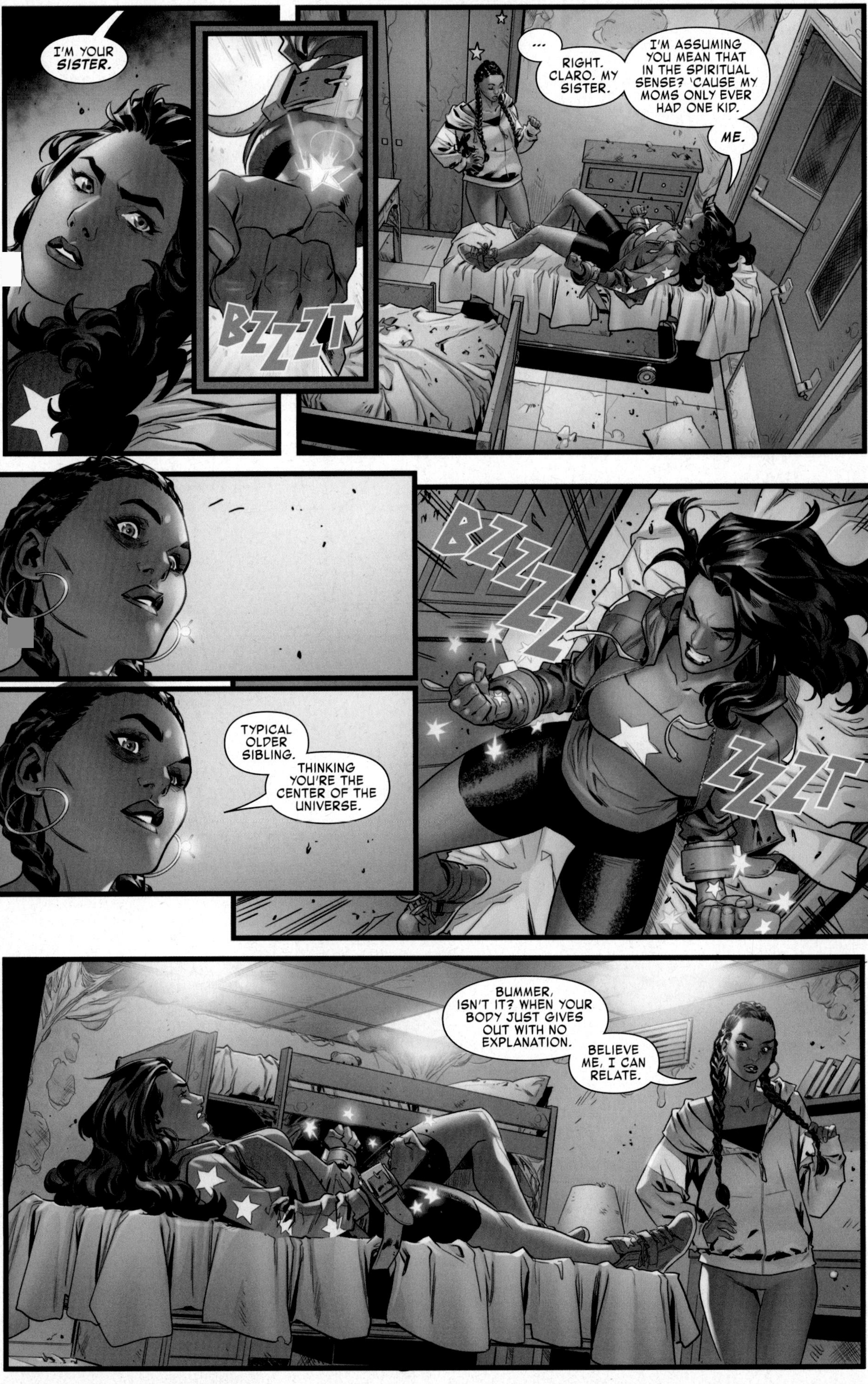
I'M YOUR SISTER.
BZZZT
...
RIGHT. CLARO. MY SISTER.
I'M ASSUMING YOU MEAN THAT IN THE SPIRITUAL SENSE? 'CAUSE MY MOMS ONLY EVER HAD ONE KID.
ME.
BZZZZ
TYPICAL OLDER SIBLING.
THINKING YOU'RE THE CENTER OF THE UNIVERSE.
ZZZZT
BUMMER, ISN'T IT? WHEN YOUR BODY JUST GIVES OUT WITH NO EXPLANATION.
BELIEVE ME, I CAN RELATE.

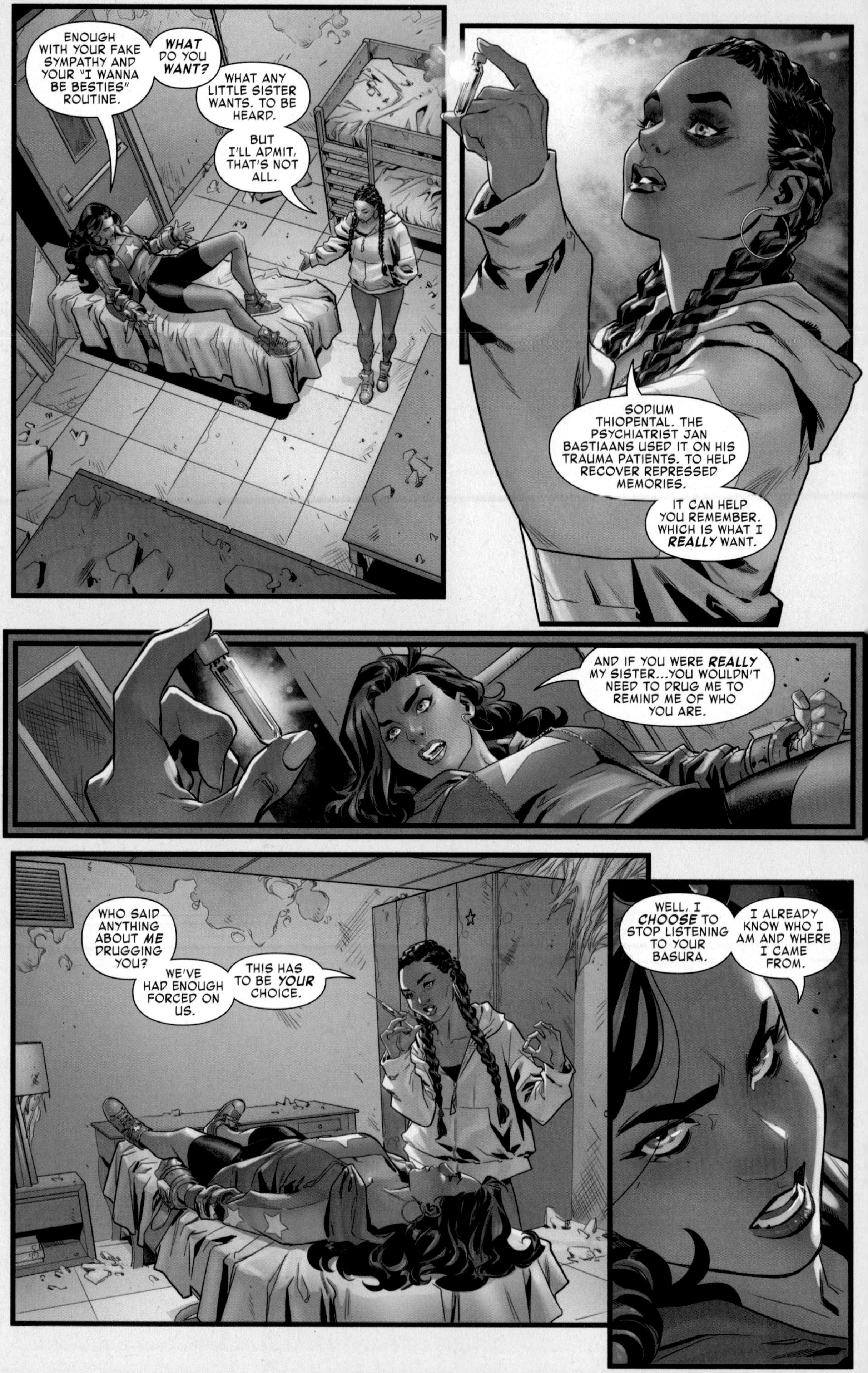
ENOUGH WITH YOUR FAKE SYMPATHY AND YOUR "I WANNA BE BESTIES" ROUTINE.
WHAT DO YOU WANT?
WHAT ANY LITTLE SISTER WANTS. TO BE HEARD.
BUT I'LL ADMIT, THAT'S NOT ALL.
SODIUM THIOPENTAL. THE PSYCHIATRIST JAN BASTIAANS USED IT ON HIS TRAUMA PATIENTS. TO HELP RECOVER REPRESSED MEMORIES.
IT CAN HELP YOU REMEMBER. WHICH IS WHAT I REALLY WANT.
AND IF YOU WERE REALLY MY SISTER...YOU WOULDN'T NEED TO DRUG ME TO REMIND ME OF WHO YOU ARE.
WHO SAID ANYTHING ABOUT ME DRUGGING YOU?
WE'VE HAD ENOUGH FORCED ON US.
THIS HAS TO BE YOUR CHOICE.
WELL, I CHOOSE TO STOP LISTENING TO YOUR BASURA.
I ALREADY KNOW WHO I AM AND WHERE I CAME FROM.

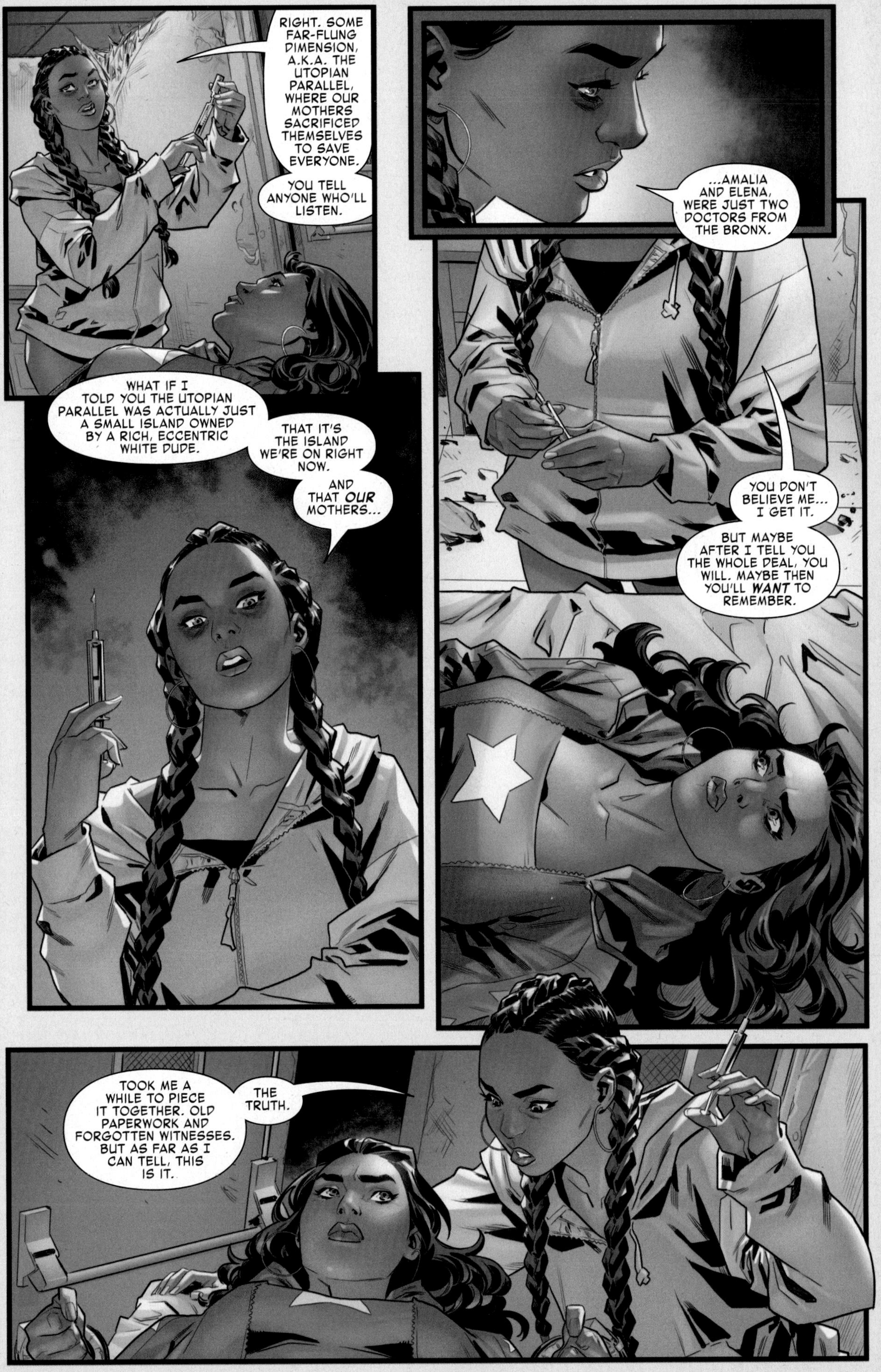
RIGHT. SOME FAR-FLUNG DIMENSION, A.K.A. THE UTOPIAN PARALLEL, WHERE OUR MOTHERS SACRIFICED THEMSELVES TO SAVE EVERYONE.
YOU TELL ANYONE WHO'LL LISTEN.
WHAT IF I TOLD YOU THE UTOPIAN PARALLEL WAS ACTUALLY JUST A SMALL ISLAND OWNED BY A RICH, ECCENTRIC WHITE DUDE.
THAT IT'S THE ISLAND WE'RE ON RIGHT NOW.
AND THAT OUR MOTHERS...
...AMALIA AND ELENA, WERE JUST TWO DOCTORS FROM THE BRONX.
YOU DON'T BELIEVE ME... I GET IT.
BUT MAYBE AFTER I TELL YOU THE WHOLE DEAL, YOU WILL. MAYBE THEN YOU'LL WANT TO REMEMBER.
TOOK ME A WHILE TO PIECE IT TOGETHER. OLD PAPERWORK AND FORGOTTEN WITNESSES. BUT AS FAR AS I CAN TELL, THIS IS IT.
THE TRUTH.

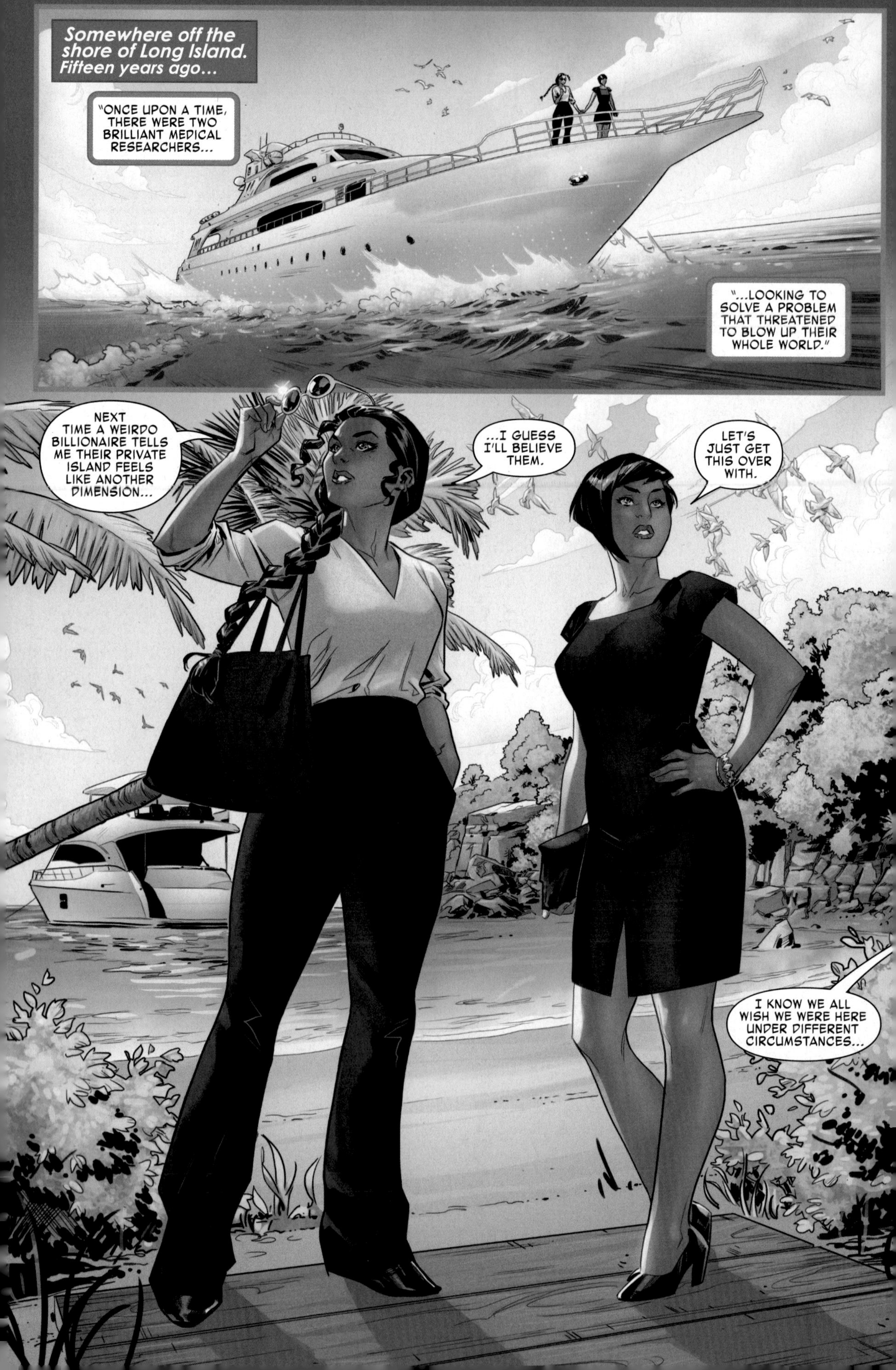
Somewhere off the shore of Long Island. Fifteen years ago...
"ONCE UPON A TIME, THERE WERE TWO BRILLIANT MEDICAL RESEARCHERS...
"...LOOKING TO SOLVE A PROBLEM THAT THREATENED TO BLOW UP THEIR WHOLE WORLD."
NEXT TIME A WEIRDO BILLIONAIRE TELLS ME THEIR PRIVATE ISLAND FEELS LIKE ANOTHER DIMENSION...
...I GUESS I'LL BELIEVE THEM.
LET'S JUST GET THIS OVER WITH.
I KNOW WE ALL WISH WE WERE HERE UNDER DIFFERENT CIRCUMSTANCES...

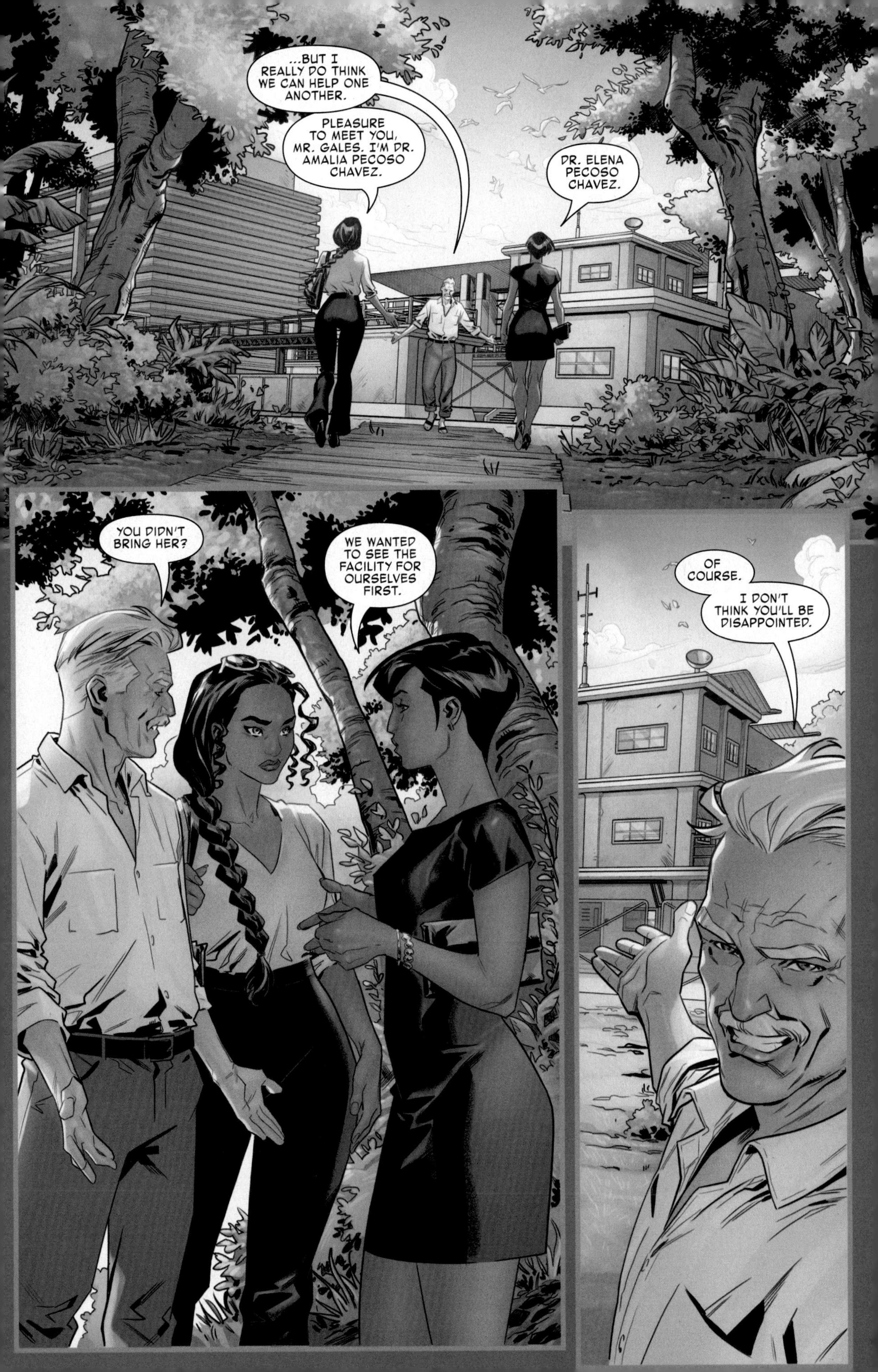
...BUT I REALLY DO THINK WE CAN HELP ONE ANOTHER.
PLEASURE TO MEET YOU, MR. GALES. I'M DR. AMALIA PECOSO CHAVEZ.
DR. ELENA PECOSO CHAVEZ.
YOU DIDN'T BRING HER?
WE WANTED TO SEE THE FACILITY FOR OURSELVES FIRST.
OF COURSE.
I DON'T THINK YOU'LL BE DISAPPOINTED.

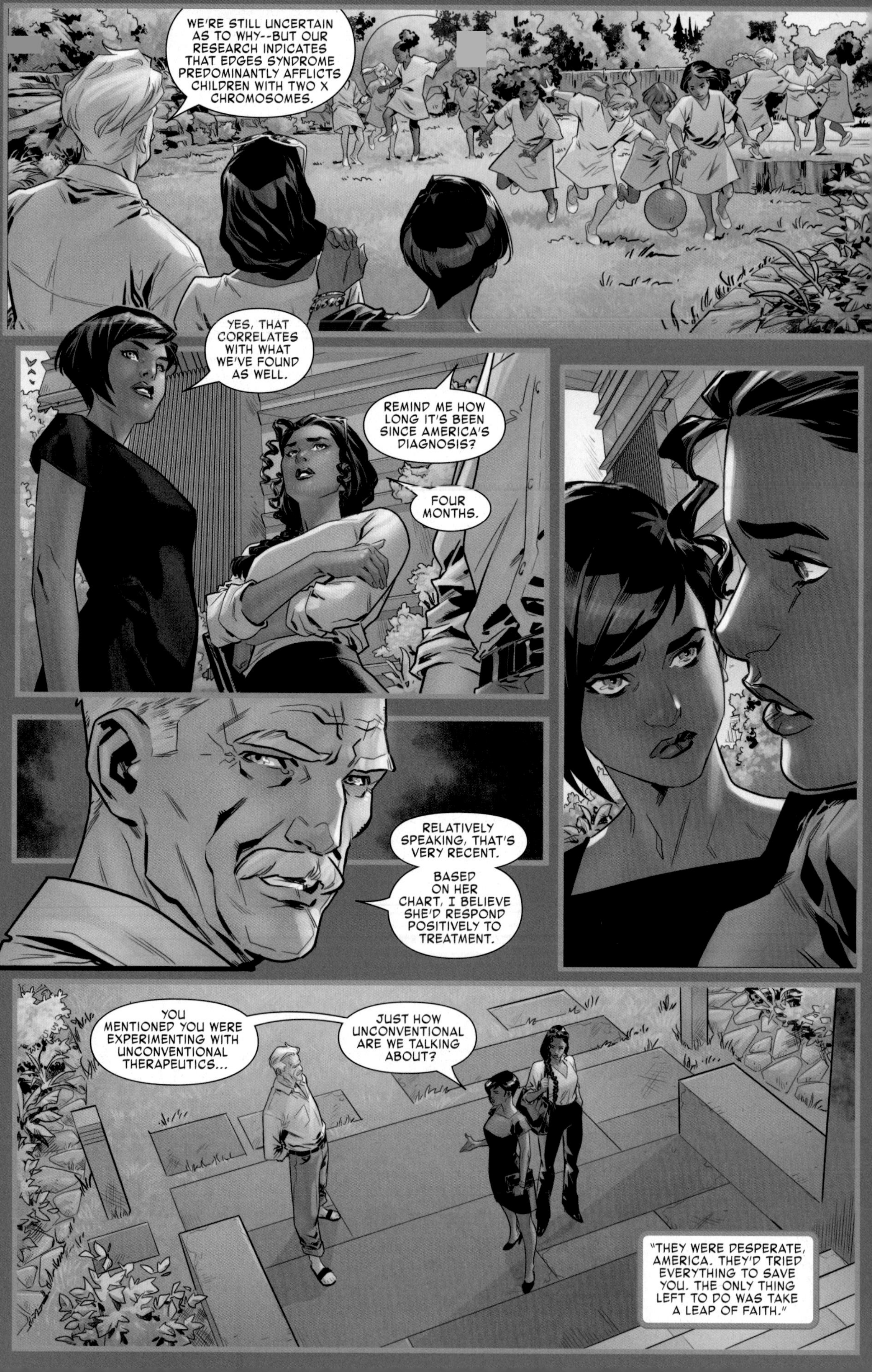
WE'RE STILL UNCERTAIN AS TO WHY--BUT OUR RESEARCH INDICATES THAT EDGES SYNDROME PREDOMINANTLY AFFLICTS CHILDREN WITH TWO X CHROMOSOMES.
YES, THAT CORRELATES WITH WHAT WE'VE FOUND AS WELL.
REMIND ME HOW LONG IT'S BEEN SINCE AMERICA'S DIAGNOSIS?
FOUR MONTHS.
RELATIVELY SPEAKING, THAT'S VERY RECENT.
BASED ON HER CHART, I BELIEVE SHE'D RESPOND POSITIVELY TO TREATMENT.
YOU MENTIONED YOU WERE EXPERIMENTING WITH UNCONVENTIONAL THERAPEUTICS...
JUST HOW UNCONVENTIONAL ARE WE TALKING ABOUT?
"THEY WERE DESPERATE, AMERICA. THEY'D TRIED EVERYTHING TO SAVE YOU. THE ONLY THING LEFT TO DO WAS TAKE A LEAP OF FAITH."

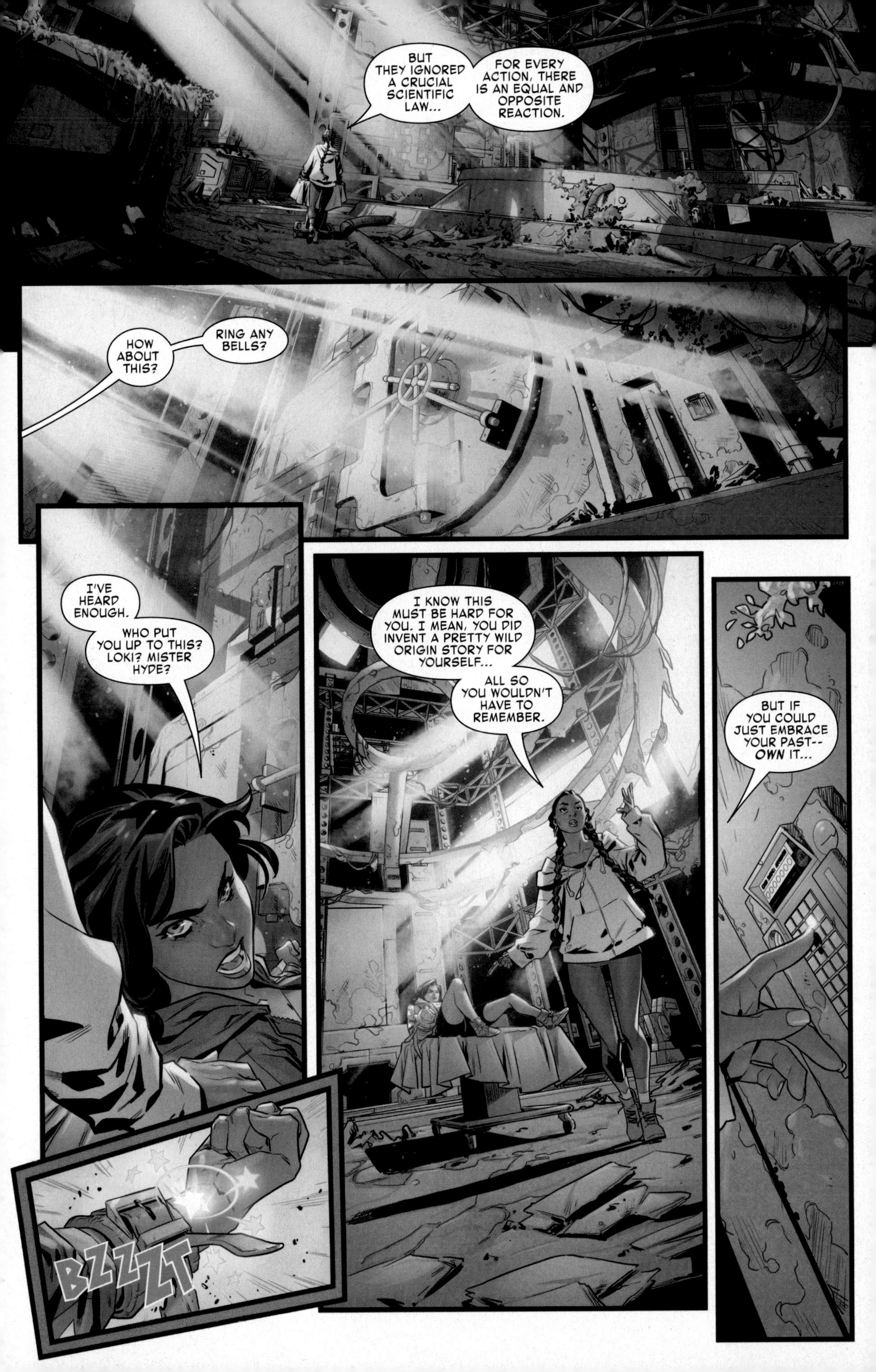

BUT THEY IGNORED A CRUCIAL SCIENTIFIC LAW...
FOR EVERY ACTION, THERE IS AN EQUAL AND OPPOSITE REACTION.
HOW ABOUT THIS?
RING ANY BELLS?
I'VE HEARD ENOUGH.
WHO PUT YOU UP TO THIS? LOKI? MISTER HYDE?
BZZZT
I KNOW THIS MUST BE HARD FOR YOU. I MEAN, YOU DID INVENT A PRETTY WILD ORIGIN STORY FOR YOURSELF...
ALL SO YOU WOULDN'T HAVE TO REMEMBER.
BUT IF YOU COULD JUST EMBRACE YOUR PAST--
OWN IT...

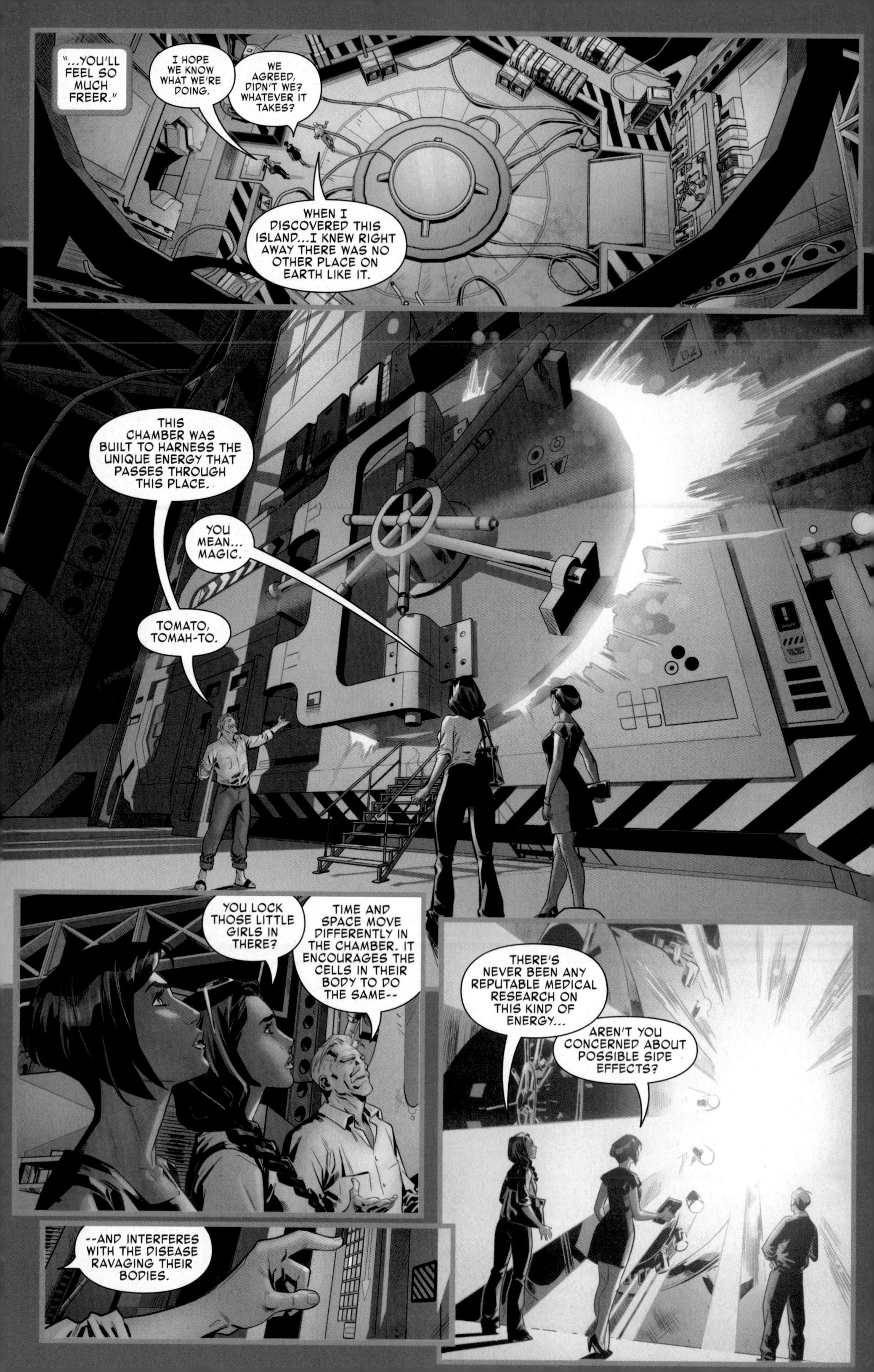
"...YOU'LL FEEL SO MUCH FREER."
I HOPE WE KNOW WHAT WE'RE DOING.
WE AGREED, DIDN'T WE? WHATEVER IT TAKES?
WHEN I DISCOVERED THIS ISLAND...I KNEW RIGHT AWAY THERE WAS NO OTHER PLACE ON EARTH LIKE IT.
THIS CHAMBER WAS BUILT TO HARNESS THE UNIQUE ENERGY THAT PASSES THROUGH THIS PLACE.
YOU MEAN... MAGIC.
TOMATO, TOMAH-TO.
YOU LOCK THOSE LITTLE GIRLS IN THERE?
TIME AND SPACE MOVE DIFFERENTLY IN THE CHAMBER. IT ENCOURAGES THE CELLS IN THEIR BODY TO DO THE SAME--
--AND INTERFERES WITH THE DISEASE RAVAGING THEIR BODIES.
THERE'S NEVER BEEN ANY REPUTABLE MEDICAL RESEARCH ON THIS KIND OF ENERGY...
AREN'T YOU CONCERNED ABOUT POSSIBLE SIDE EFFECTS?

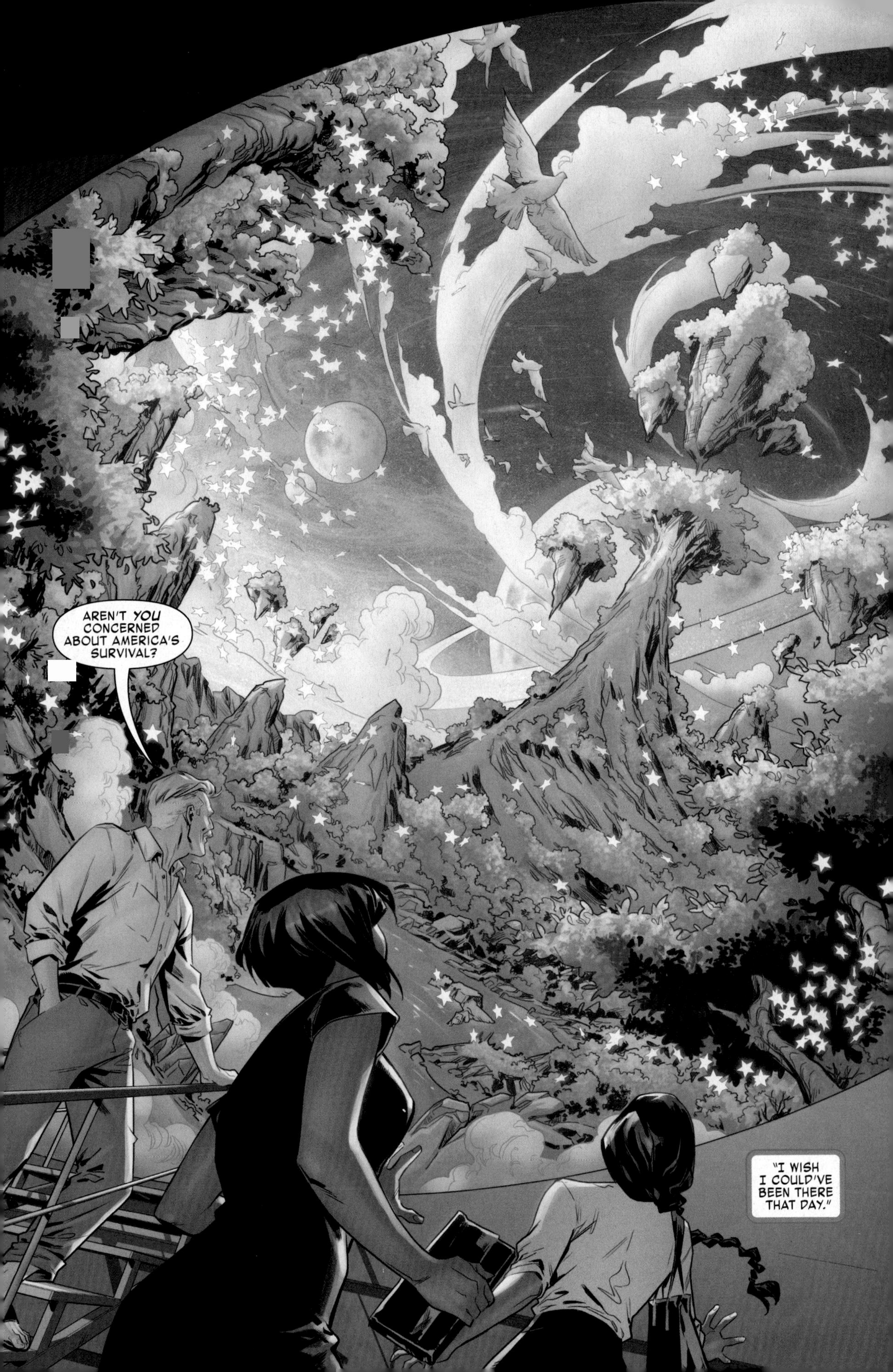
ARE'NT YOU CONCERNED ABOUT AMERICA'S SURVIVAL?
"I WISH I COULD'VE BEEN THERE THAT DAY."

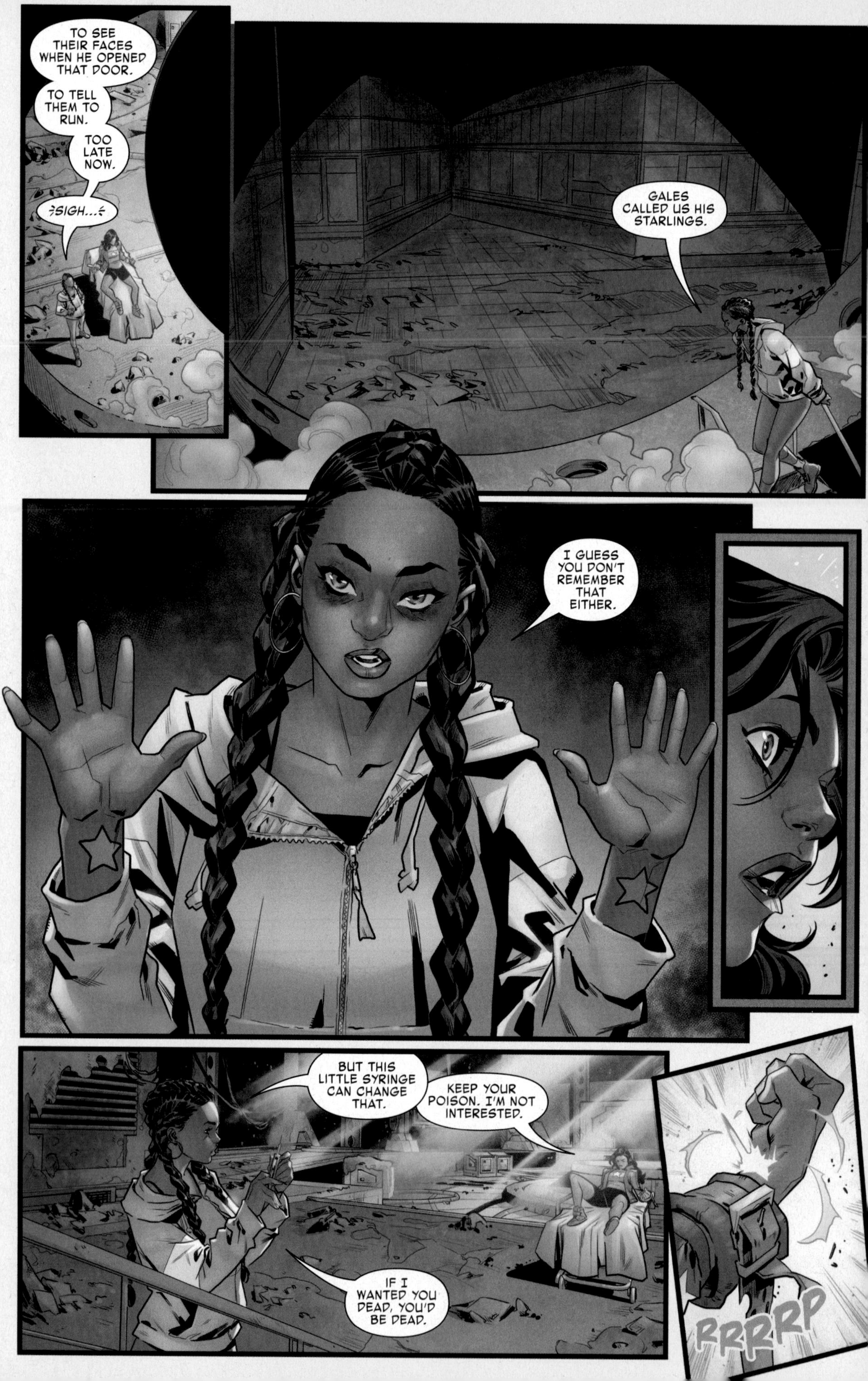
TO SEE THEIR FACES WHEN HE OPENED THAT DOOR.
TO TELL THEM TO RUN.
TOO LATE NOW.
SIGH...
GALES CALLED US HIS STARLINGS.
I GUESS YOU DON'T REMEMBER THAT EITHER.
BUT THIS LITTLE SYRINGE CAN CHANGE THAT.
KEEP YOUR POISON. I'M NOT INTERESTED.
IF I WANTED YOU DEAD, YOU'D BE DEAD.
RRRRP

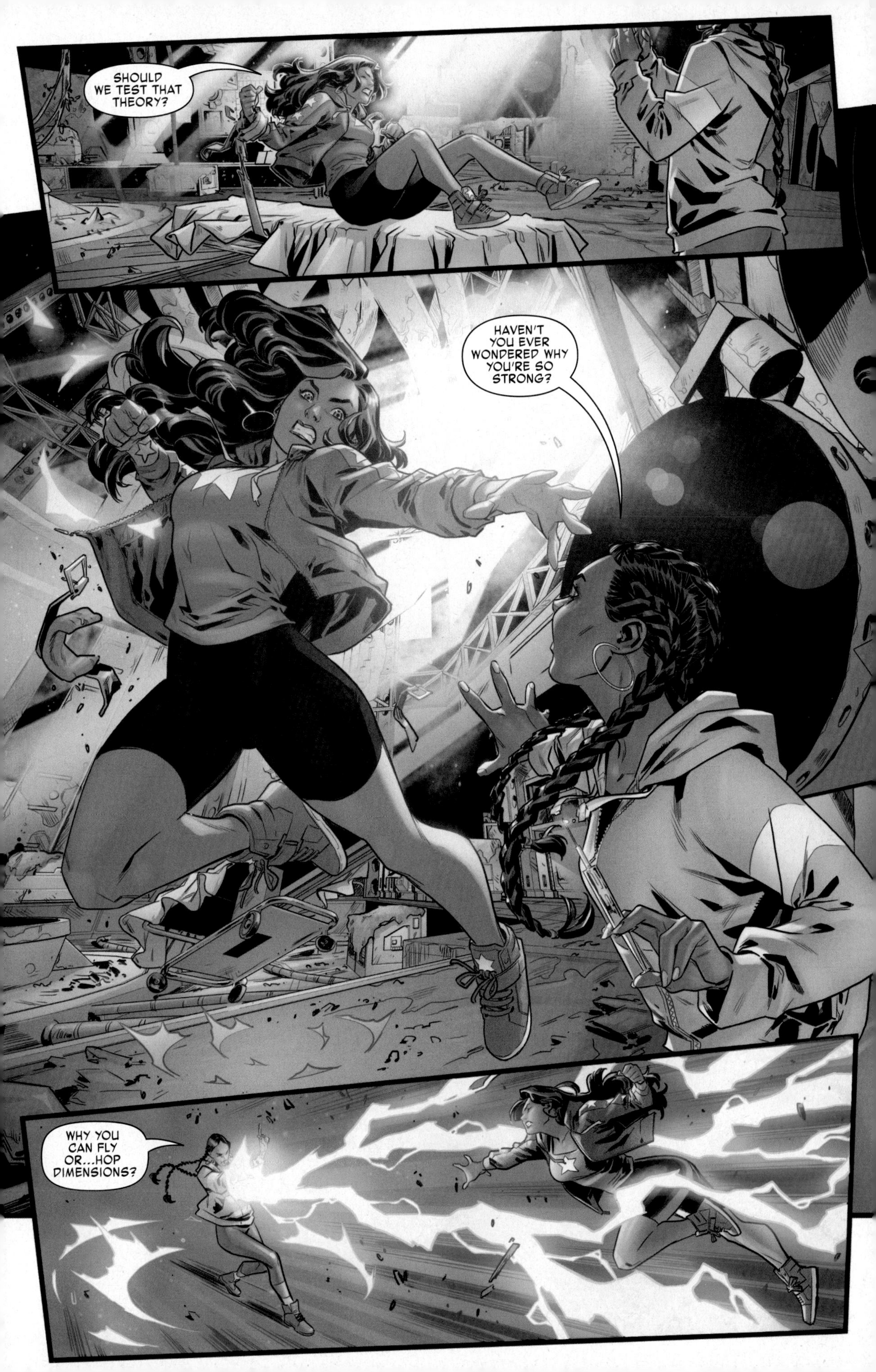
SHOULD WE TEST THAT THEORY?
HAVEN'T YOU EVER WONDERED WHY YOU'RE SO STRONG?
WHY YOU CAN FLY OR...HOP DIMENSIONS?

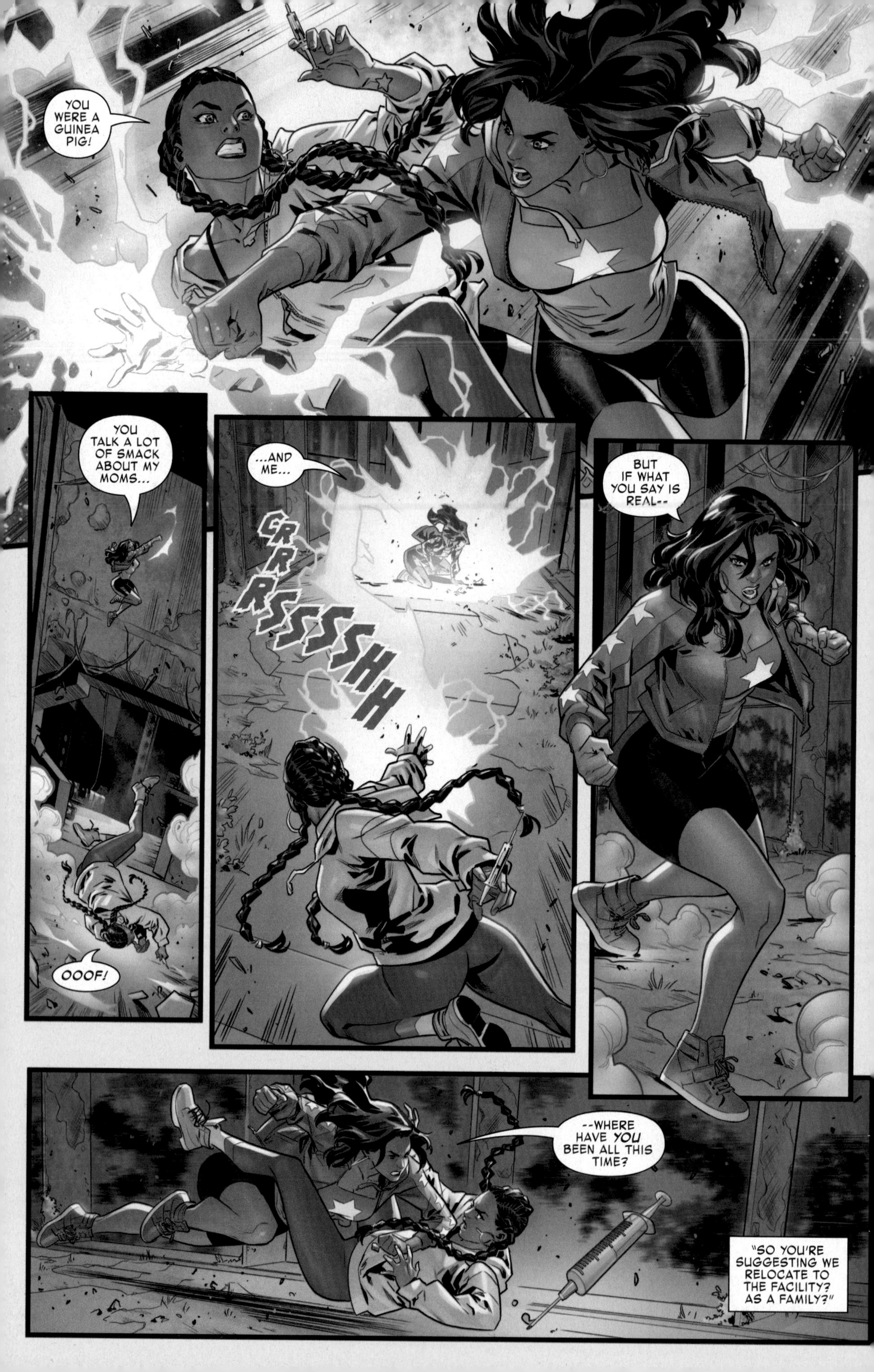
YOU WERE A GUINEA PIG!
YOU TALK A LOT OF SMACK ABOUT MY MOMS...
OOOF!
...AND ME...
CRRRSSSSHH
BUT IF WHAT YOU SAY IS REAL--
--WHERE HAVE *YOU* BEEN ALL THIS TIME?
"SO YOU'RE SUGGESTING WE RELOCATE TO THE FACILITY? AS A FAMILY?"

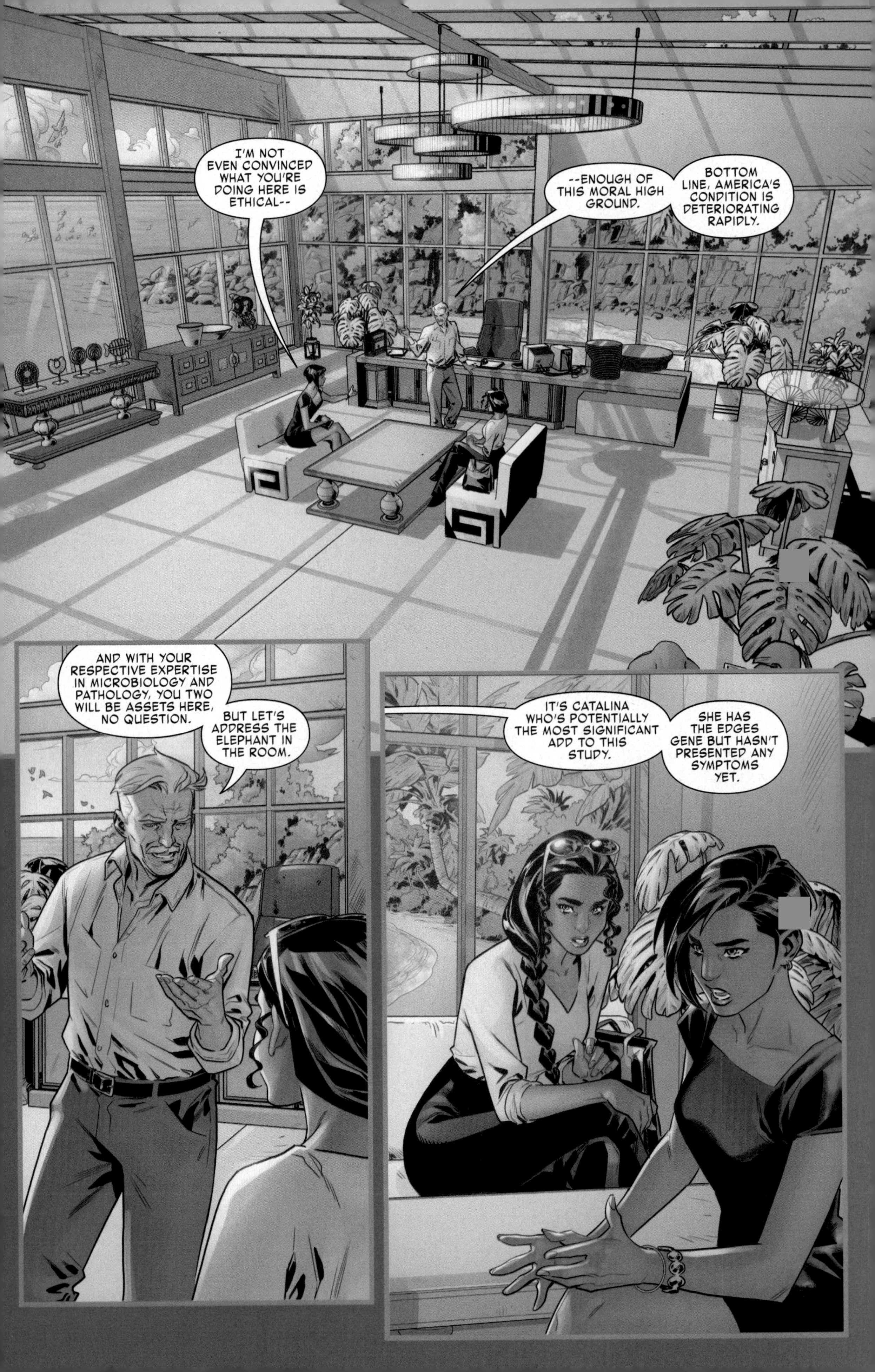
I'M NOT EVEN CONVINCED WHAT YOU'RE DOING HERE IS ETHICAL--
--ENOUGH OF THIS MORAL HIGH GROUND.
BOTTOM LINE, AMERICA'S CONDITION IS DETERIORATING RAPIDLY.
AND WITH YOUR RESPECTIVE EXPERTISE IN MICROBIOLOGY AND PATHOLOGY, YOU TWO WILL BE ASSETS HERE, NO QUESTION.
BUT LET'S ADDRESS THE ELEPHANT IN THE ROOM.
IT'S CATALINA WHO'S POTENTIALLY THE MOST SIGNIFICANT ADD TO THIS STUDY.
SHE HAS THE EDGES GENE BUT HASN'T PRESENTED ANY SYMPTOMS YET.

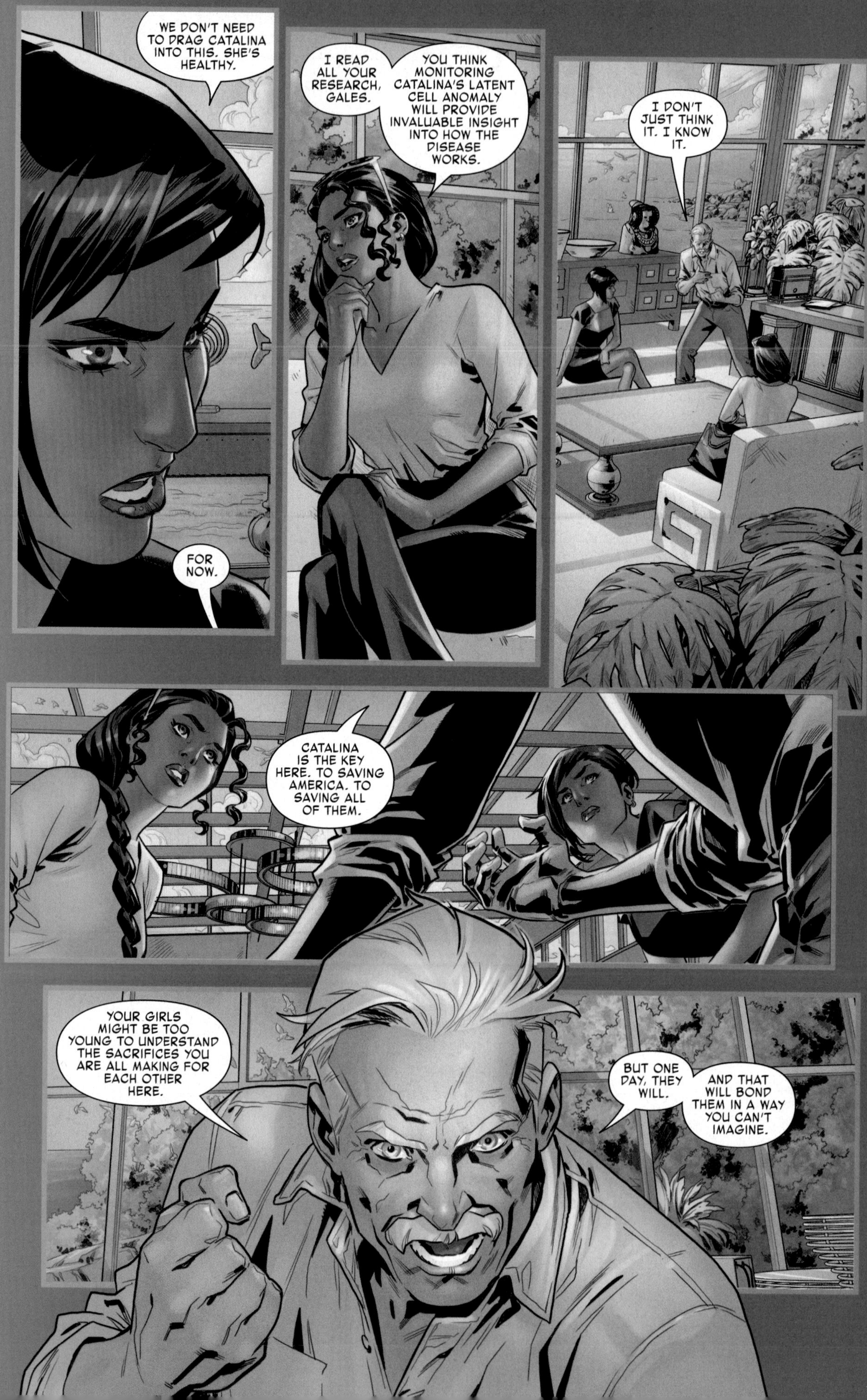
WE DON'T NEED TO DRAG CATALINA INTO THIS. SHE'S HEALTHY.
FOR NOW.
I READ ALL YOUR RESEARCH, GALES.
YOU THINK MONITORING CATALINA'S LATENT CELL ANOMALY WILL PROVIDE INVALUABLE INSIGHT INTO HOW THE DISEASE WORKS.
I DON'T JUST THINK IT. I KNOW IT.
CATALINA IS THE KEY HERE. TO SAVING AMERICA. TO SAVING ALL OF THEM.
YOUR GIRLS MIGHT BE TOO YOUNG TO UNDERSTAND THE SACRIFICES YOU ARE ALL MAKING FOR EACH OTHER HERE.
BUT ONE DAY, THEY WILL.
AND THAT WILL BOND THEM IN A WAY YOU CAN'T IMAGINE.

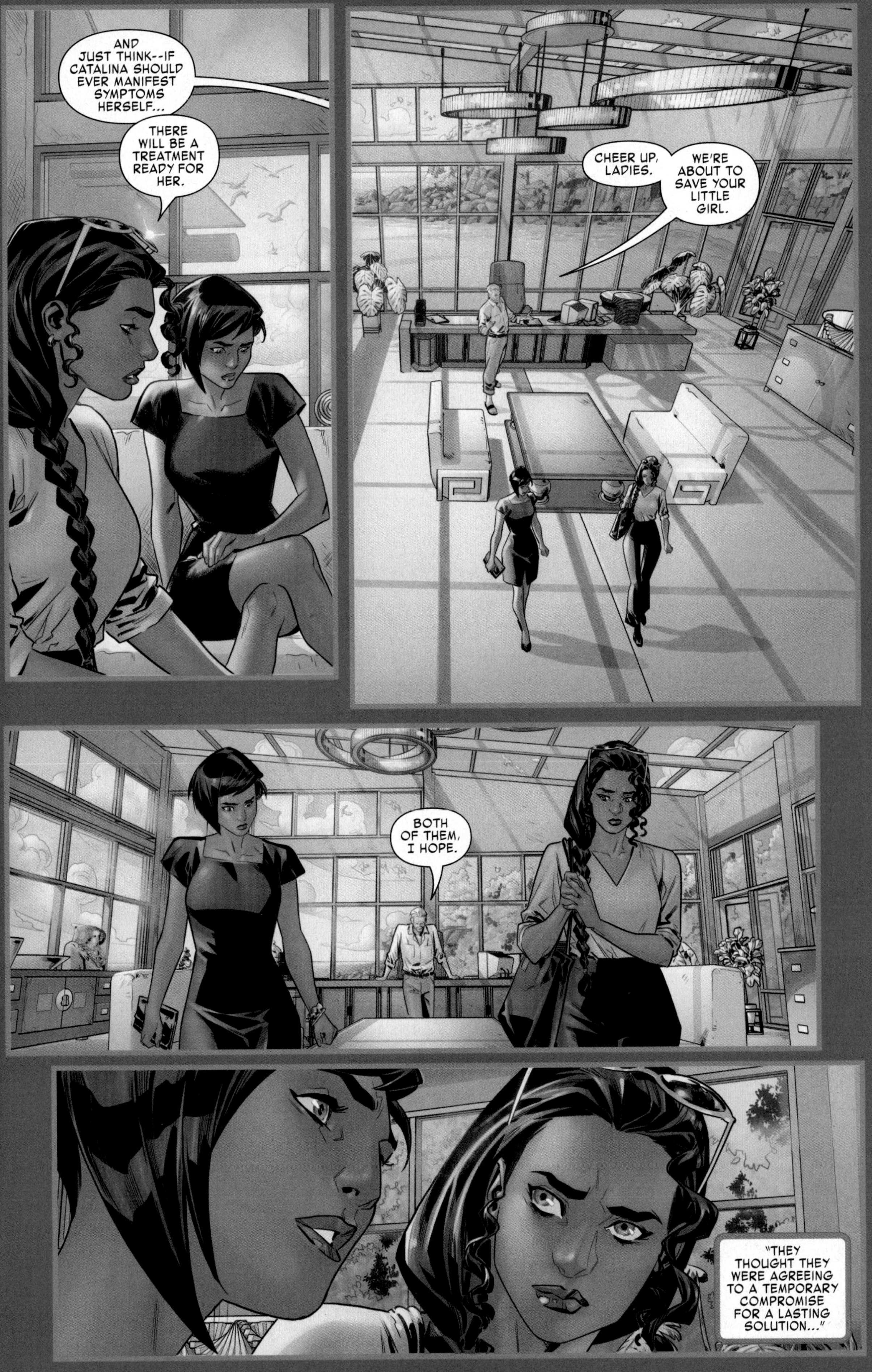

AND JUST THINK--IF CATALINA SHOULD EVER MANIFEST SYMPTOMS HERSELF...
THERE WILL BE A TREATMENT READY FOR HER.
CHEER UP, LADIES.
WE'RE ABOUT TO SAVE YOUR LITTLE GIRL.
BOTH OF THEM, I HOPE.
"THEY THOUGHT THEY WERE AGREEING TO A TEMPORARY COMPROMISE FOR A LASTING SOLUTION..."

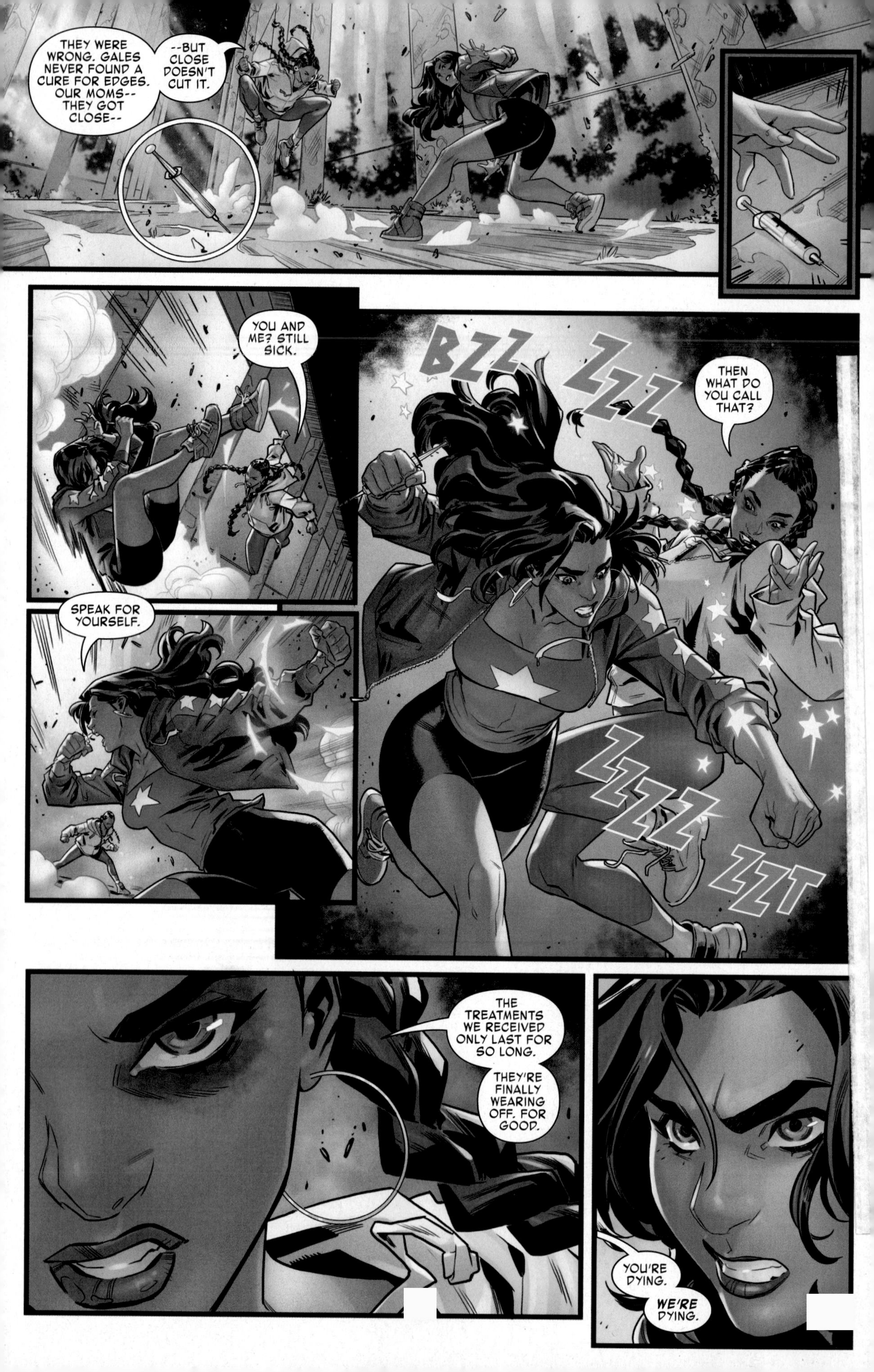
THEY WERE WRONG. GALES NEVER FOUND A CURE FOR EDGES. OUR MOMS-- THEY GOT CLOSE--
--BUT CLOSE DOESN'T CUT IT.
YOU AND ME? STILL SICK.
SPEAK FOR YOURSELF.
BZZ
ZZZ
THEN WHAT DO YOU CALL THAT?
ZZZZZT
THE TREATMENTS WE RECEIVED ONLY LAST FOR SO LONG.
THEY'RE FINALLY WEARING OFF. FOR GOOD.
YOU'RE DYING.
WE'RE DYING.

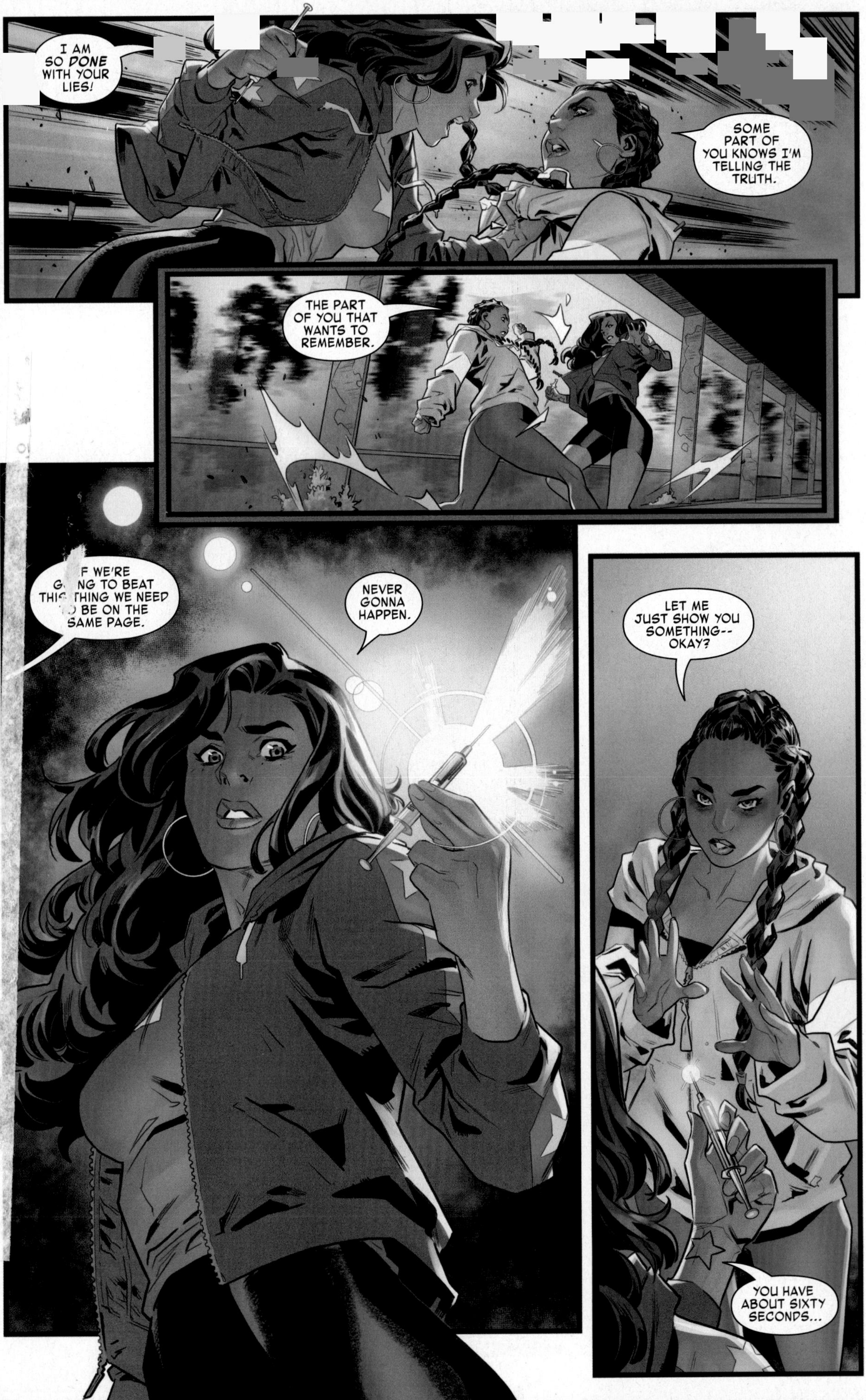
I AM SO DONE WITH YOUR LIES!
SOME PART OF YOU KNOWS I'M TELLING THE TRUTH.
THE PART OF YOU THAT WANTS TO REMEMBER.
F WE'RE G NG TO BEAT THIS THING WE NEED O BE ON THE SAME PAGE.
NEVER GONNA HAPPEN.
LET ME JUST SHOW YOU SOMETHING-- OKAY?
YOU HAVE ABOUT SIXTY SECONDS...

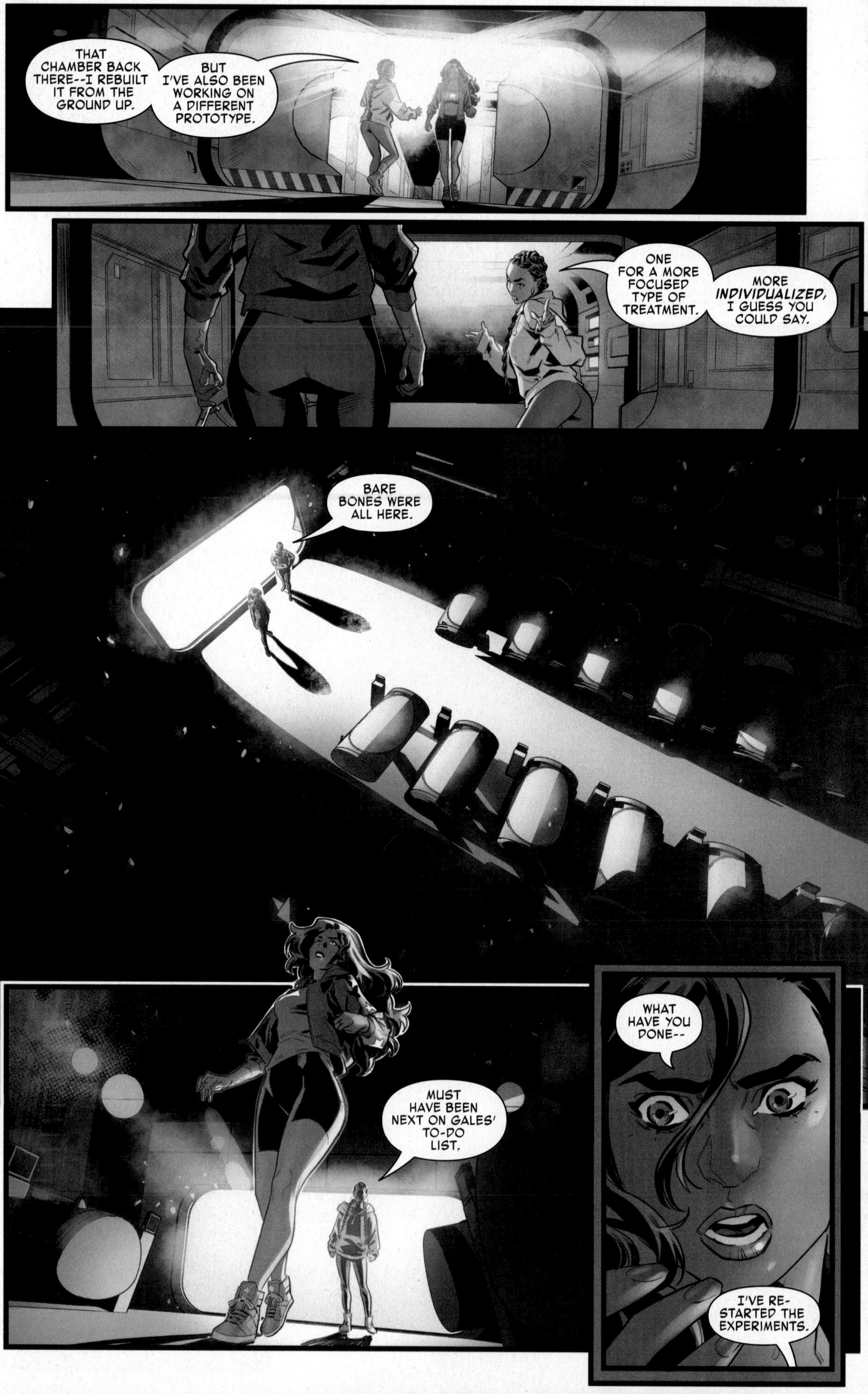
THAT CHAMBER BACK THERE--I REBUILT IT FROM THE GROUND UP.
BUT I'VE ALSO BEEN WORKING ON A DIFFERENT PROTOTYPE.
ONE FOR A MORE FOCUSED TYPE OF TREATMENT.
MORE *INDIVIDUALIZED*, I GUESS YOU COULD SAY.
BARE BONES WERE ALL HERE.
MUST HAVE BEEN NEXT ON GALES' TO-DO LIST.
WHAT HAVE YOU DONE--
I'VE RE-STARTED THE EXPERIMENTS.

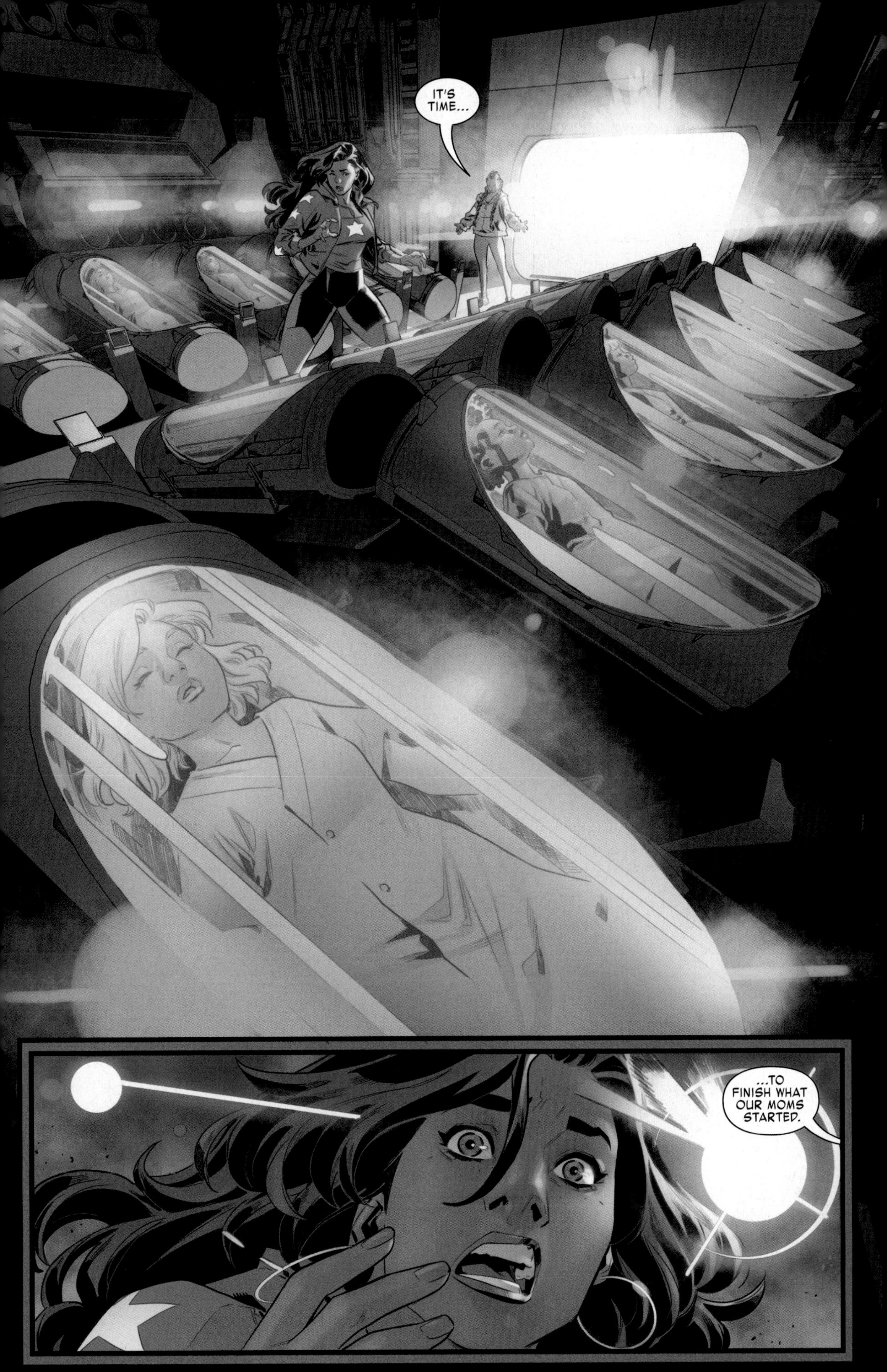
IT'S TIME...
...TO FINISH WHAT OUR MOMS STARTED.

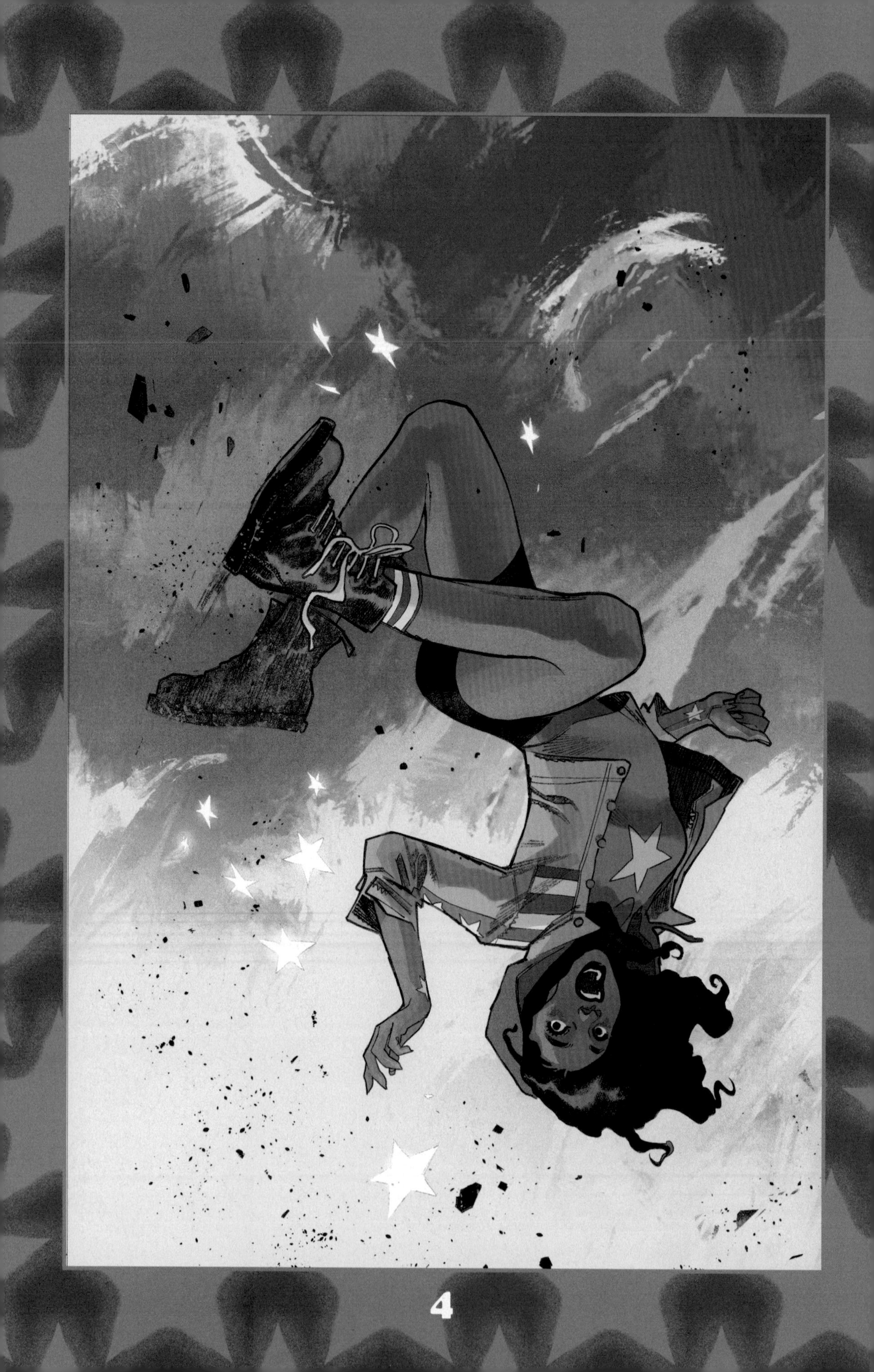

4

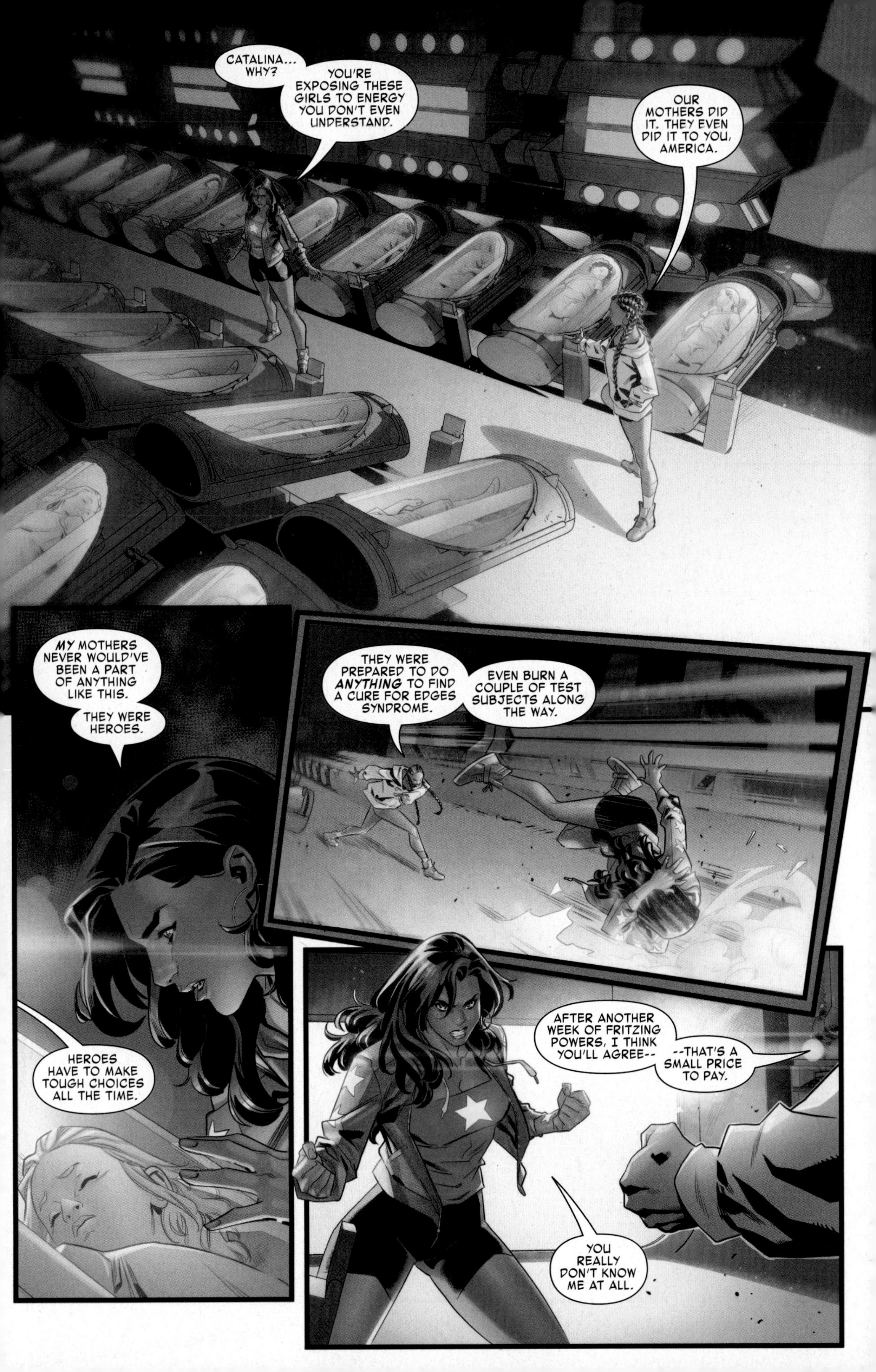
CATALINA... WHY?
YOU'RE EXPOSING THESE GIRLS TO ENERGY YOU DON'T EVEN UNDERSTAND.
OUR MOTHERS DID IT. THEY EVEN DID IT TO YOU, AMERICA.
MY MOTHERS NEVER WOULD'VE BEEN A PART OF ANYTHING LIKE THIS.
THEY WERE HEROES.
THEY WERE PREPARED TO DO ANYTHING TO FIND A CURE FOR EDGES SYNDROME.
EVEN BURN A COUPLE OF TEST SUBJECTS ALONG THE WAY.
HEROES HAVE TO MAKE TOUGH CHOICES ALL THE TIME.
AFTER ANOTHER WEEK OF FRITZING POWERS, I THINK YOU'LL AGREE--
--THAT'S A SMALL PRICE TO PAY.
YOU REALLY DON'T KNOW ME AT ALL.

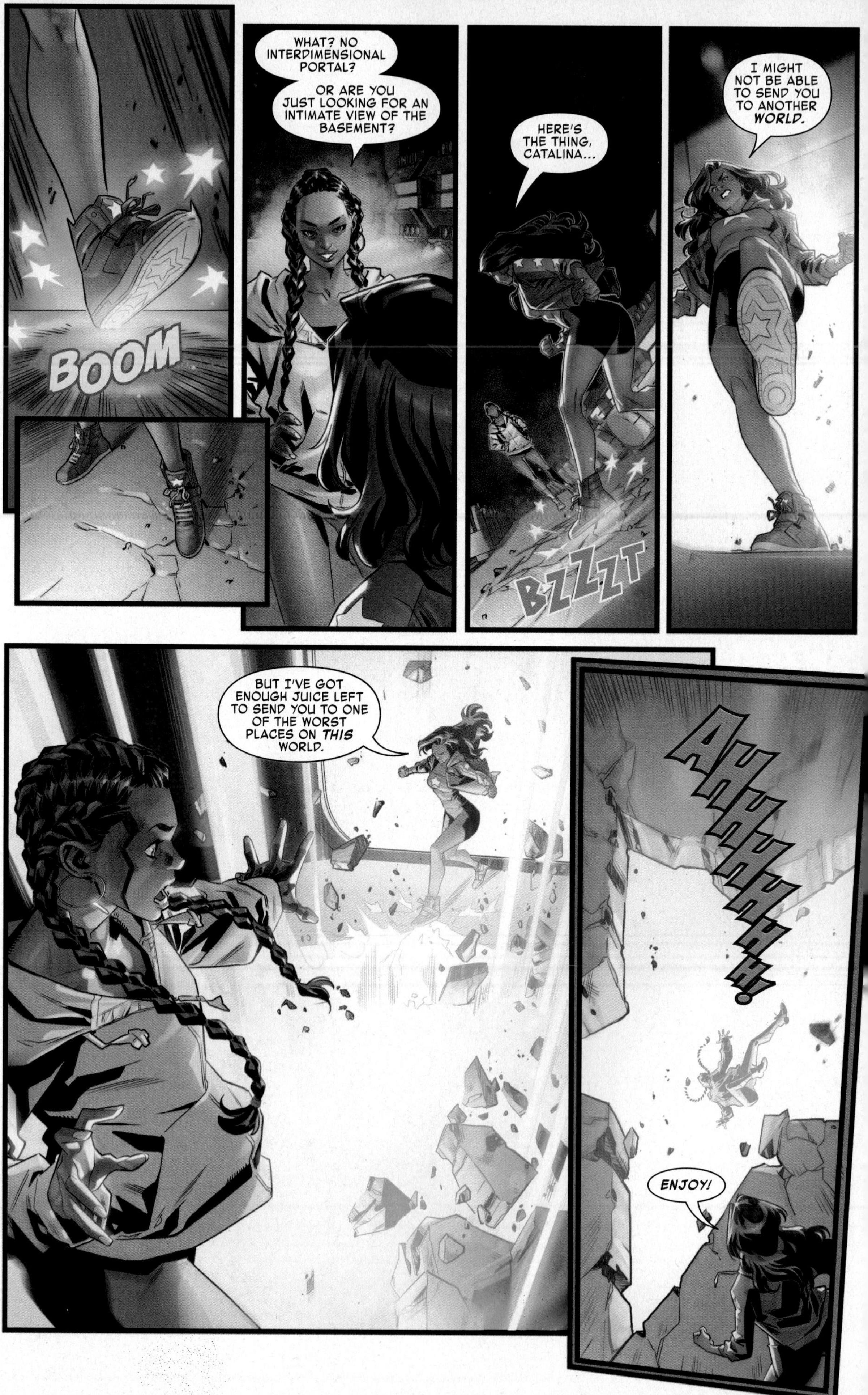
BOOM
WHAT? NO INTERDIMENSIONAL PORTAL?
OR ARE YOU JUST LOOKING FOR AN INTIMATE VIEW OF THE BASEMENT?
HERE'S THE THING, CATALINA...
BZZZZT
I MIGHT NOT BE ABLE TO SEND YOU TO ANOTHER WORLD.
BUT I'VE GOT ENOUGH JUICE LEFT TO SEND YOU TO ONE OF THE WORST PLACES ON THIS WORLD.
AHHHHHHH!
ENJOY!

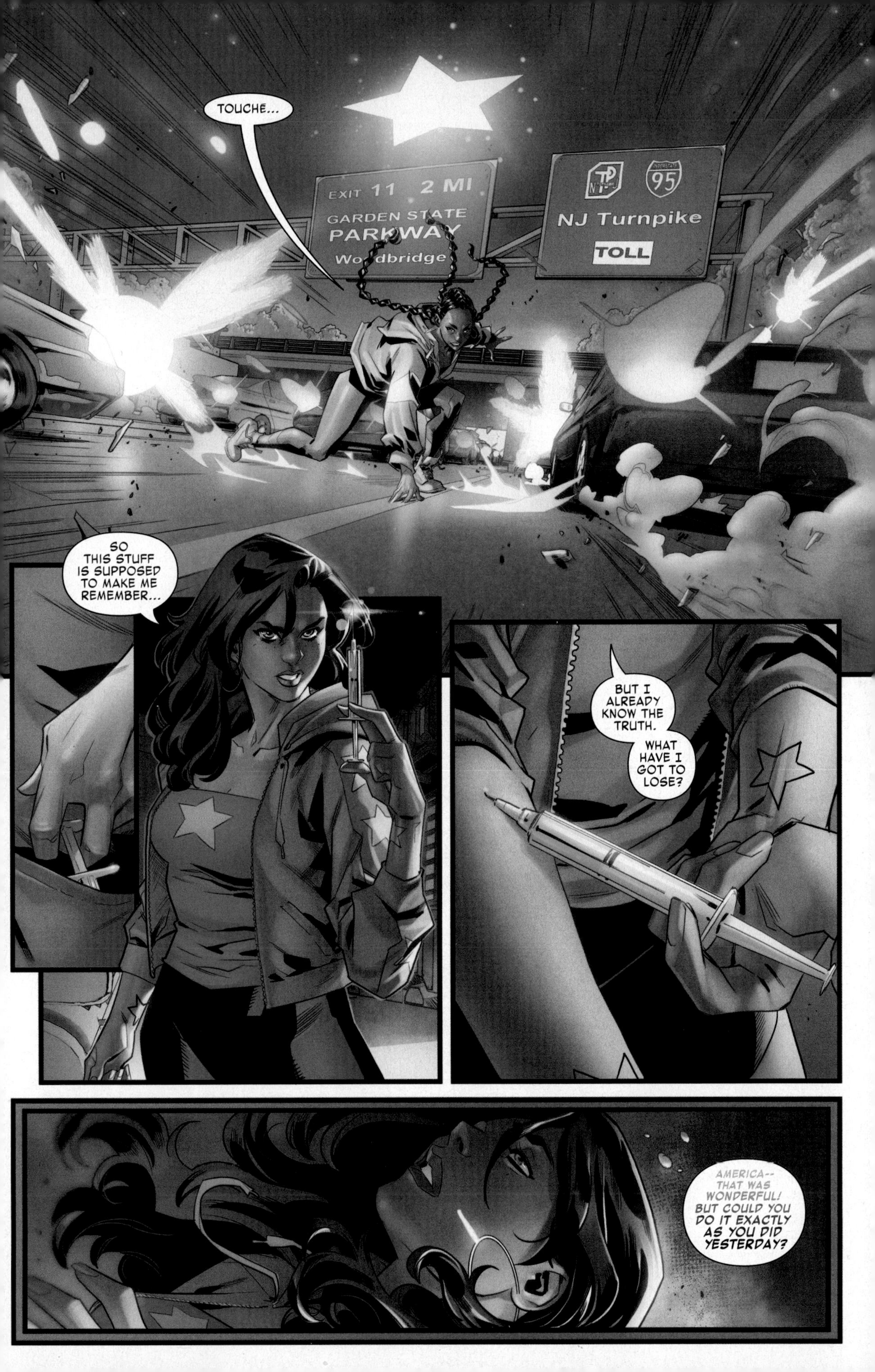
TOUCHE...
EXIT 11 2 MI
GARDEN STATE
PARKWAY
Woodbridge
95
NJ Turnpike
TOLL
SO THIS STUFF IS SUPPOSED TO MAKE ME REMEMBER...
BUT I ALREADY KNOW THE TRUTH.
WHAT HAVE I GOT TO LOSE?
AMERICA-- THAT WAS WONDERFUL! BUT COULD YOU DO IT EXACTLY AS YOU DID YESTERDAY?

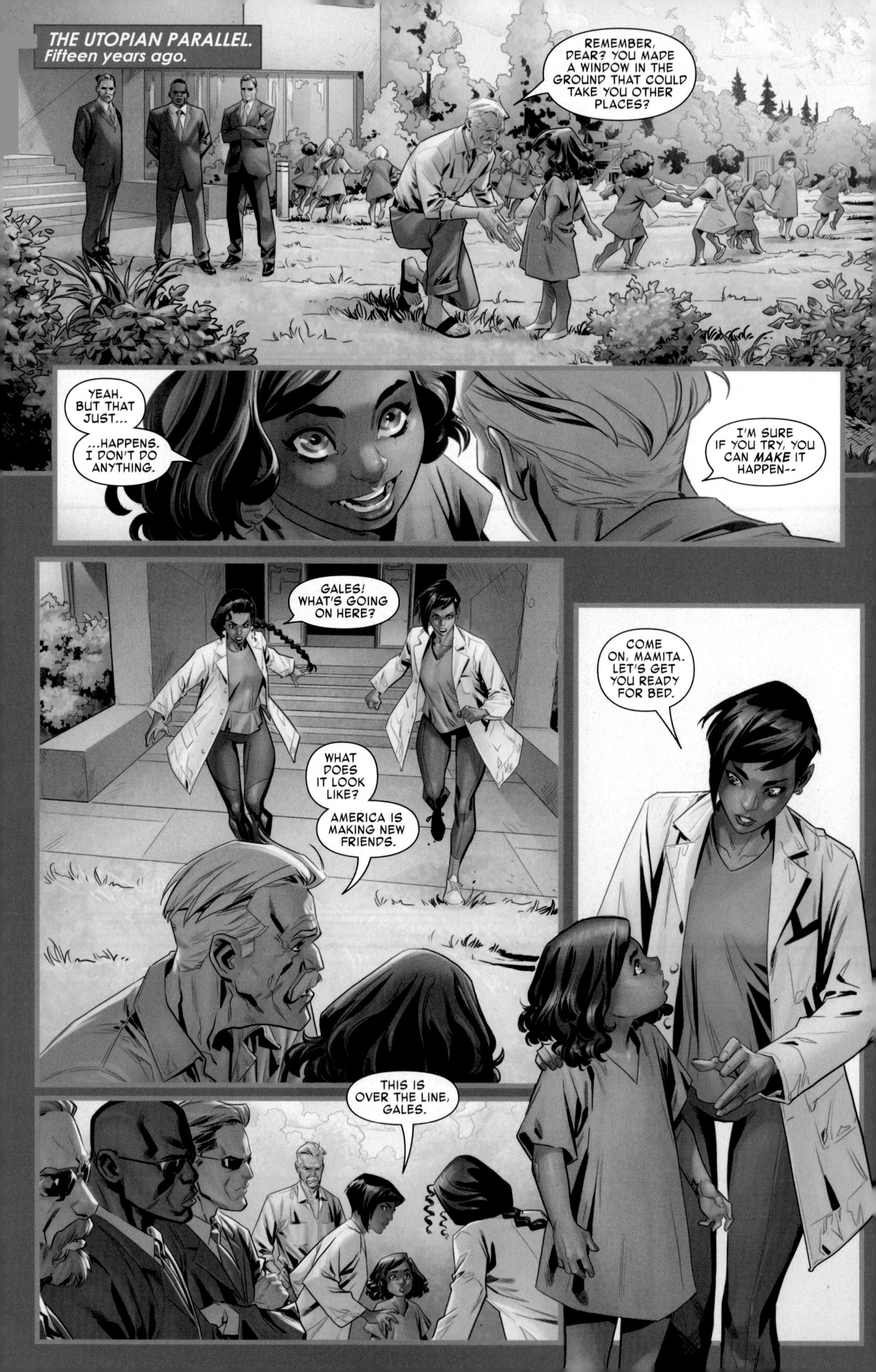
THE UTOPIAN PARALLEL.
Fifteen years ago.
REMEMBER, DEAR? YOU MADE A WINDOW IN THE GROUND THAT COULD TAKE YOU OTHER PLACES?
YEAH. BUT THAT JUST...
...HAPPENS. I DON'T DO ANYTHING.
I'M SURE IF YOU TRY, YOU CAN MAKE IT HAPPEN--
GALES! WHAT'S GOING ON HERE?
WHAT DOES IT LOOK LIKE?
AMERICA IS MAKING NEW FRIENDS.
COME ON, MAMITA. LET'S GET YOU READY FOR BED.
THIS IS OVER THE LINE, GALES.

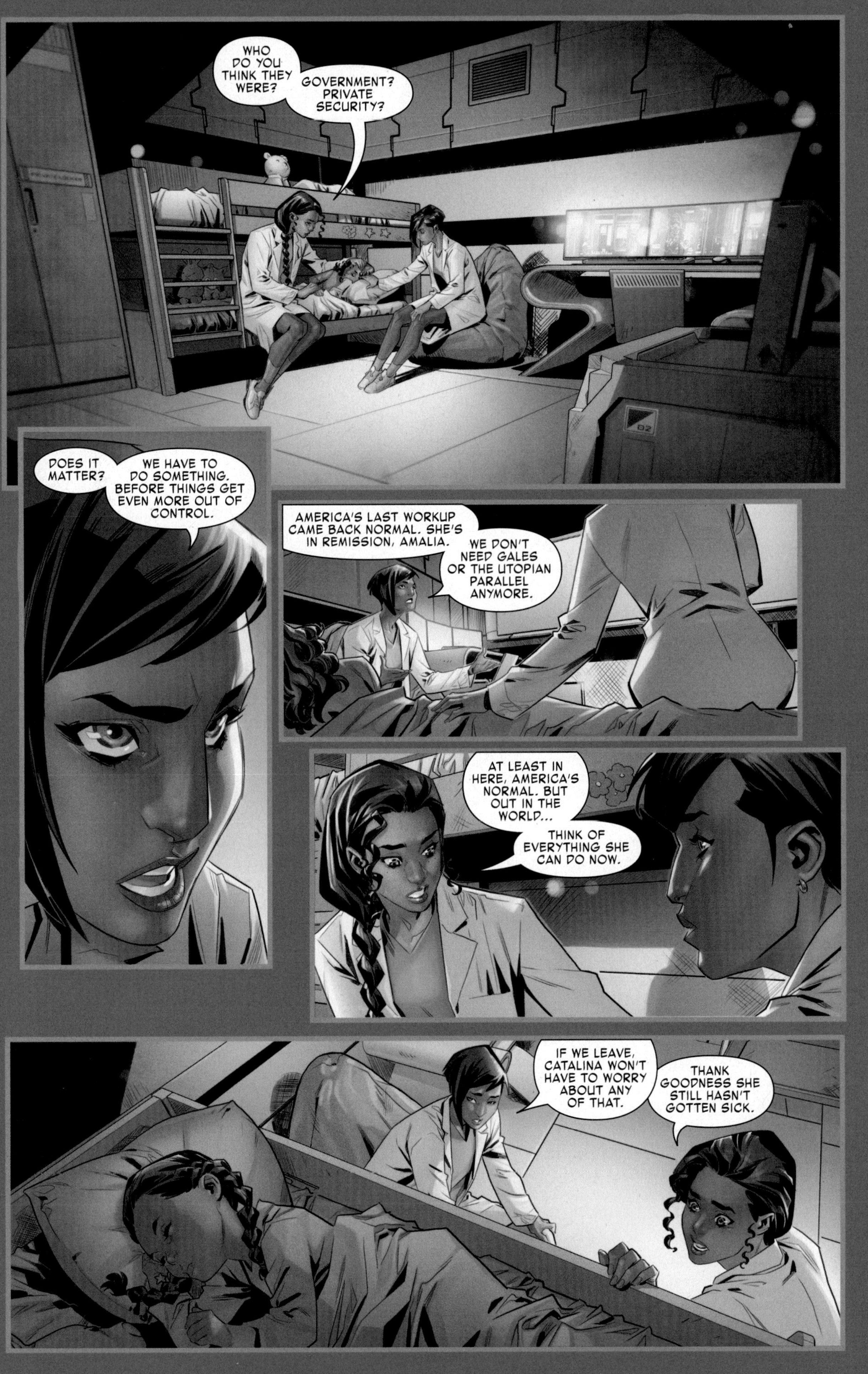
WHO DO YOU THINK THEY WERE?
GOVERNMENT? PRIVATE SECURITY?
DOES IT MATTER?
WE HAVE TO DO SOMETHING. BEFORE THINGS GET EVEN MORE OUT OF CONTROL.
AMERICA'S LAST WORKUP CAME BACK NORMAL. SHE'S IN REMISSION, AMALIA.
WE DON'T NEED GALES OR THE UTOPIAN PARALLEL ANYMORE.
AT LEAST IN HERE, AMERICA'S NORMAL. BUT OUT IN THE WORLD...
THINK OF EVERYTHING SHE CAN DO NOW.
IF WE LEAVE, CATALINA WON'T HAVE TO WORRY ABOUT ANY OF THAT.
THANK GOODNESS SHE STILL HASN'T GOTTEN SICK.

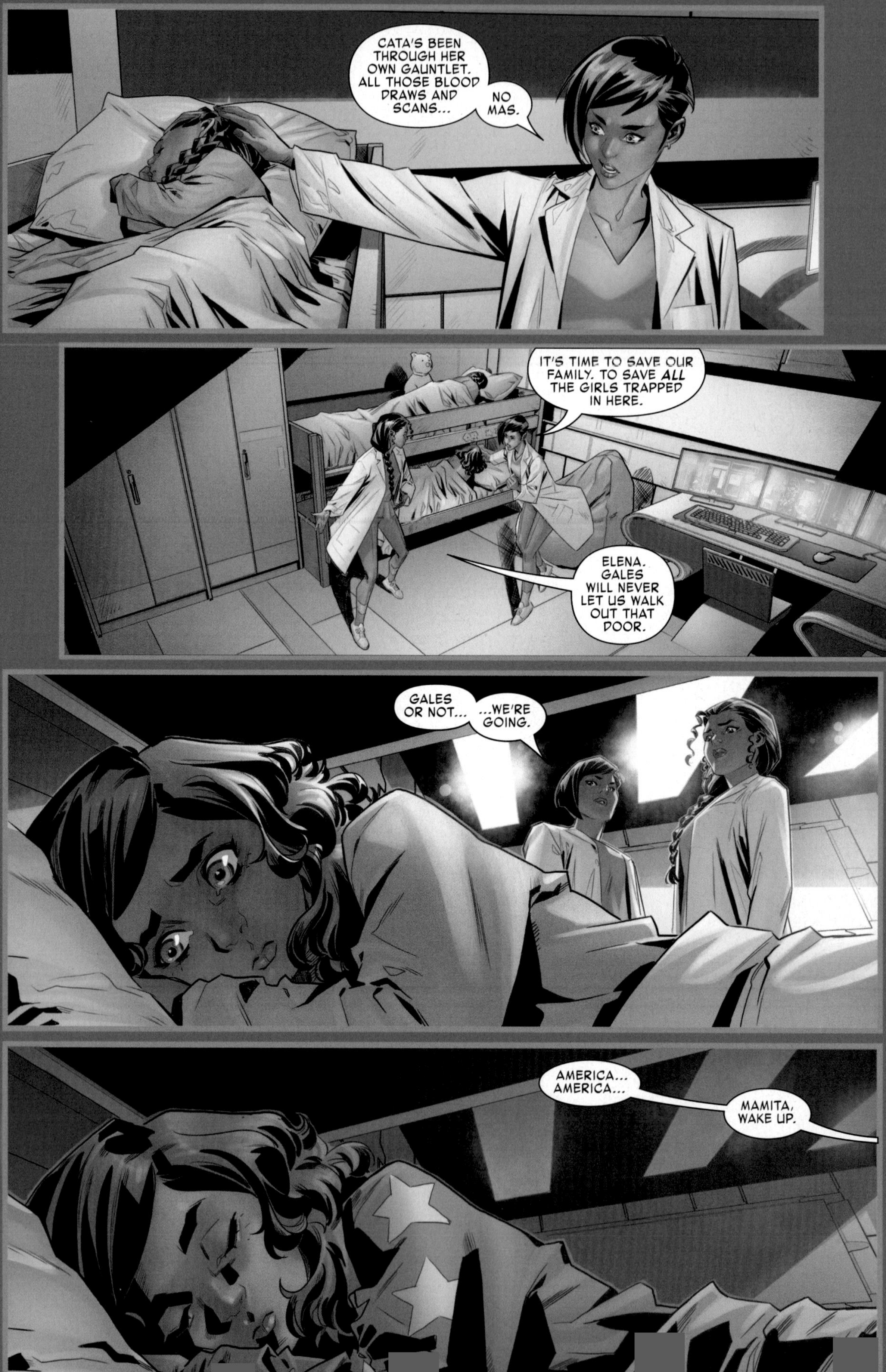
CATA'S BEEN THROUGH HER OWN GAUNTLET. ALL THOSE BLOOD DRAWS AND SCANS...
NO MAS.
IT'S TIME TO SAVE OUR FAMILY. TO SAVE ALL THE GIRLS TRAPPED IN HERE.
ELENA. GALES WILL NEVER LET US WALK OUT THAT DOOR.
GALES OR NOT...
...WE'RE GOING.
AMERICA... AMERICA...
MAMITA, WAKE UP.

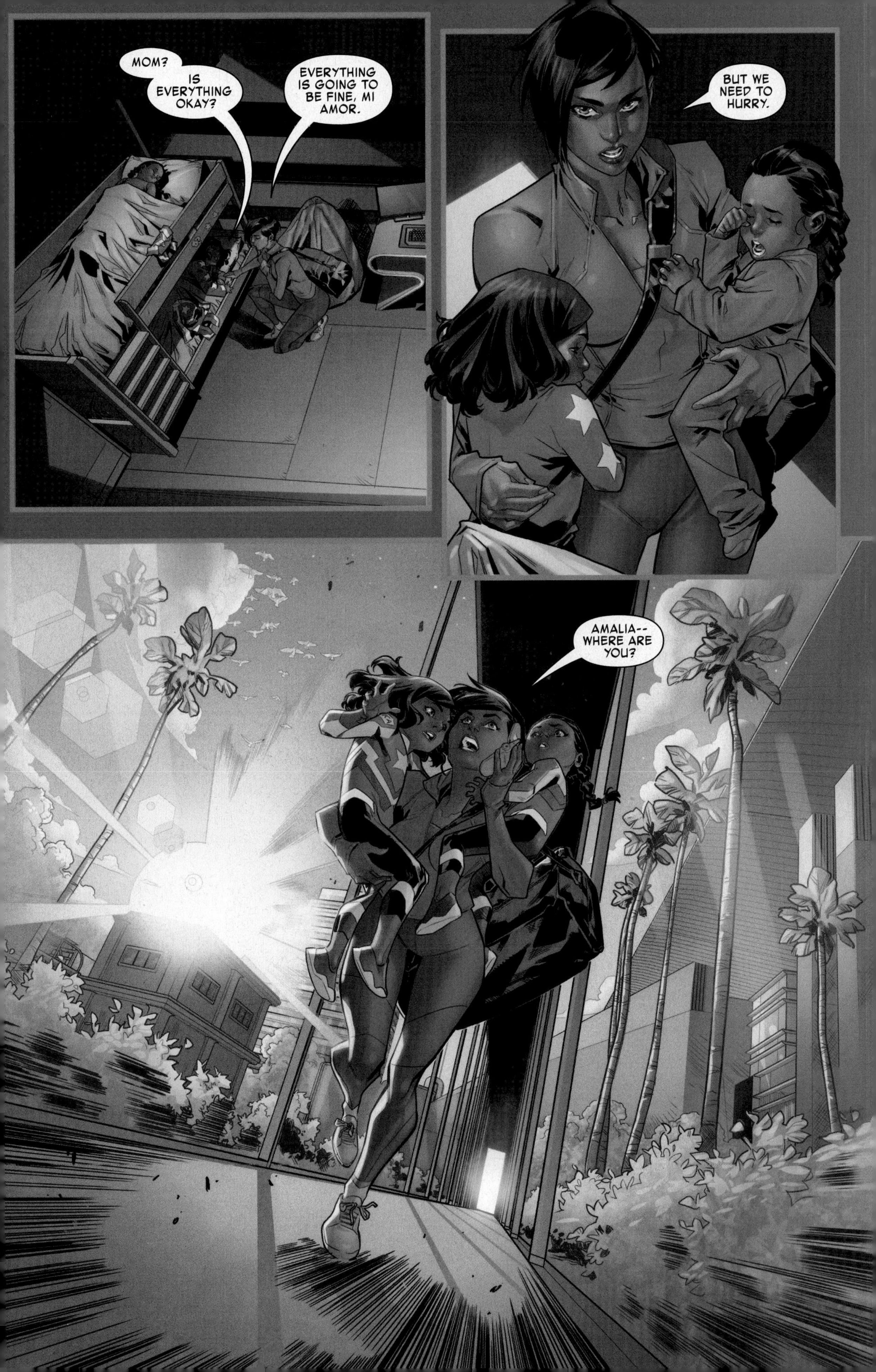
MOM?
IS EVERYTHING OKAY?
EVERYTHING IS GOING TO BE FINE, MI AMOR.
BUT WE NEED TO HURRY.
AMALIA-- WHERE ARE YOU?

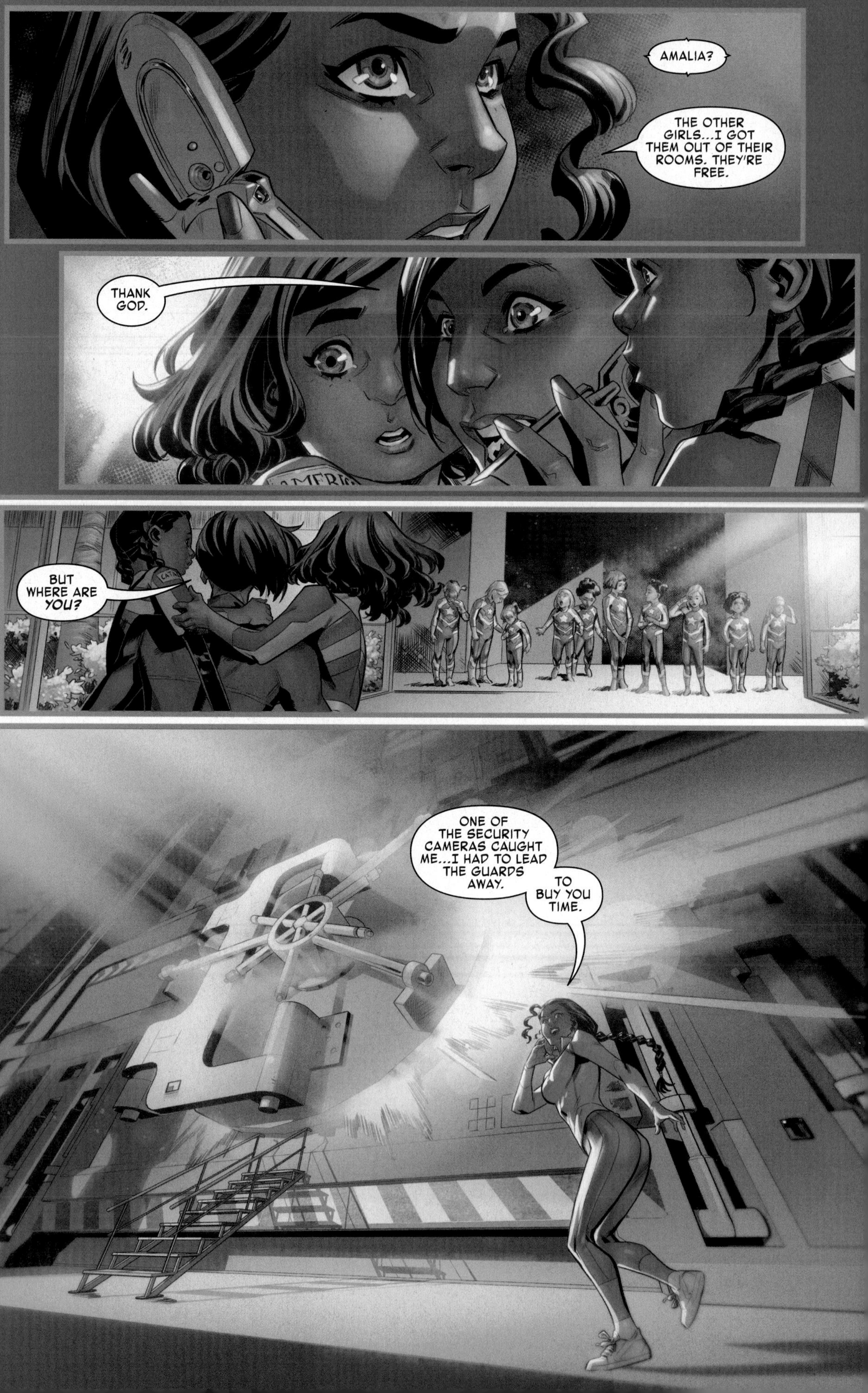

AMALIA?
THE OTHER GIRLS...I GOT THEM OUT OF THEIR ROOMS. THEY'RE FREE.
THANK GOD.
BUT WHERE ARE YOU?
ONE OF THE SECURITY CAMERAS CAUGHT ME...I HAD TO LEAD THE GUARDS AWAY.
TO BUY YOU TIME.

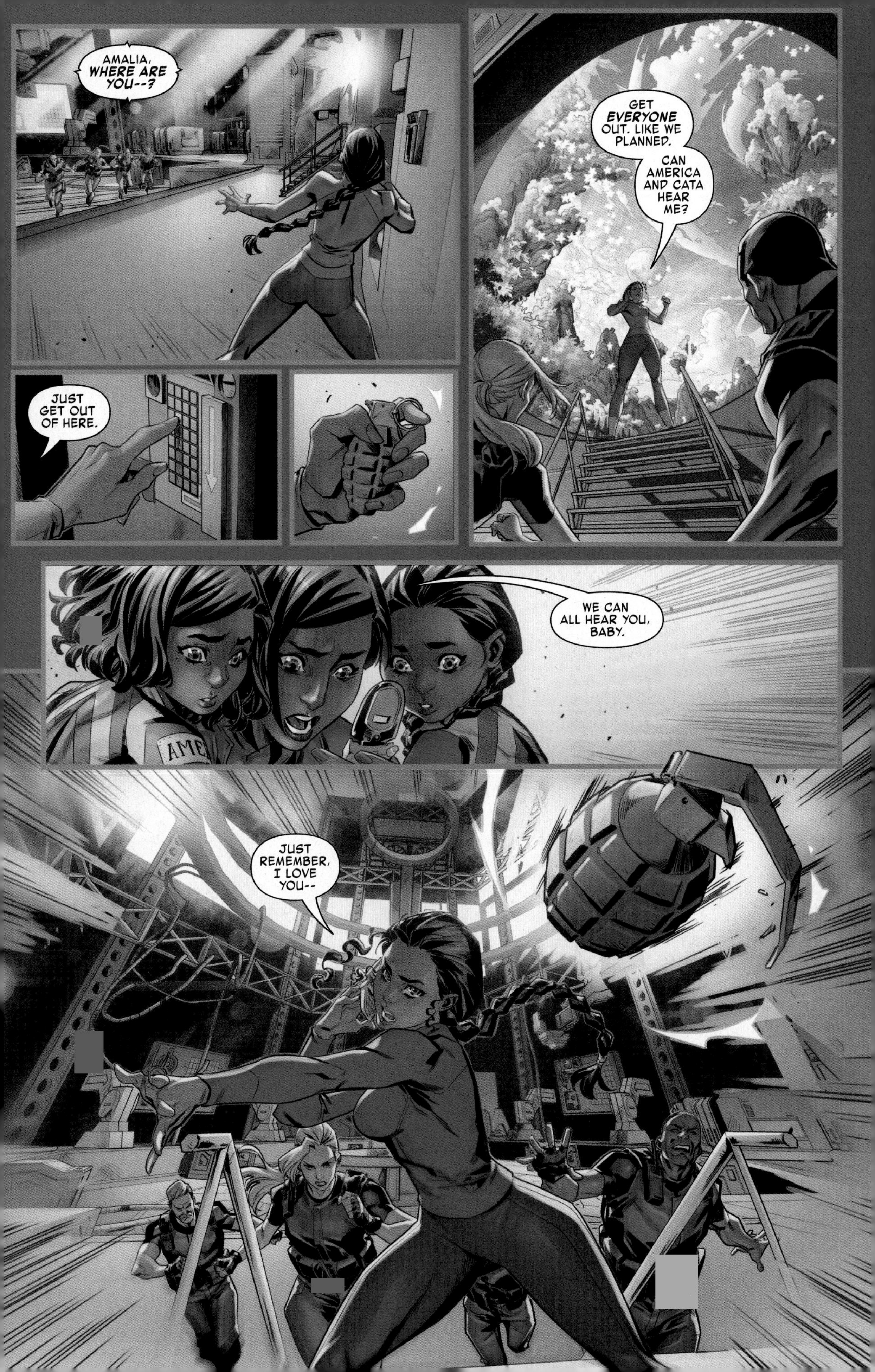
AMALIA, WHERE ARE YOU--?
GET EVERYONE OUT. LIKE WE PLANNED.
CAN AMERICA AND CATA HEAR ME?
JUST GET OUT OF HERE.
WE CAN ALL HEAR YOU, BABY.
AME
JUST REMEMBER, I LOVE YOU--

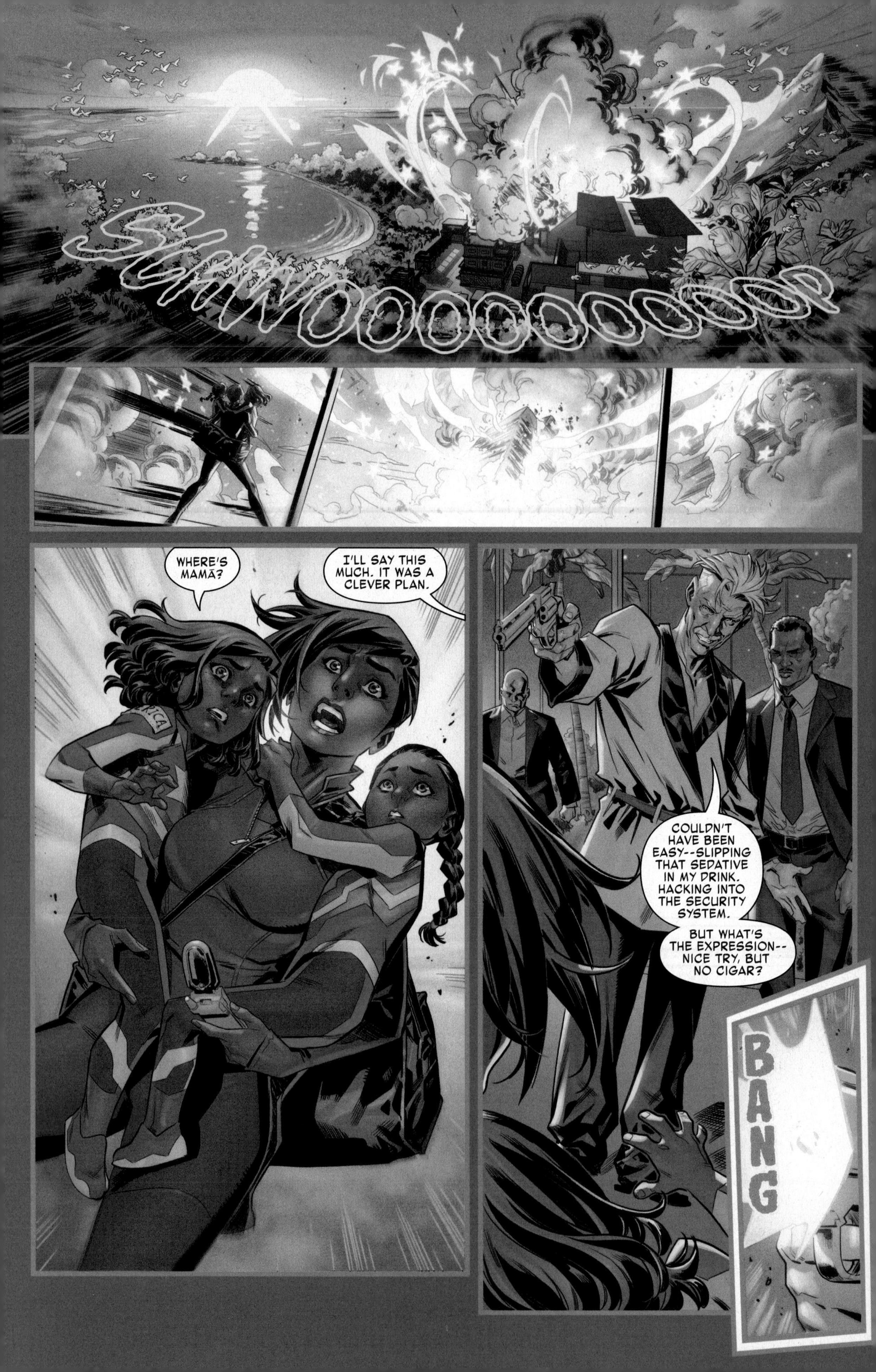
SHHWOOOOOOOOOOP
WHERE'S MAMÁ?
I'LL SAY THIS MUCH. IT WAS A CLEVER PLAN.
COULDN'T HAVE BEEN EASY--SLIPPING THAT SEDATIVE IN MY DRINK. HACKING INTO THE SECURITY SYSTEM.
BUT WHAT'S THE EXPRESSION--NICE TRY, BUT NO CIGAR?
BANG

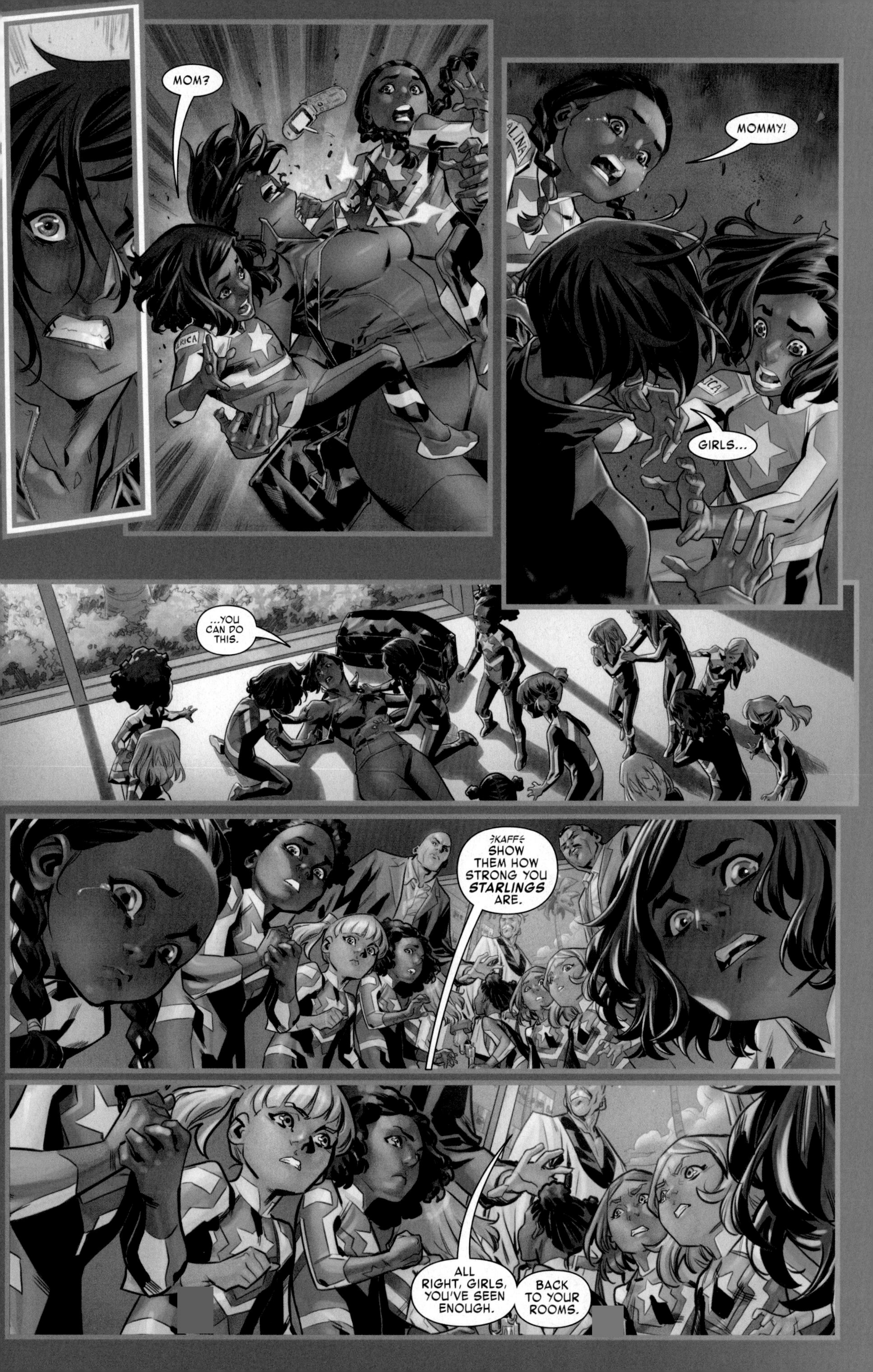
MOM?
MOMMY!
GIRLS...
...YOU CAN DO THIS.
KAFF SHOW THEM HOW STRONG YOU STARLINGS ARE.
ALL RIGHT, GIRLS, YOU'VE SEEN ENOUGH.
BACK TO YOUR ROOMS.

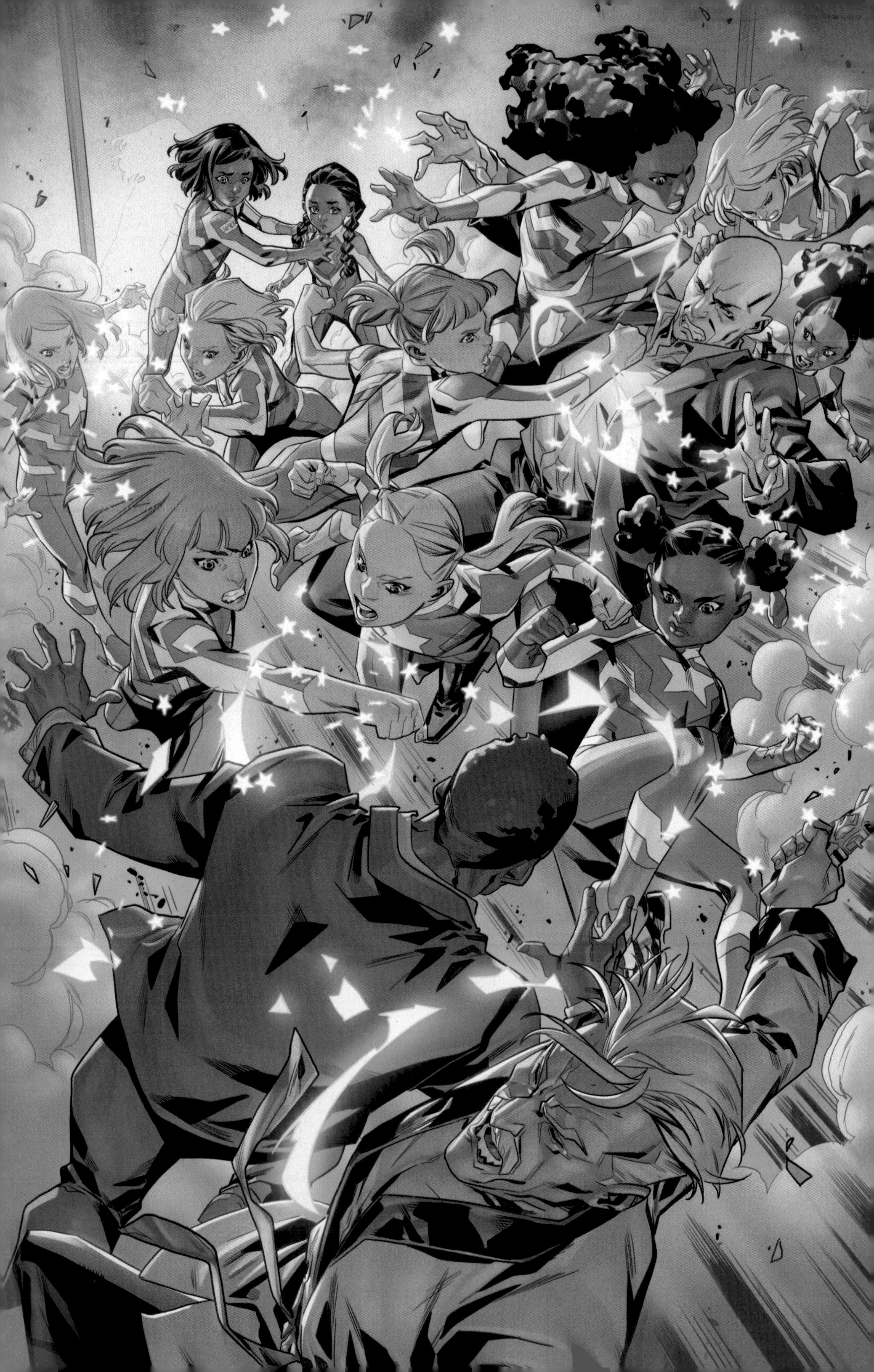

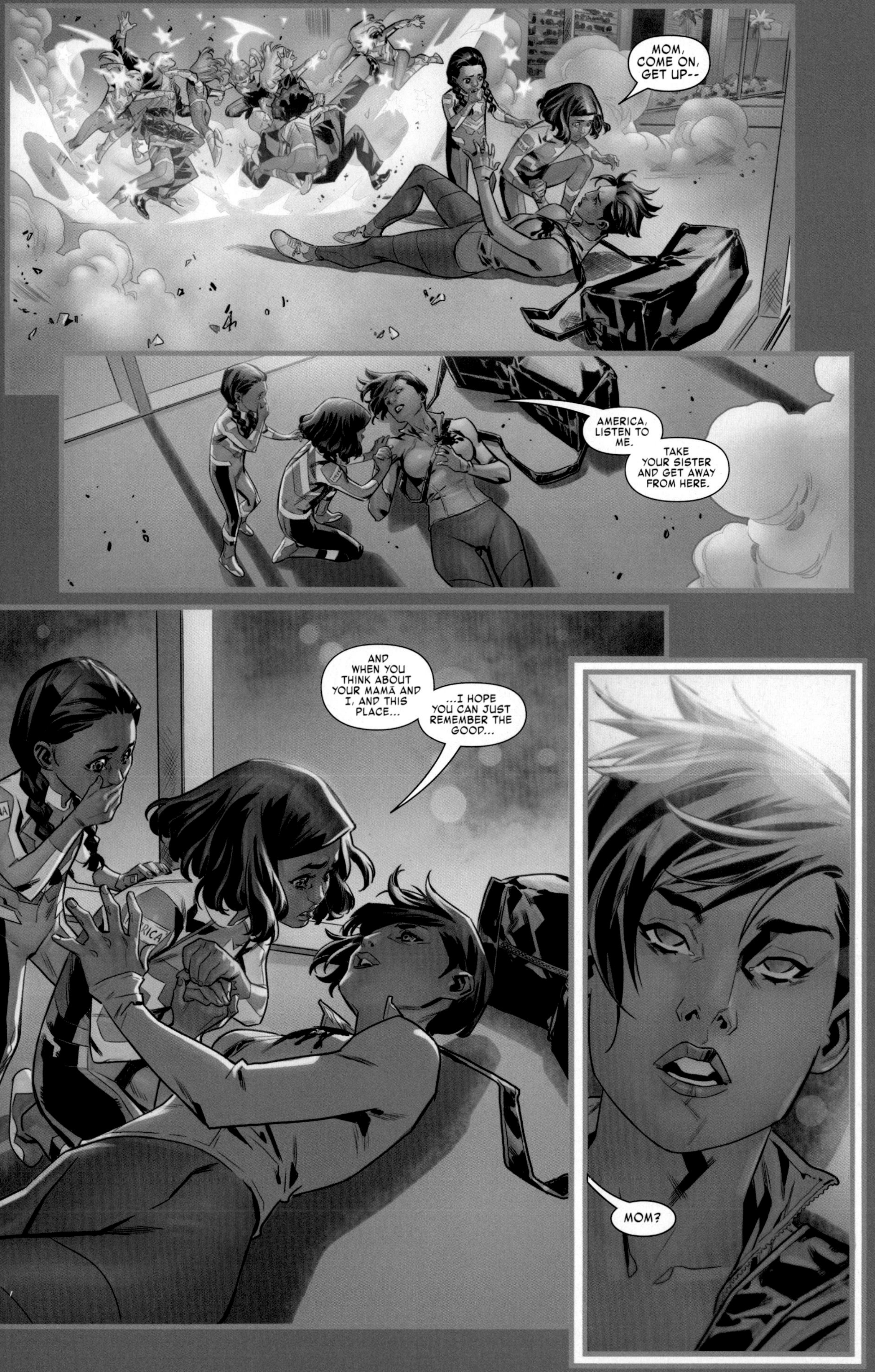
MOM, COME ON, GET UP--
AMERICA, LISTEN TO ME.
TAKE YOUR SISTER AND GET AWAY FROM HERE.
AND WHEN YOU THINK ABOUT YOUR MAMÁ AND I, AND THIS PLACE...
...I HOPE YOU CAN JUST REMEMBER THE GOOD...
MOM?

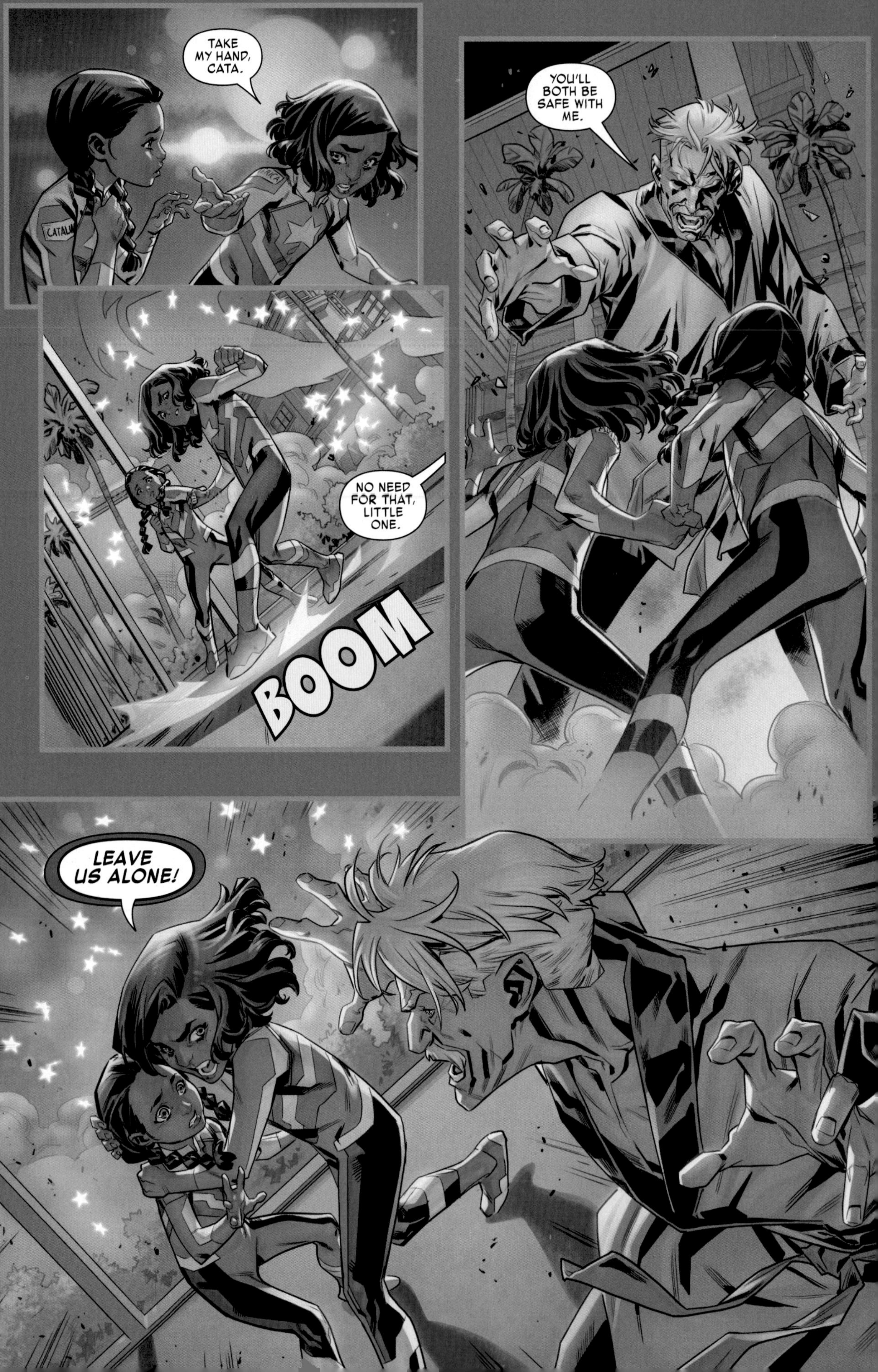
TAKE MY HAND, CATA.
YOU'LL BOTH BE SAFE WITH ME.
NO NEED FOR THAT, LITTLE ONE.
BOOM
LEAVE US ALONE!

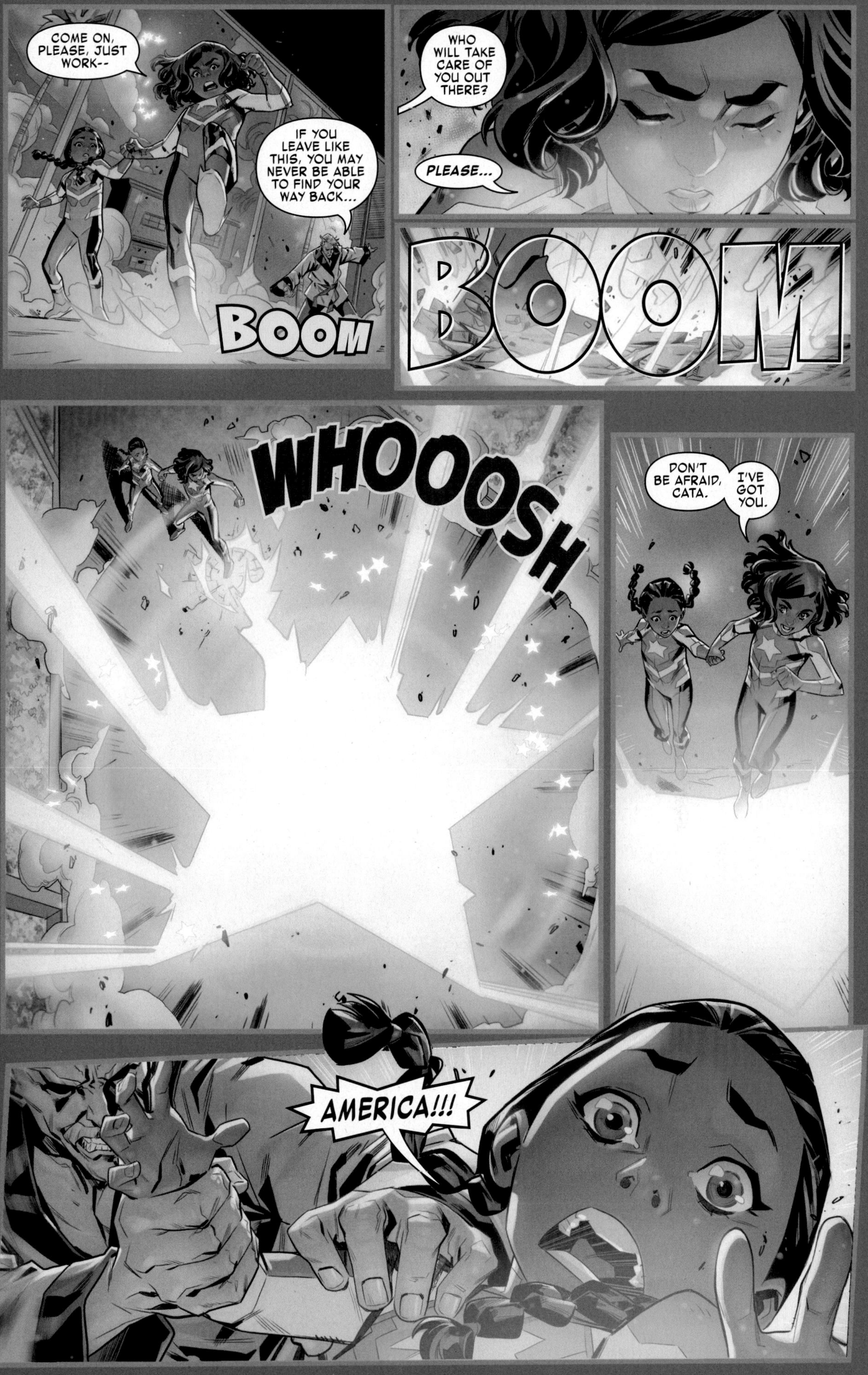
COME ON, PLEASE, JUST WORK--
IF YOU LEAVE LIKE THIS, YOU MAY NEVER BE ABLE TO FIND YOUR WAY BACK...
BOOM
WHO WILL TAKE CARE OF YOU OUT THERE?
PLEASE...
BOOM
WHOOOSH
DON'T BE AFRAID, CATA.
I'VE GOT YOU.
AMERICA!!!

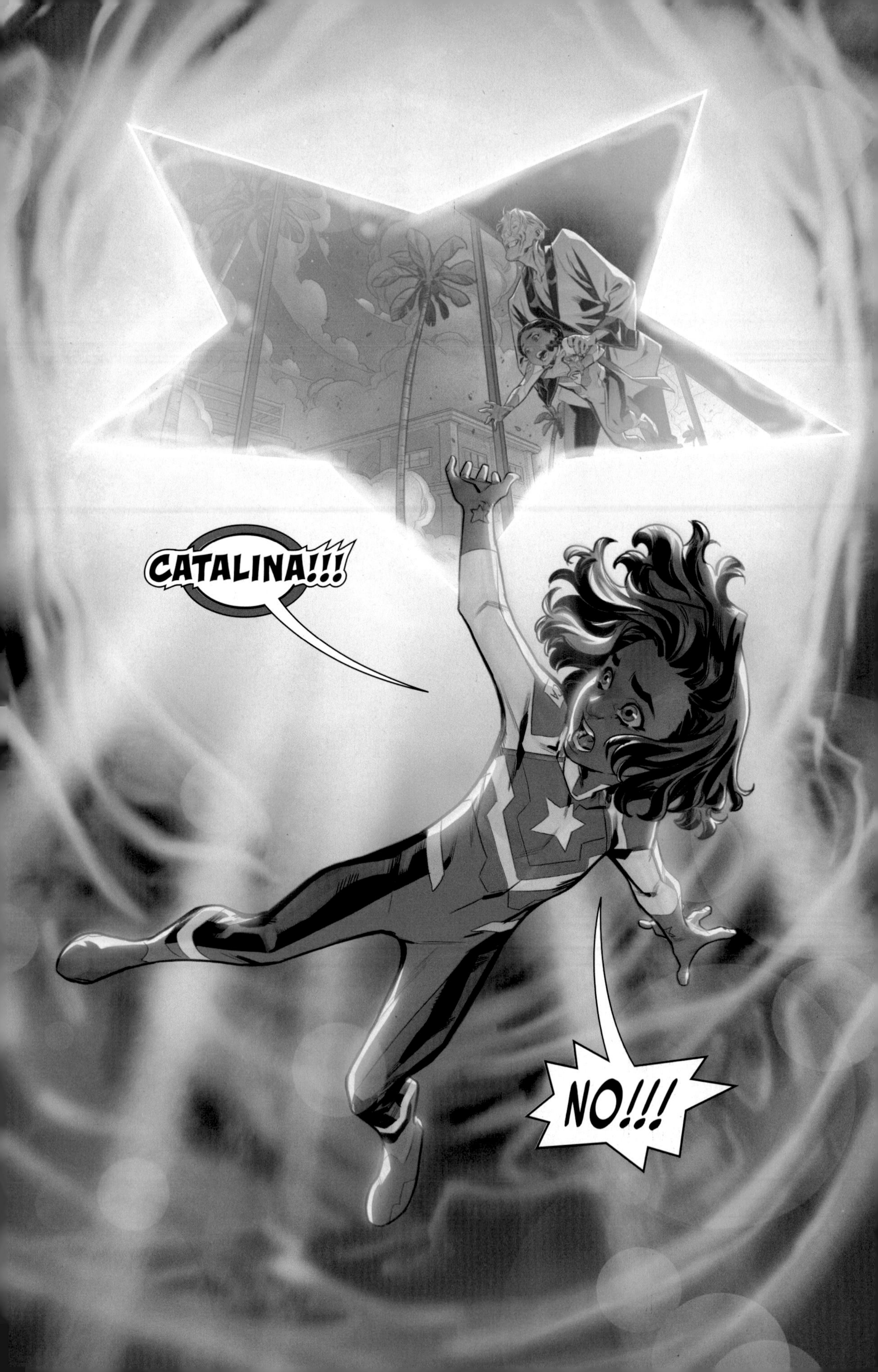
CATALINA!!!
NO!!!

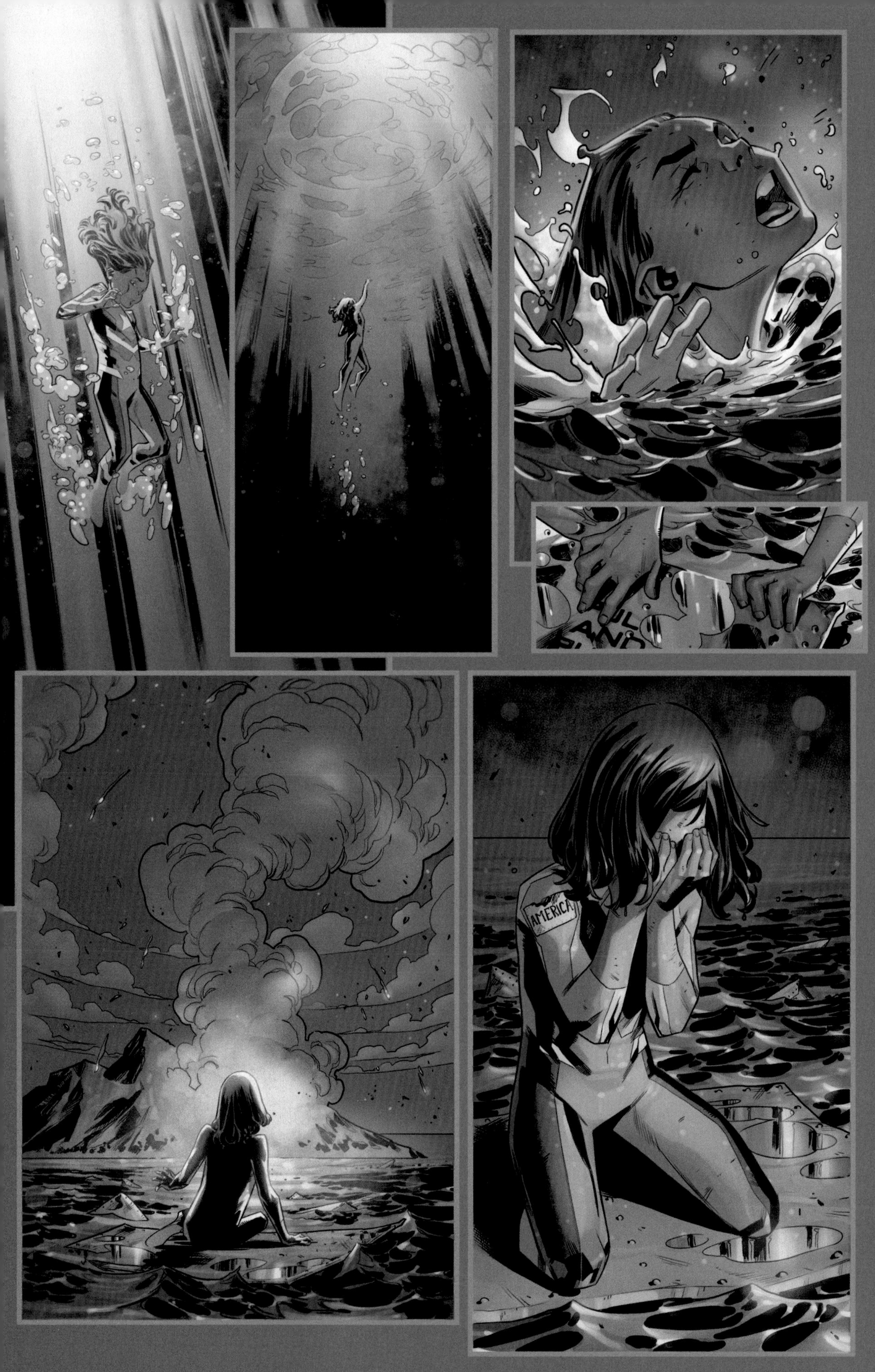
AMERICA

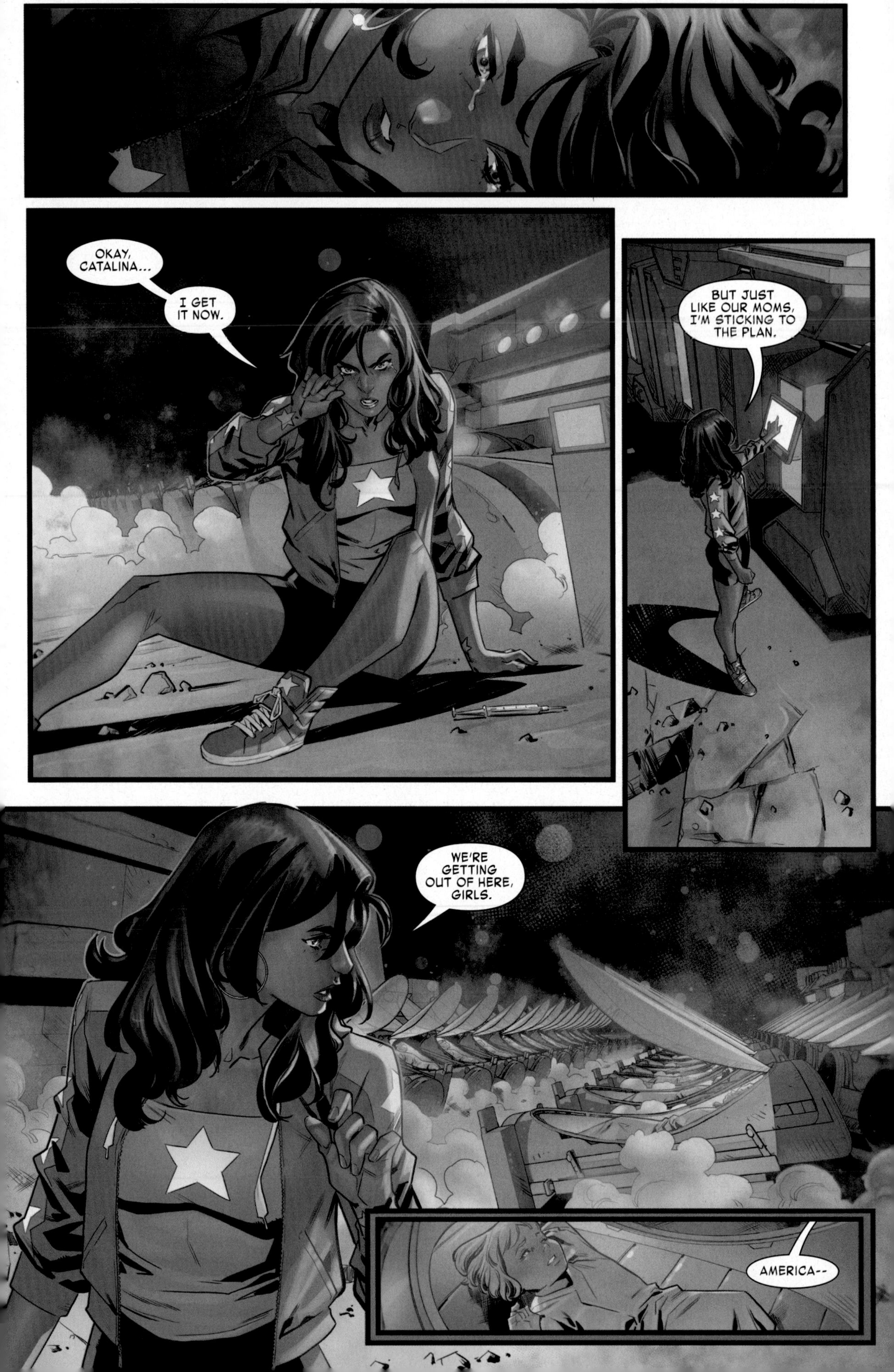
OKAY, CATALINA...
I GET IT NOW.
BUT JUST LIKE OUR MOMS, I'M STICKING TO THE PLAN.
WE'RE GETTING OUT OF HERE, GIRLS.
AMERICA--

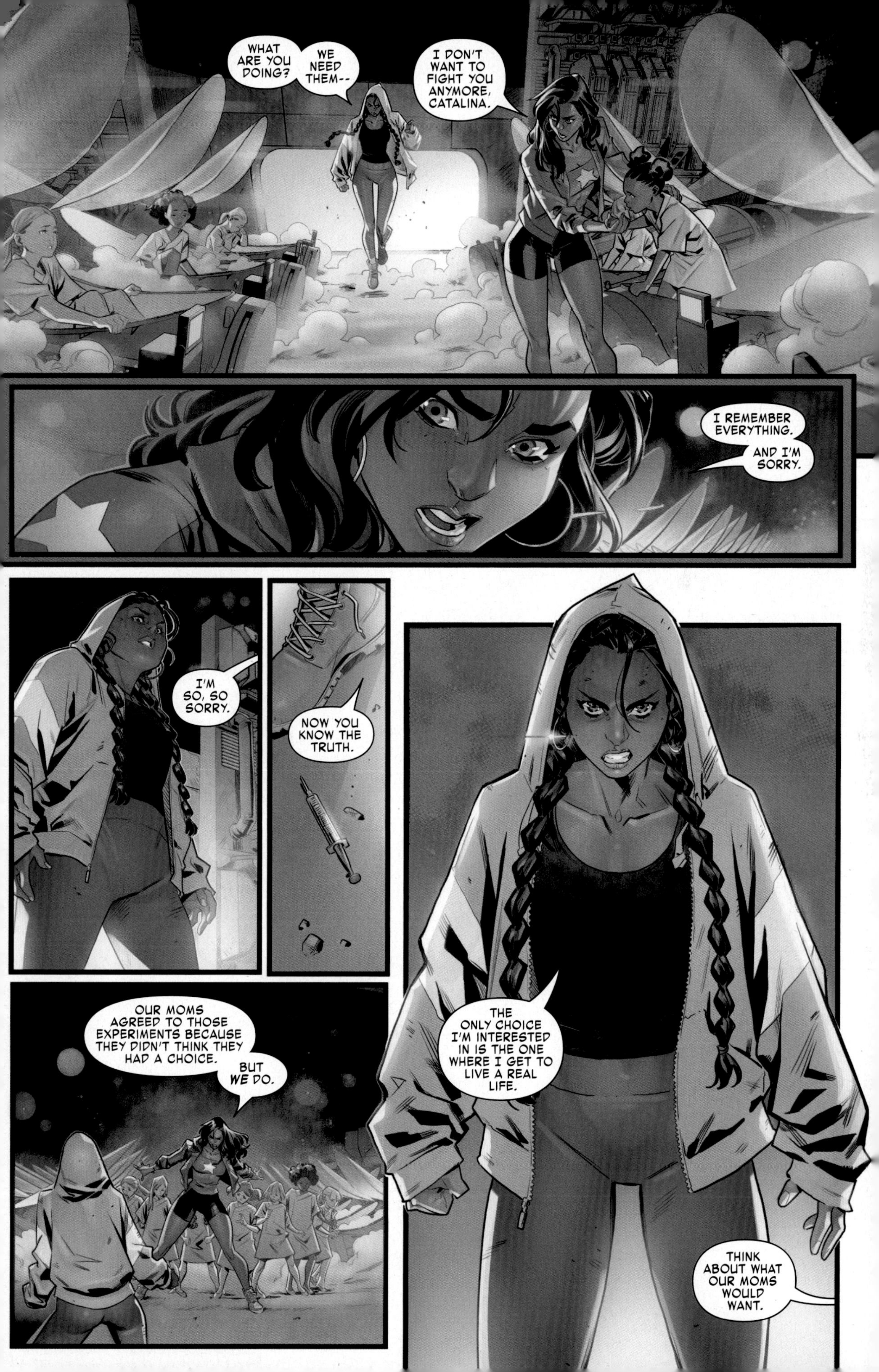
WHAT ARE YOU DOING?
WE NEED THEM--
I DON'T WANT TO FIGHT YOU ANYMORE, CATALINA.
I REMEMBER EVERYTHING.
AND I'M SORRY.
I'M SO, SO SORRY.
NOW YOU KNOW THE TRUTH.
THE ONLY CHOICE I'M INTERESTED IN IS THE ONE WHERE I GET TO LIVE A REAL LIFE.
OUR MOMS AGREED TO THOSE EXPERIMENTS BECAUSE THEY DIDN'T THINK THEY HAD A CHOICE.
BUT WE DO.
THINK ABOUT WHAT OUR MOMS WOULD WANT.

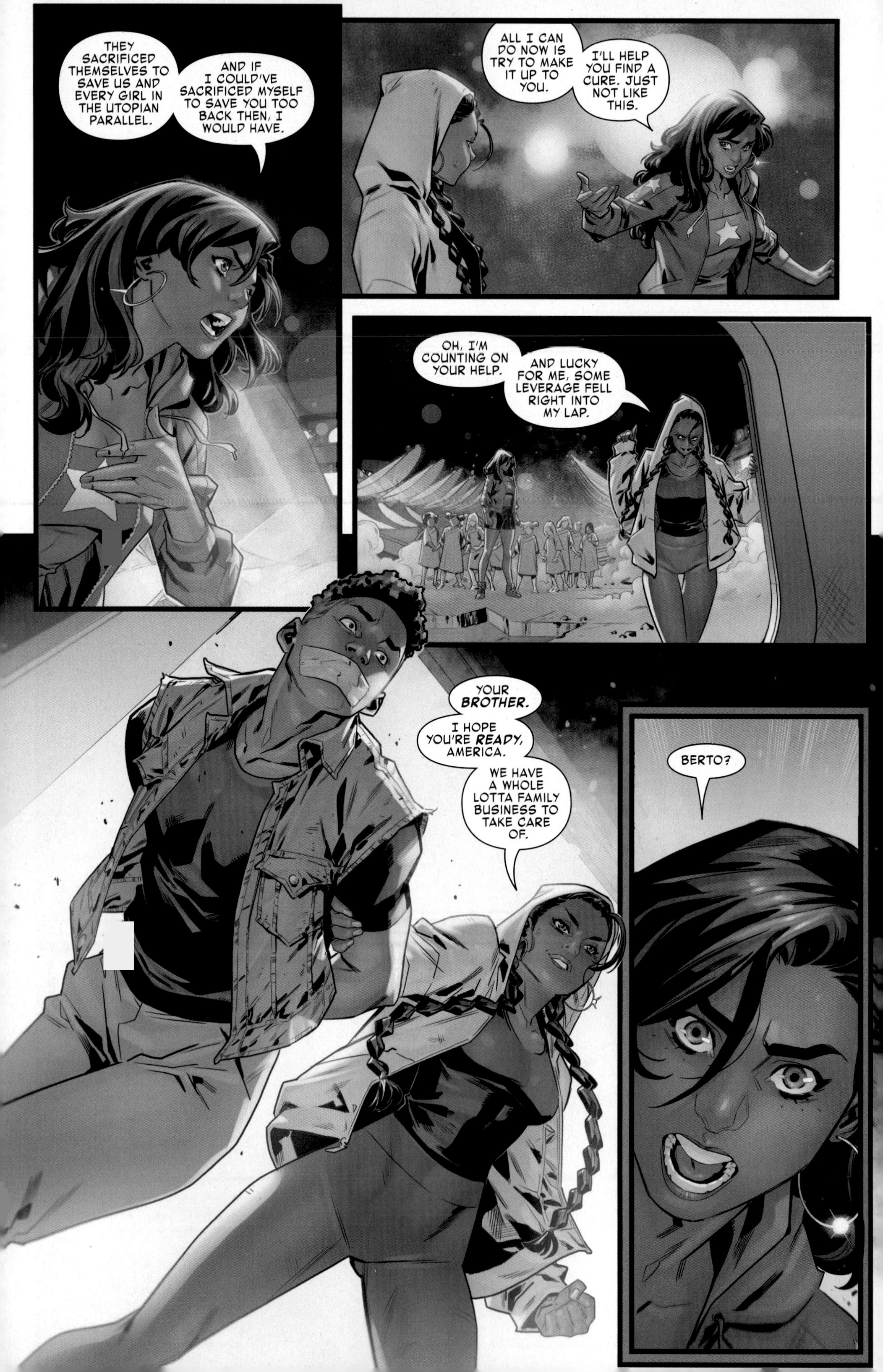
THEY SACRIFICED THEMSELVES TO SAVE US AND EVERY GIRL IN THE UTOPIAN PARALLEL.
AND IF I COULD'VE SACRIFICED MYSELF TO SAVE YOU TOO BACK THEN, I WOULD HAVE.
ALL I CAN DO NOW IS TRY TO MAKE IT UP TO YOU.
I'LL HELP YOU FIND A CURE. JUST NOT LIKE THIS.
OH, I'M COUNTING ON YOUR HELP.
AND LUCKY FOR ME, SOME LEVERAGE FELL RIGHT INTO MY LAP.
YOUR BROTHER.
I HOPE YOU'RE READY, AMERICA.
WE HAVE A WHOLE LOTTA FAMILY BUSINESS TO TAKE CARE OF.
BERTO?

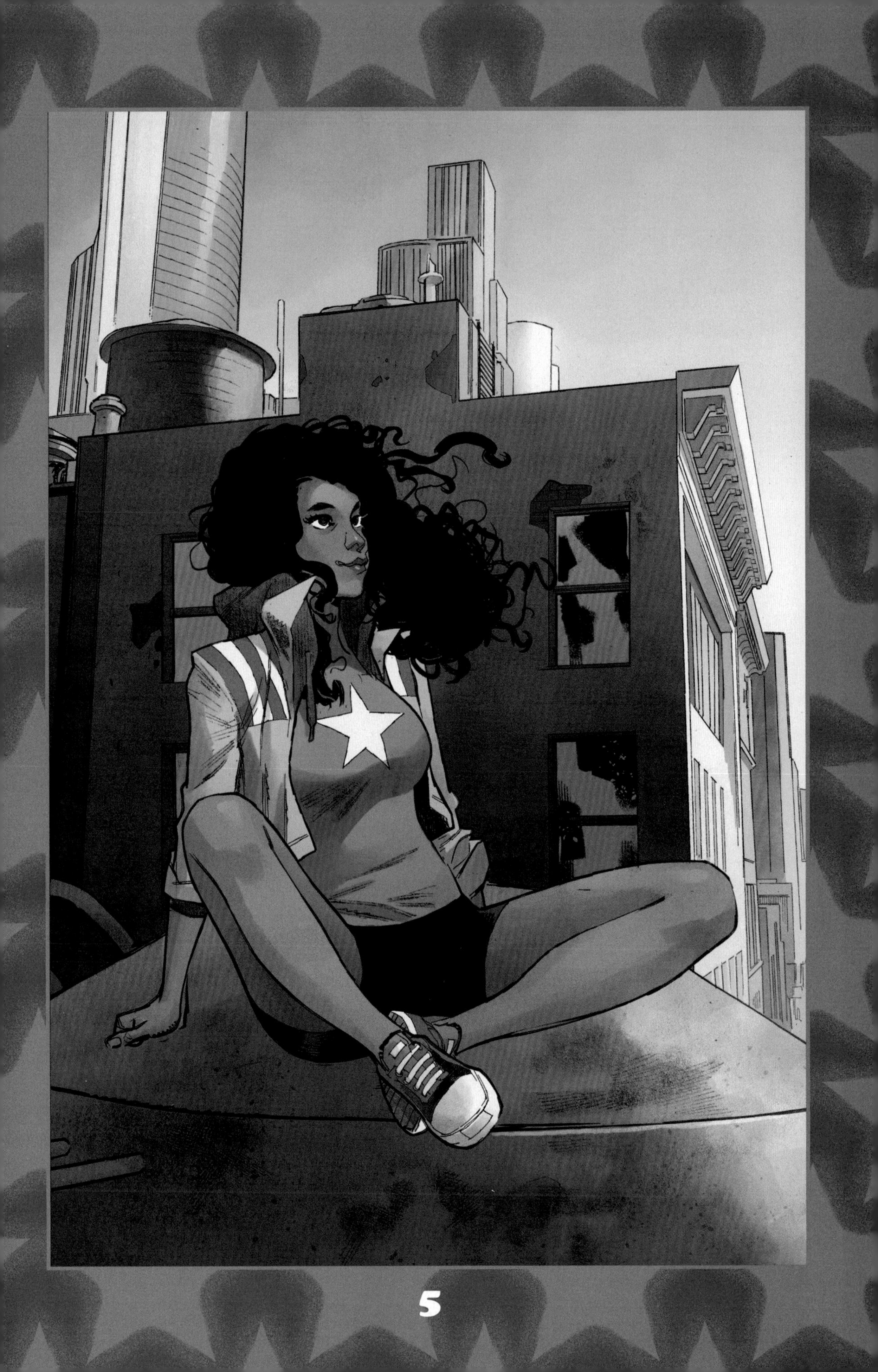

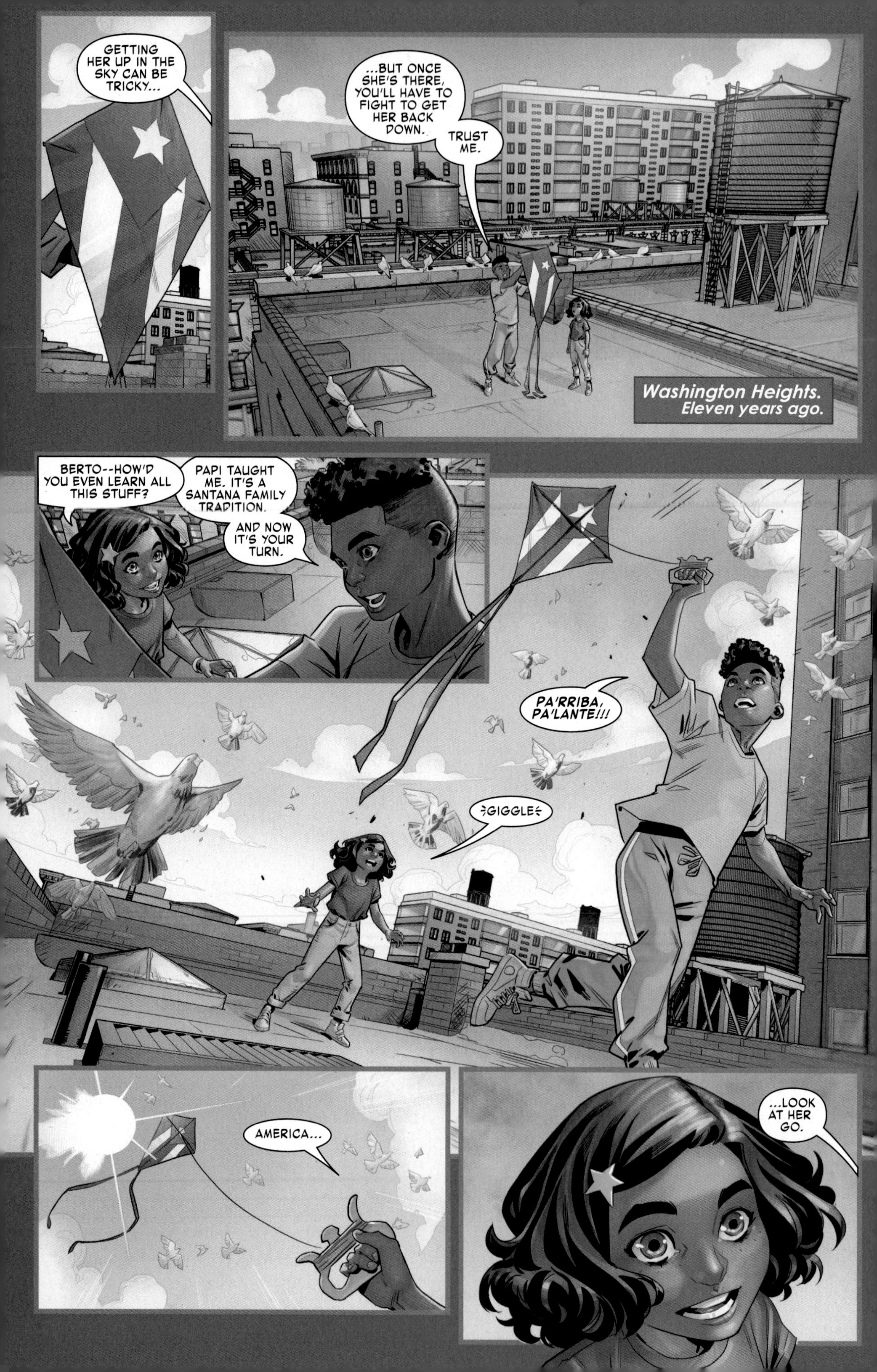
GETTING HER UP IN THE SKY CAN BE TRICKY...
...BUT ONCE SHE'S THERE, YOU'LL HAVE TO FIGHT TO GET HER BACK DOWN.
TRUST ME.
Washington Heights. Eleven years ago.
BERTO--HOW'D YOU EVEN LEARN ALL THIS STUFF?
PAPI TAUGHT ME. IT'S A SANTANA FAMILY TRADITION.
AND NOW IT'S YOUR TURN.
PA'RRIBA, PA'LANTE!!!
GIGGLE
AMERICA...
...LOOK AT HER GO.

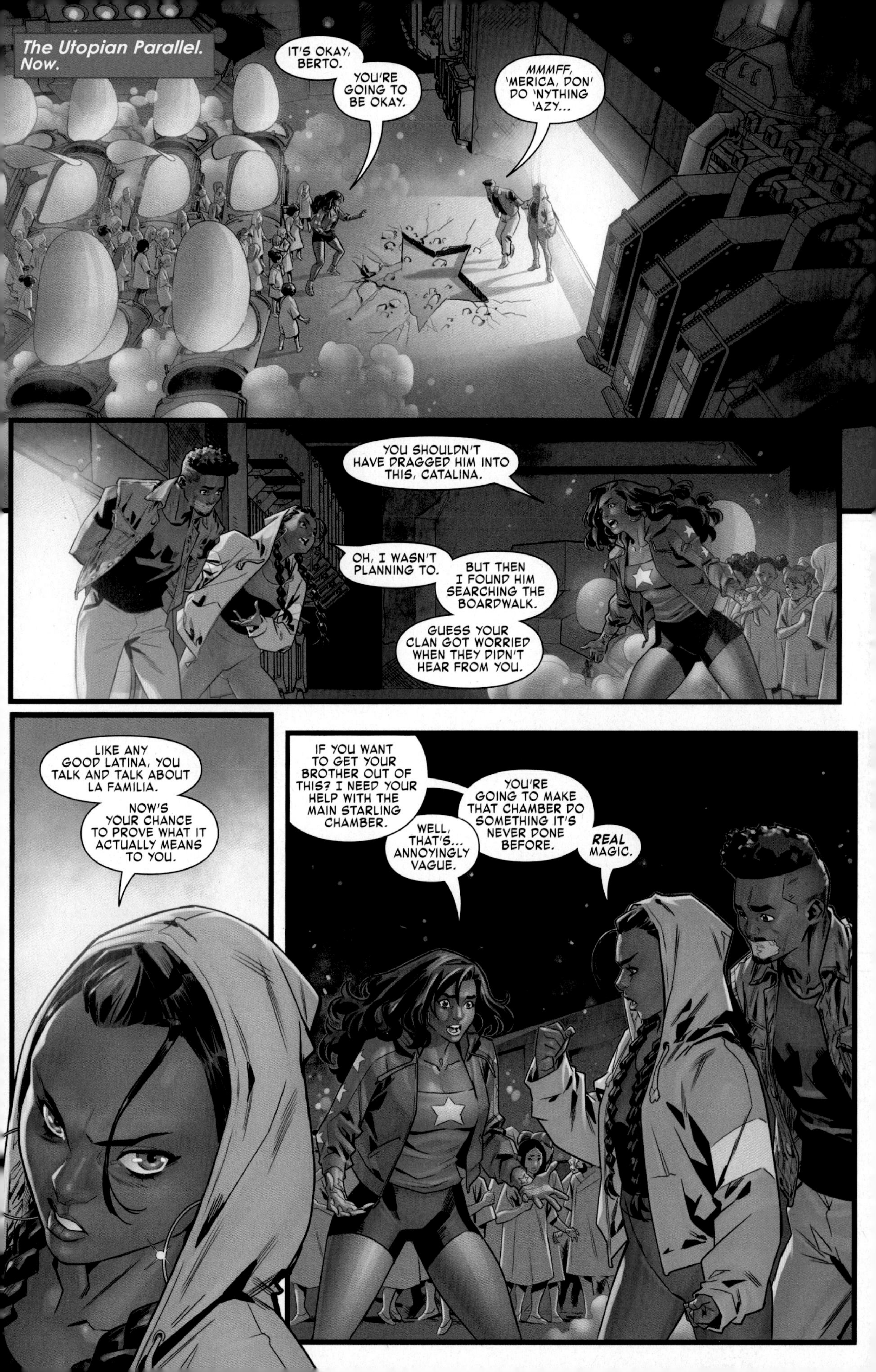

The Utopian Parallel. Now.
IT'S OKAY, BERTO.
YOU'RE GOING TO BE OKAY.
MMMFF, 'MERICA, DON' DO 'NYTHING 'AZY...
YOU SHOULDN'T HAVE DRAGGED HIM INTO THIS, CATALINA.
OH, I WASN'T PLANNING TO.
BUT THEN I FOUND HIM SEARCHING THE BOARDWALK.
GUESS YOUR CLAN GOT WORRIED WHEN THEY DIDN'T HEAR FROM YOU.
LIKE ANY GOOD LATINA, YOU TALK AND TALK ABOUT LA FAMILIA.
NOW'S YOUR CHANCE TO PROVE WHAT IT ACTUALLY MEANS TO YOU.
IF YOU WANT TO GET YOUR BROTHER OUT OF THIS? I NEED YOUR HELP WITH THE MAIN STARLING CHAMBER.
WELL, THAT'S... ANNOYINGLY VAGUE.
YOU'RE GOING TO MAKE THAT CHAMBER DO SOMETHING IT'S NEVER DONE BEFORE.
REAL MAGIC.

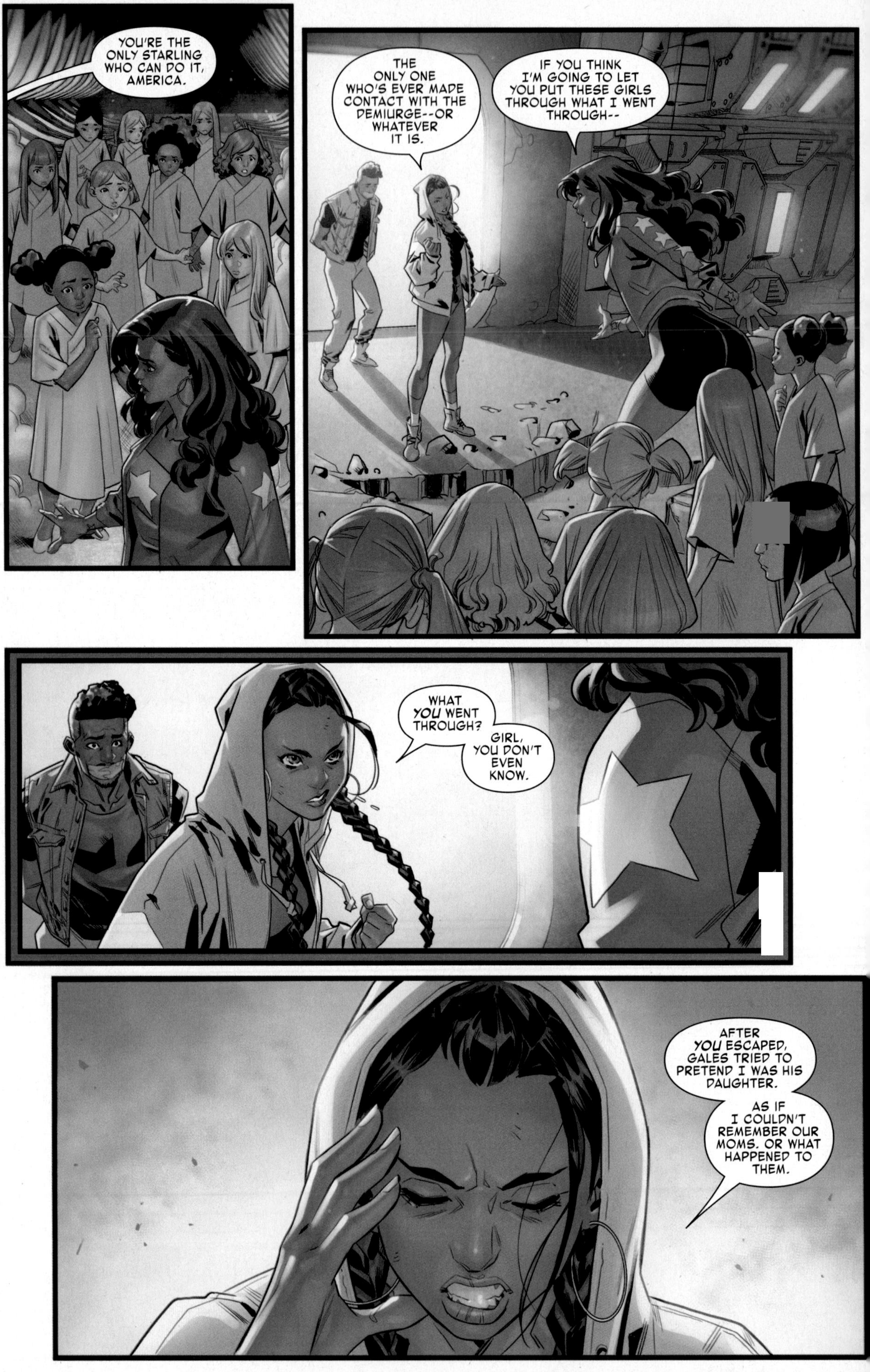
YOU'RE THE ONLY STARLING WHO CAN DO IT, AMERICA.
THE ONLY ONE WHO'S EVER MADE CONTACT WITH THE DEMIURGE--OR WHATEVER IT IS.
IF YOU THINK I'M GOING TO LET YOU PUT THESE GIRLS THROUGH WHAT I WENT THROUGH--
WHAT YOU WENT THROUGH?
GIRL, YOU DON'T EVEN KNOW.
AFTER YOU ESCAPED, GALES TRIED TO PRETEND I WAS HIS DAUGHTER.
AS IF I COULDN'T REMEMBER OUR MOMS. OR WHAT HAPPENED TO THEM.

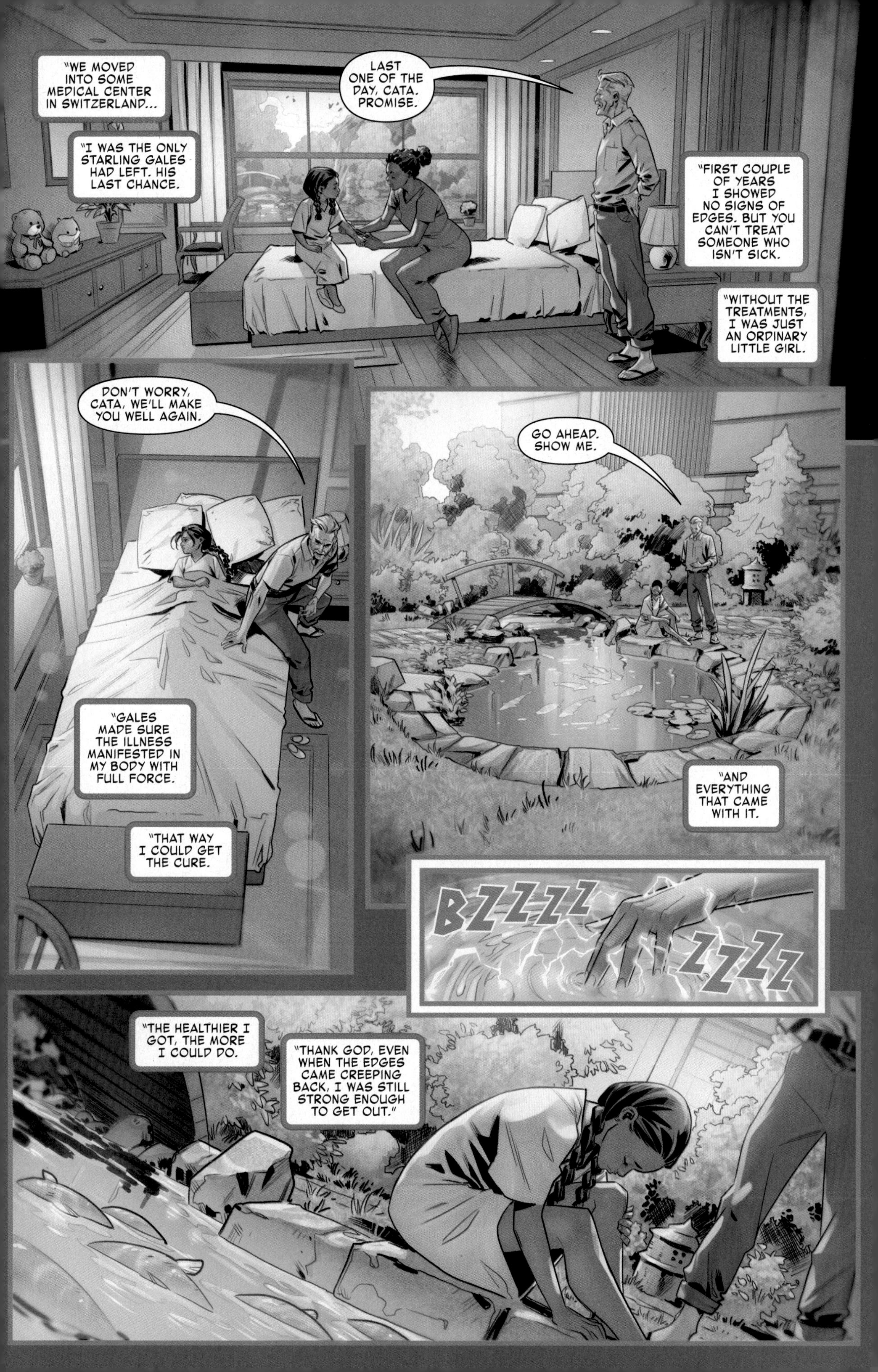
"WE MOVED INTO SOME MEDICAL CENTER IN SWITZERLAND...
"I WAS THE ONLY STARLING GALES HAD LEFT. HIS LAST CHANCE.
LAST ONE OF THE DAY, CATA. PROMISE.
"FIRST COUPLE OF YEARS I SHOWED NO SIGNS OF EDGES. BUT YOU CAN'T TREAT SOMEONE WHO ISN'T SICK.
"WITHOUT THE TREATMENTS, I WAS JUST AN ORDINARY LITTLE GIRL.
DON'T WORRY, CATA, WE'LL MAKE YOU WELL AGAIN.
"GALES MADE SURE THE ILLNESS MANIFESTED IN MY BODY WITH FULL FORCE.
"THAT WAY I COULD GET THE CURE.
GO AHEAD. SHOW ME.
"AND EVERYTHING THAT CAME WITH IT.
BZZZZZ ZZZZ
"THE HEALTHIER I GOT, THE MORE I COULD DO.
"THANK GOD, EVEN WHEN THE EDGES CAME CREEPING BACK, I WAS STILL STRONG ENOUGH TO GET OUT."

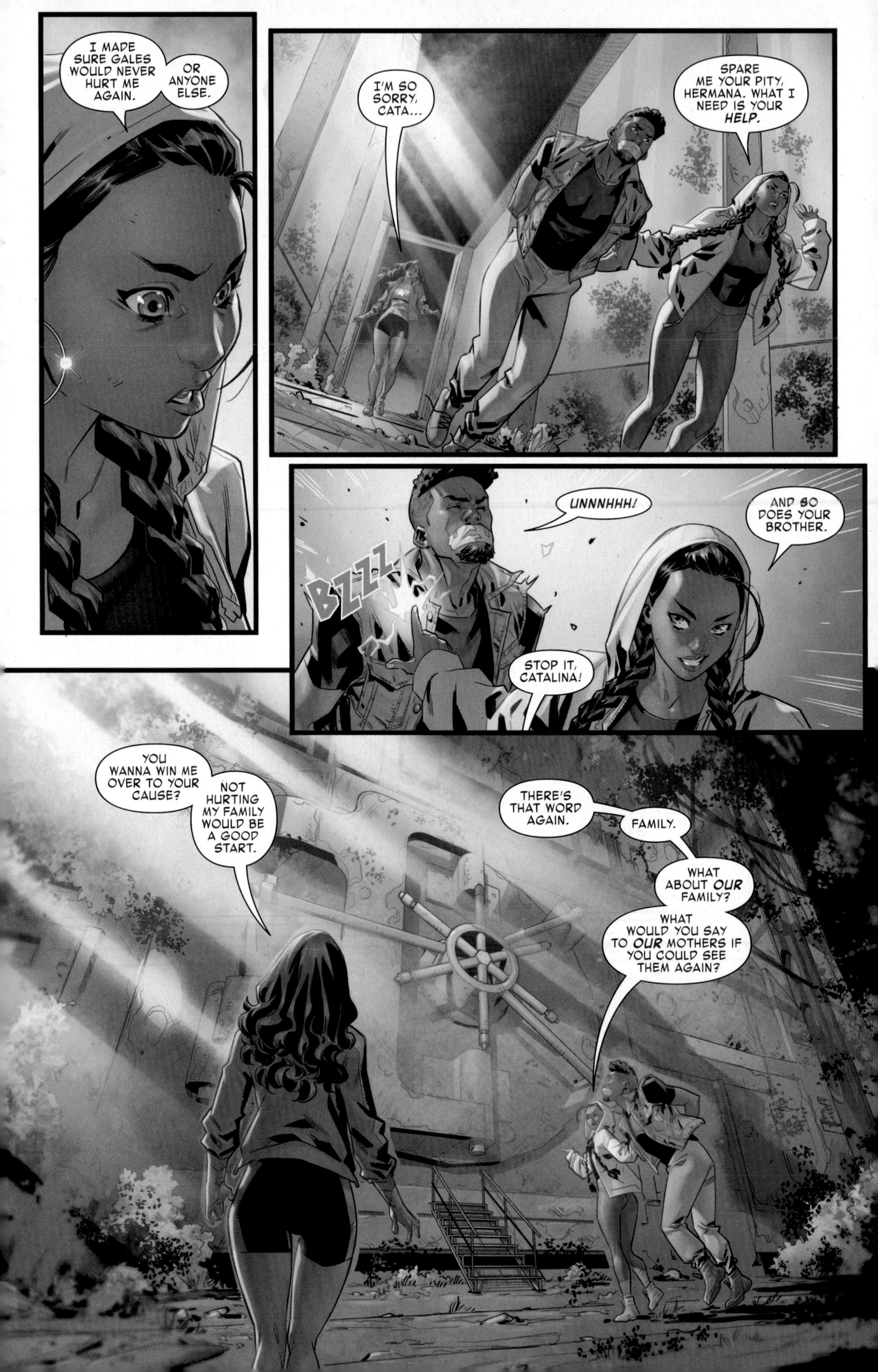
I MADE SURE GALES WOULD NEVER HURT ME AGAIN.
OR ANYONE ELSE.
I'M SO SORRY, CATA...
SPARE ME YOUR PITY, HERMANA. WHAT I NEED IS YOUR HELP.
UNNNHHH!
AND SO DOES YOUR BROTHER.
BZZZ
STOP IT, CATALINA!
YOU WANNA WIN ME OVER TO YOUR CAUSE?
NOT HURTING MY FAMILY WOULD BE A GOOD START.
THERE'S THAT WORD AGAIN.
FAMILY.
WHAT ABOUT OUR FAMILY?
WHAT WOULD YOU SAY TO OUR MOTHERS IF YOU COULD SEE THEM AGAIN?

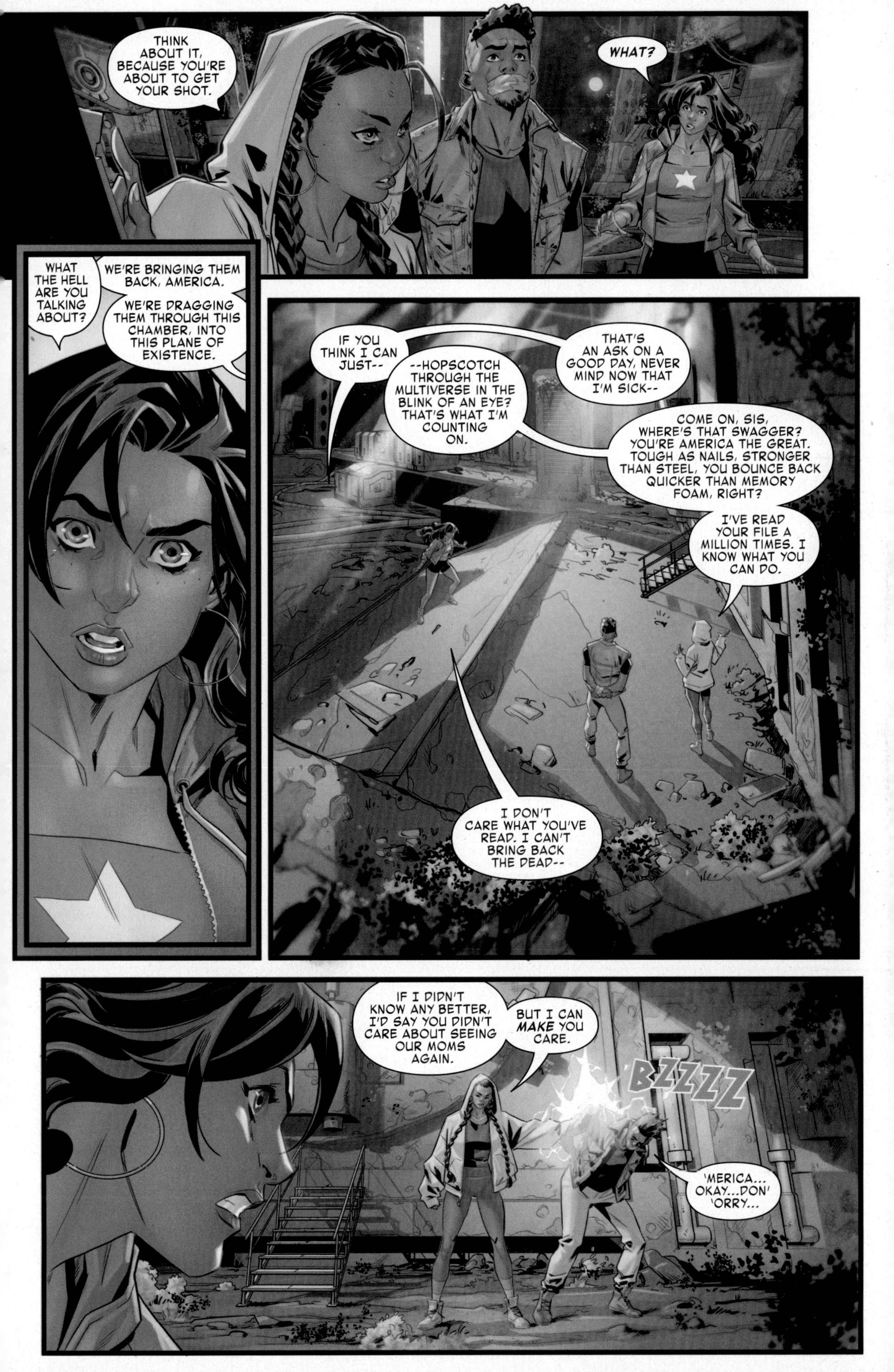
THINK ABOUT IT, BECAUSE YOU'RE ABOUT TO GET YOUR SHOT.
WHAT?
WHAT THE HELL ARE YOU TALKING ABOUT?
WE'RE BRINGING THEM BACK, AMERICA.
WE'RE DRAGGING THEM THROUGH THIS CHAMBER, INTO THIS PLANE OF EXISTENCE.
IF YOU THINK I CAN JUST--
THAT'S AN ASK ON A GOOD DAY, NEVER MIND NOW THAT I'M SICK--
--HOPSCOTCH THROUGH THE MULTIVERSE IN THE BLINK OF AN EYE? THAT'S WHAT I'M COUNTING ON.
COME ON, SIS, WHERE'S THAT SWAGGER? YOU'RE AMERICA THE GREAT. TOUGH AS NAILS, STRONGER THAN STEEL, YOU BOUNCE BACK QUICKER THAN MEMORY FOAM, RIGHT?
I'VE READ YOUR FILE A MILLION TIMES. I KNOW WHAT YOU CAN DO.
I DON'T CARE WHAT YOU'VE READ. I CAN'T BRING BACK THE DEAD--
IF I DIDN'T KNOW ANY BETTER, I'D SAY YOU DIDN'T CARE ABOUT SEEING OUR MOMS AGAIN.
BUT I CAN MAKE YOU CARE.
BZZZZ
'MERICA... OKAY...DON' 'ORRY...

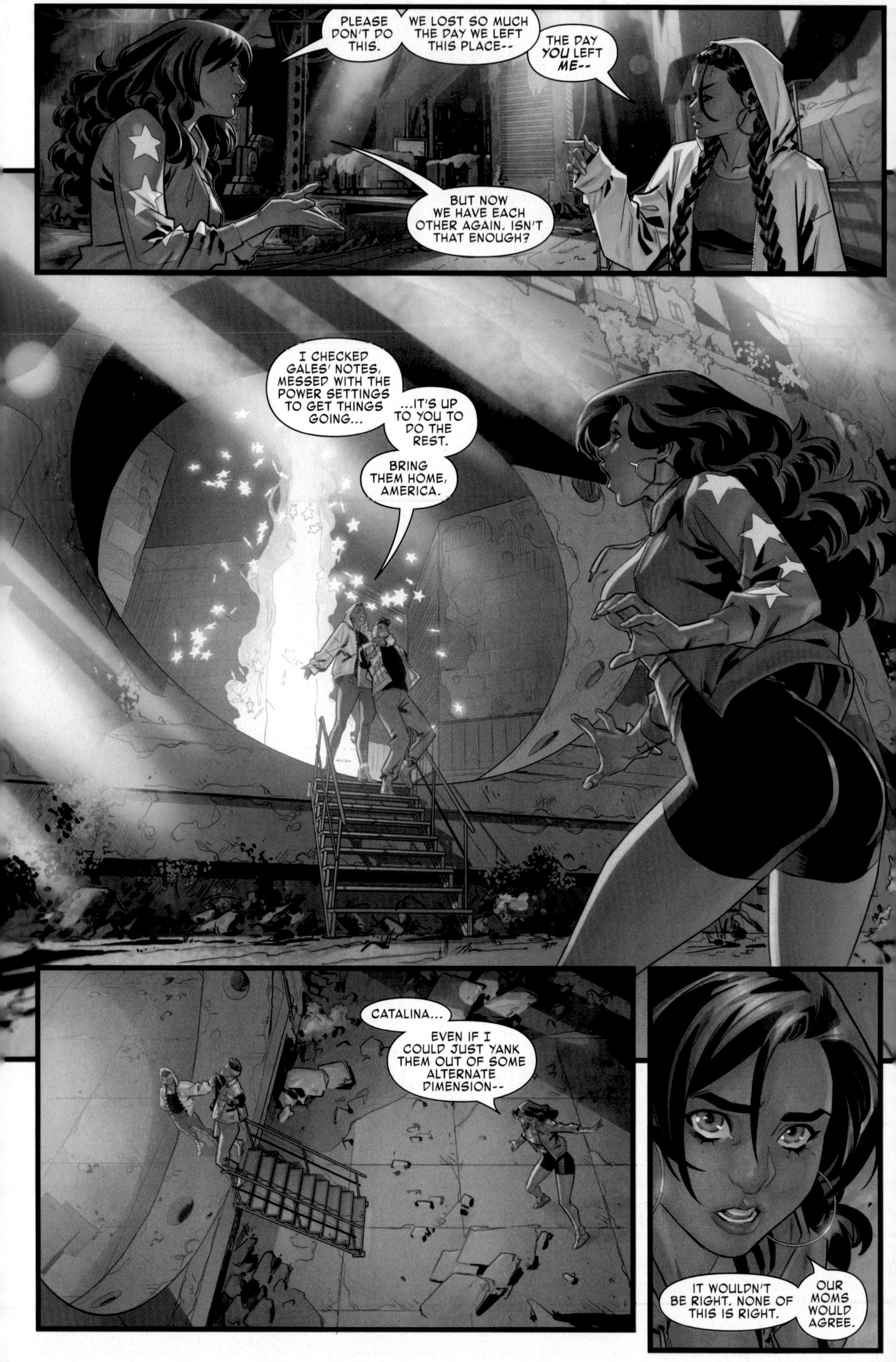

PLEASE DON'T DO THIS.
WE LOST SO MUCH THE DAY WE LEFT THIS PLACE--
THE DAY YOU LEFT ME--
BUT NOW WE HAVE EACH OTHER AGAIN. ISN'T THAT ENOUGH?
I CHECKED GALES' NOTES, MESSED WITH THE POWER SETTINGS TO GET THINGS GOING...
...IT'S UP TO YOU TO DO THE REST.
BRING THEM HOME, AMERICA.
CATALINA...
EVEN IF I COULD JUST YANK THEM OUT OF SOME ALTERNATE DIMENSION--
IT WOULDN'T BE RIGHT. NONE OF THIS IS RIGHT.
OUR MOMS WOULD AGREE.

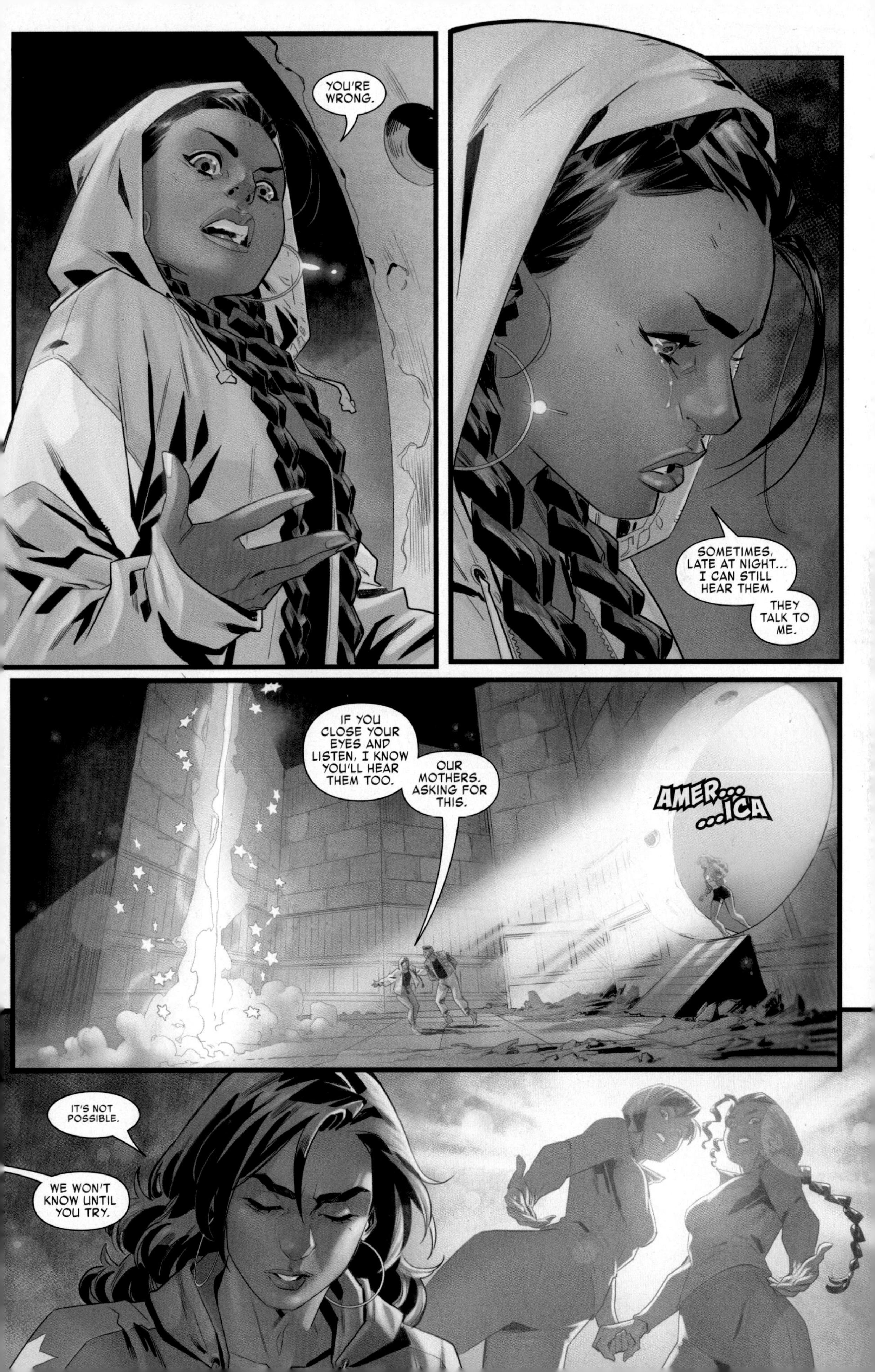

YOU'RE WRONG.
SOMETIMES, LATE AT NIGHT... I CAN STILL HEAR THEM.
THEY TALK TO ME.
IF YOU CLOSE YOUR EYES AND LISTEN, I KNOW YOU'LL HEAR THEM TOO.
OUR MOTHERS. ASKING FOR THIS.
AMER... ...ICA
IT'S NOT POSSIBLE.
WE WON'T KNOW UNTIL YOU TRY.

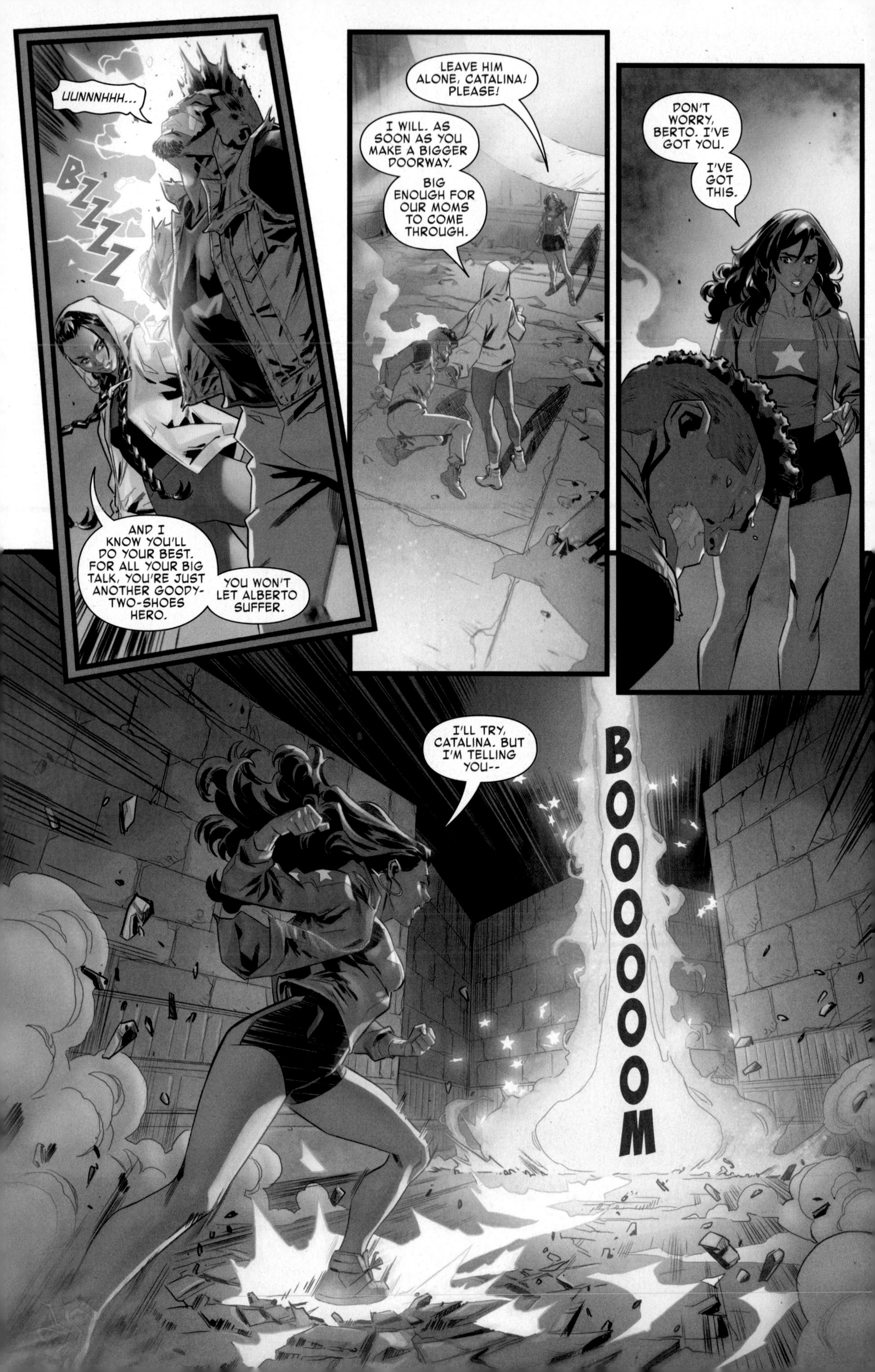
UUNNNHHH...
BZZZZ
AND I KNOW YOU'LL DO YOUR BEST. FOR ALL YOUR BIG TALK, YOU'RE JUST ANOTHER GOODY-TWO-SHOES HERO.
YOU WON'T LET ALBERTO SUFFER.
LEAVE HIM ALONE, CATALINA! PLEASE!
I WILL. AS SOON AS YOU MAKE A BIGGER DOORWAY.
BIG ENOUGH FOR OUR MOMS TO COME THROUGH.
DON'T WORRY, BERTO. I'VE GOT YOU.
I'VE GOT THIS.
I'LL TRY, CATALINA. BUT I'M TELLING YOU--
BOOOOOOM

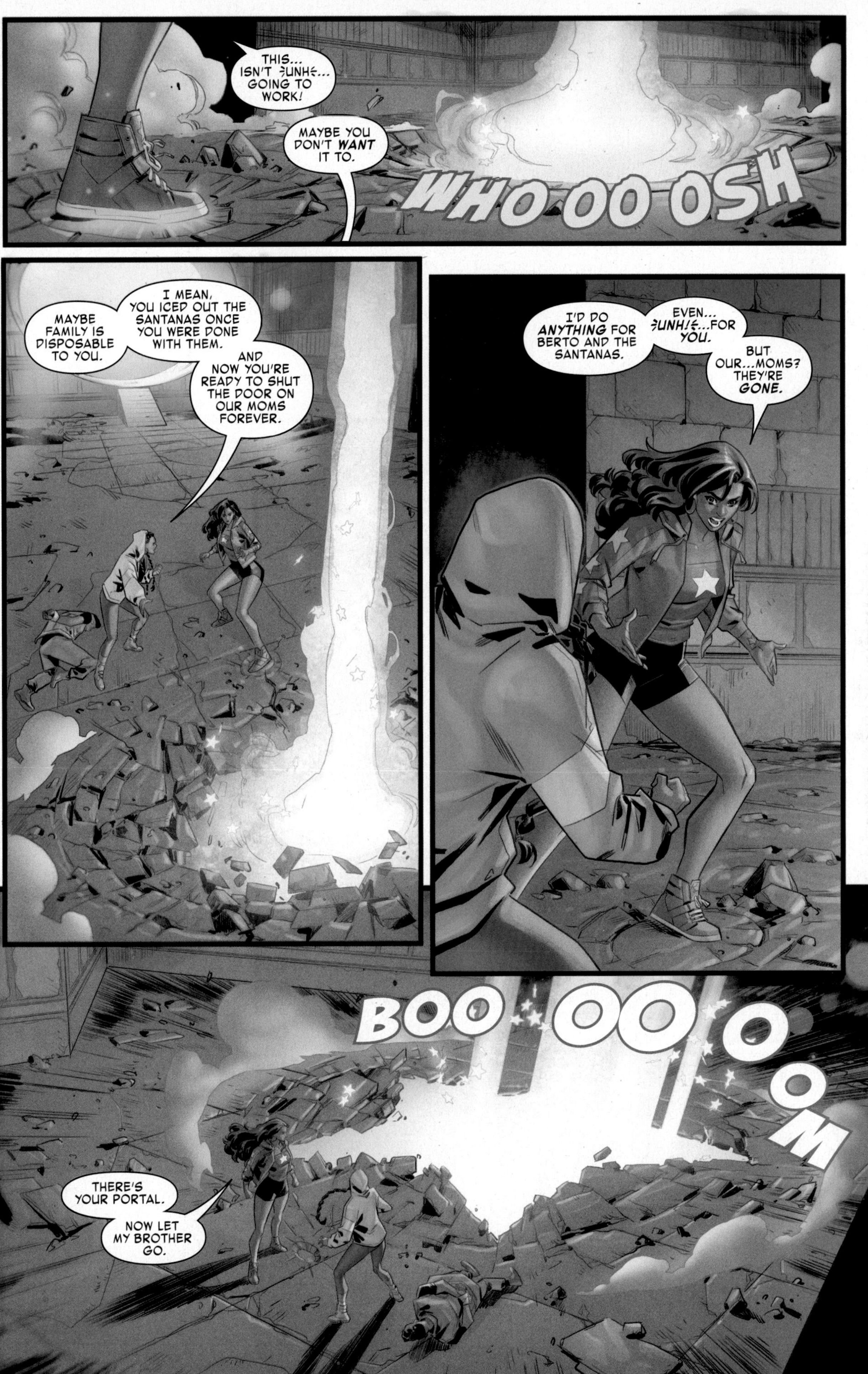
THIS... ISN'T ƎUNHƐ... GOING TO WORK!
MAYBE YOU DON'T WANT IT TO.
WHO OO OSH
MAYBE FAMILY IS DISPOSABLE TO YOU.
I MEAN, YOU ICED OUT THE SANTANAS ONCE YOU WERE DONE WITH THEM.
AND NOW YOU'RE READY TO SHUT THE DOOR ON OUR MOMS FOREVER.
I'D DO ANYTHING FOR BERTO AND THE SANTANAS.
EVEN... ƎUNH!Ɛ...FOR YOU.
BUT OUR...MOMS? THEY'RE GONE.
BOO OO O O M
THERE'S YOUR PORTAL.
NOW LET MY BROTHER GO.

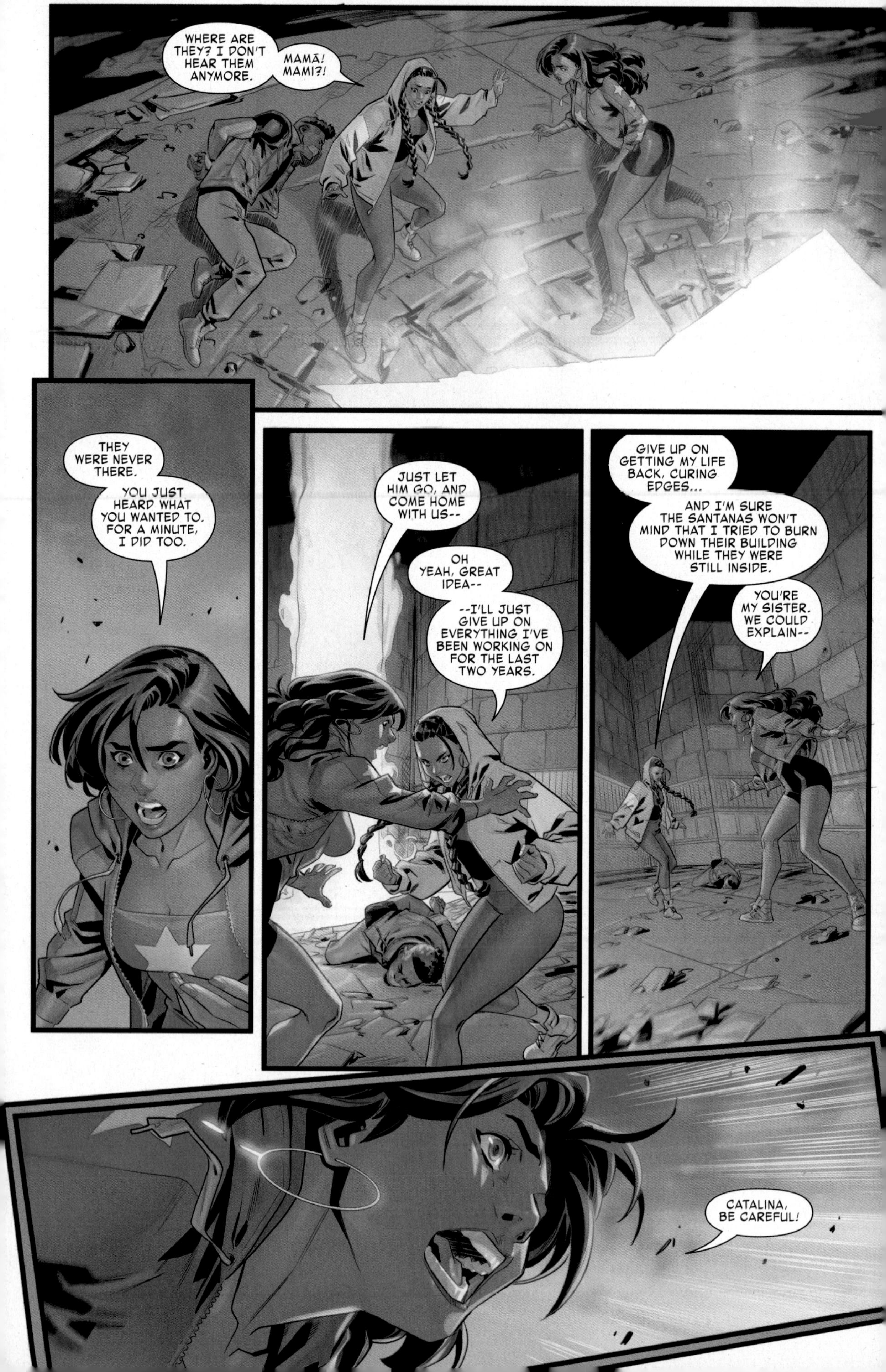
WHERE ARE THEY? I DON'T HEAR THEM ANYMORE.
MAMÁ! MAMI?!
THEY WERE NEVER THERE.
YOU JUST HEARD WHAT YOU WANTED TO. FOR A MINUTE, I DID TOO.
JUST LET HIM GO, AND COME HOME WITH US--
OH YEAH, GREAT IDEA--
--I'LL JUST GIVE UP ON EVERYTHING I'VE BEEN WORKING ON FOR THE LAST TWO YEARS.
GIVE UP ON GETTING MY LIFE BACK, CURING EDGES...
AND I'M SURE THE SANTANAS WON'T MIND THAT I TRIED TO BURN DOWN THEIR BUILDING WHILE THEY WERE STILL INSIDE.
YOU'RE MY SISTER. WE COULD EXPLAIN--
CATALINA, BE CAREFUL!

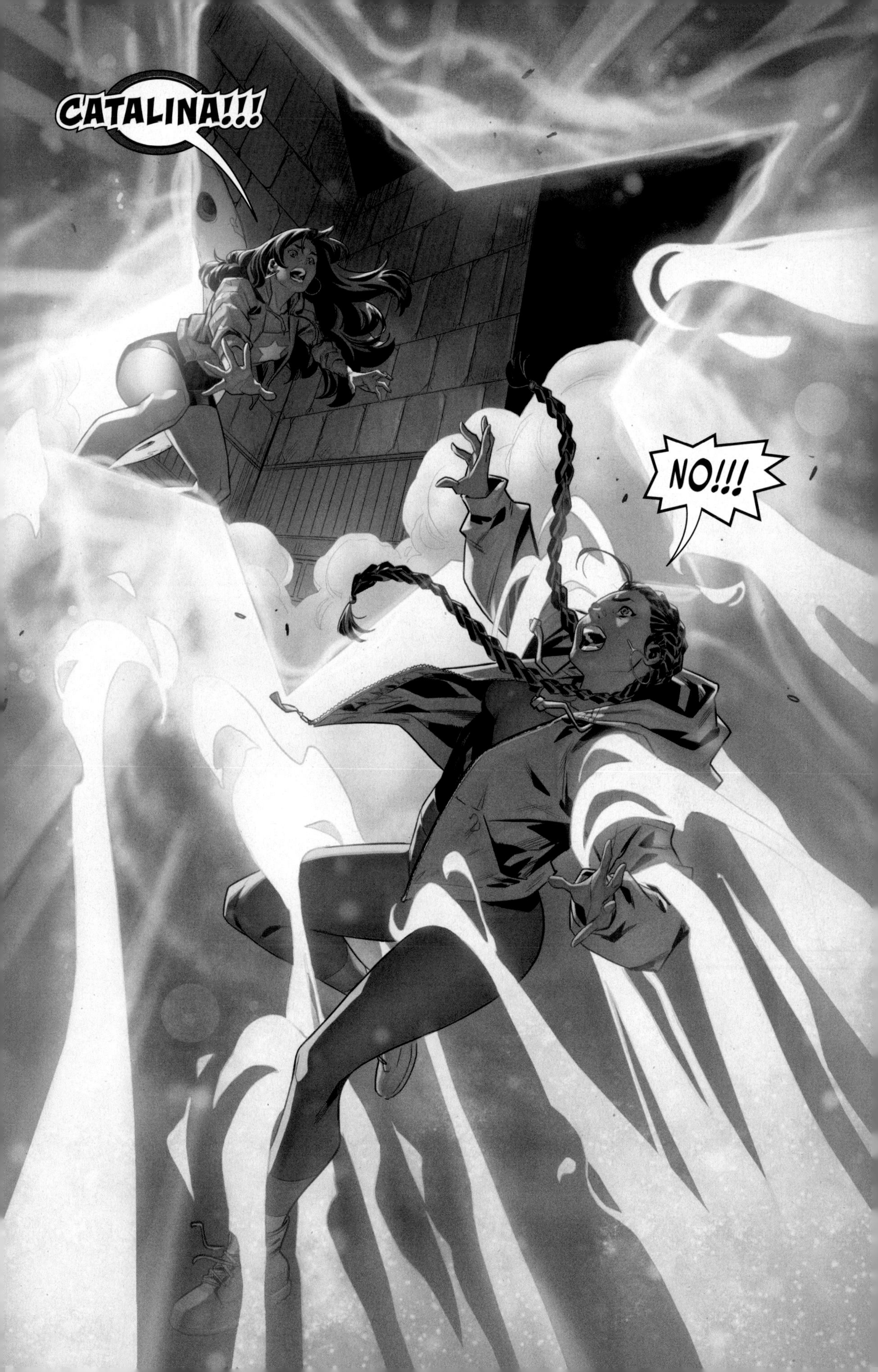
CATALINA!!!
NO!!!

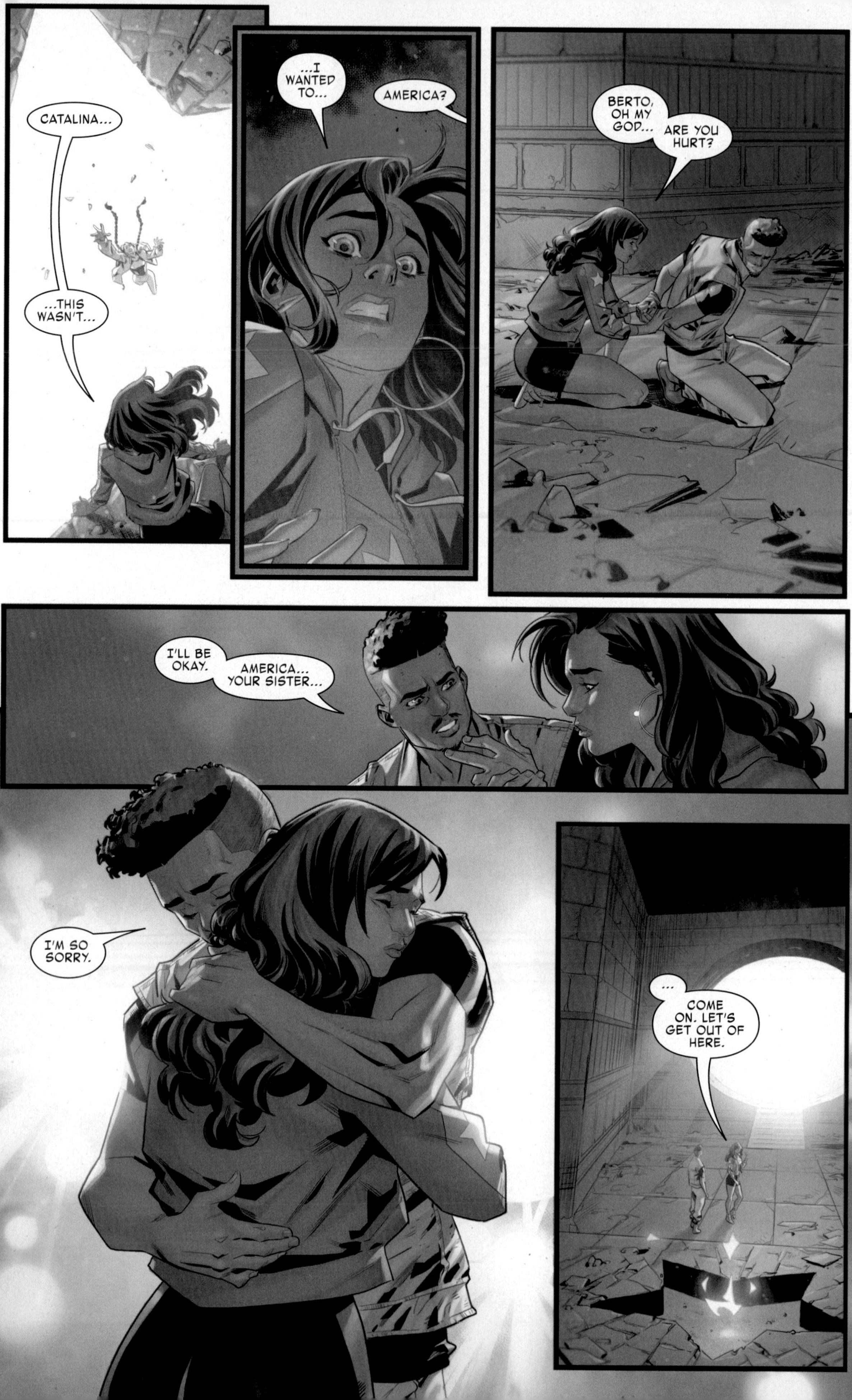
CATALINA...
...THIS WASN'T...
...I WANTED TO...
AMERICA?
BERTO, OH MY GOD...
ARE YOU HURT?
I'LL BE OKAY.
AMERICA... YOUR SISTER...
I'M SO SORRY.
...
COME ON. LET'S GET OUT OF HERE.

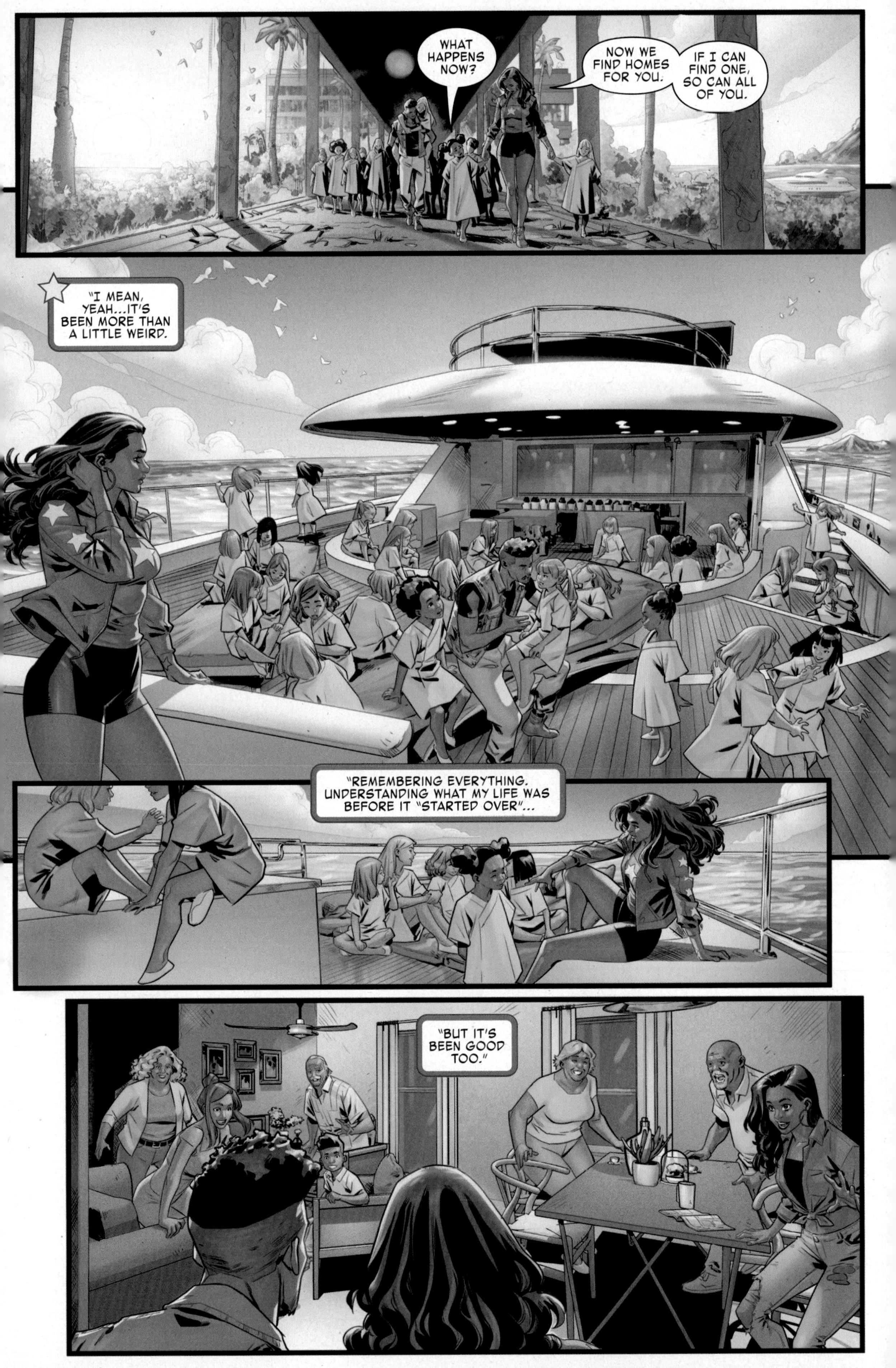
WHAT HAPPENS NOW?
NOW WE FIND HOMES FOR YOU.
IF I CAN FIND ONE, SO CAN ALL OF YOU.
"I MEAN, YEAH...IT'S BEEN MORE THAN A LITTLE WEIRD.
"REMEMBERING EVERYTHING. UNDERSTANDING WHAT MY LIFE WAS BEFORE IT "STARTED OVER"...
"BUT IT'S BEEN GOOD TOO."

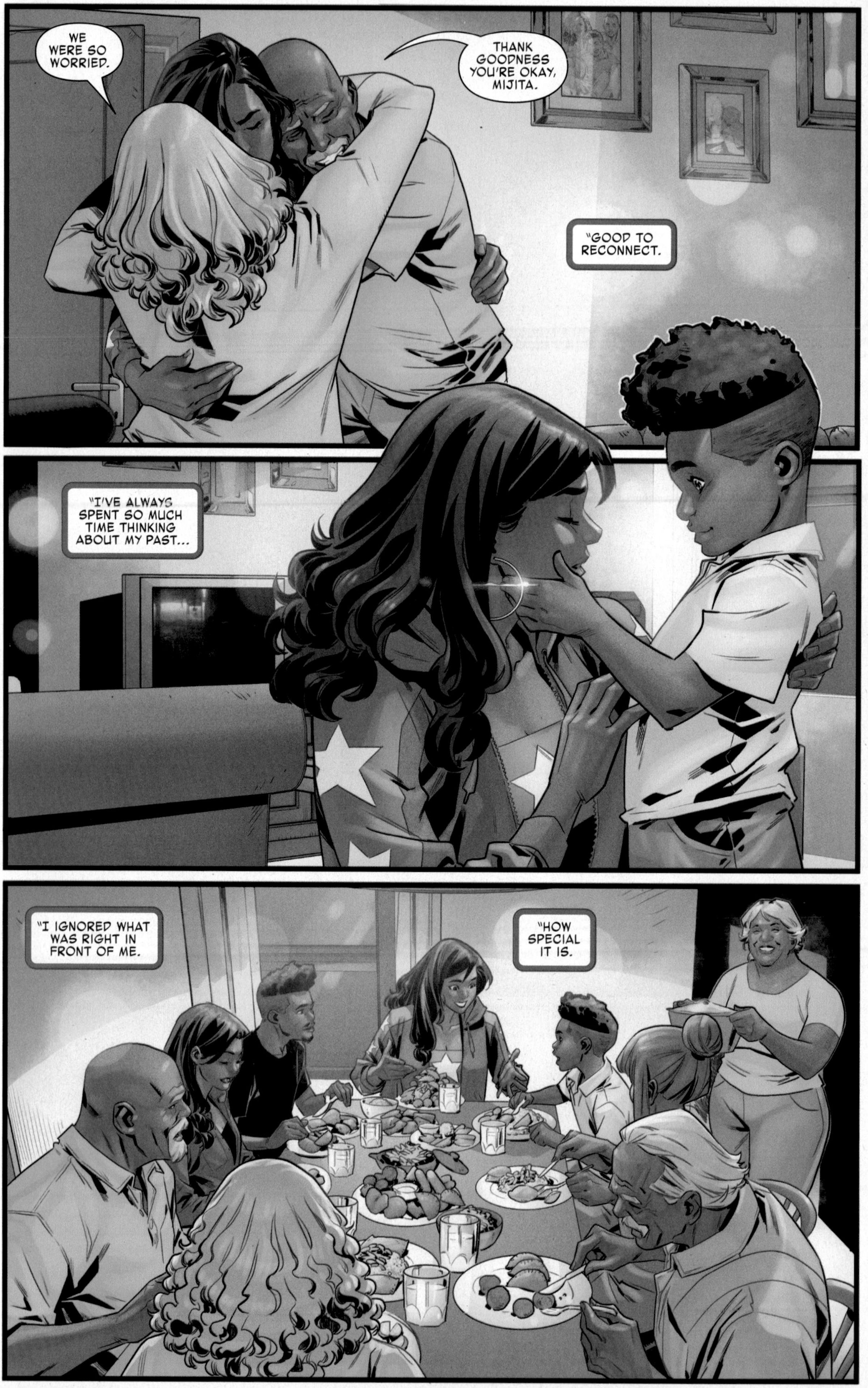

WE WERE SO WORRIED.
THANK GOODNESS YOU'RE OKAY, MIJITA.
"GOOD TO RECONNECT.
"I'VE ALWAYS SPENT SO MUCH TIME THINKING ABOUT MY PAST...
"I IGNORED WHAT WAS RIGHT IN FRONT OF ME.
"HOW SPECIAL IT IS.

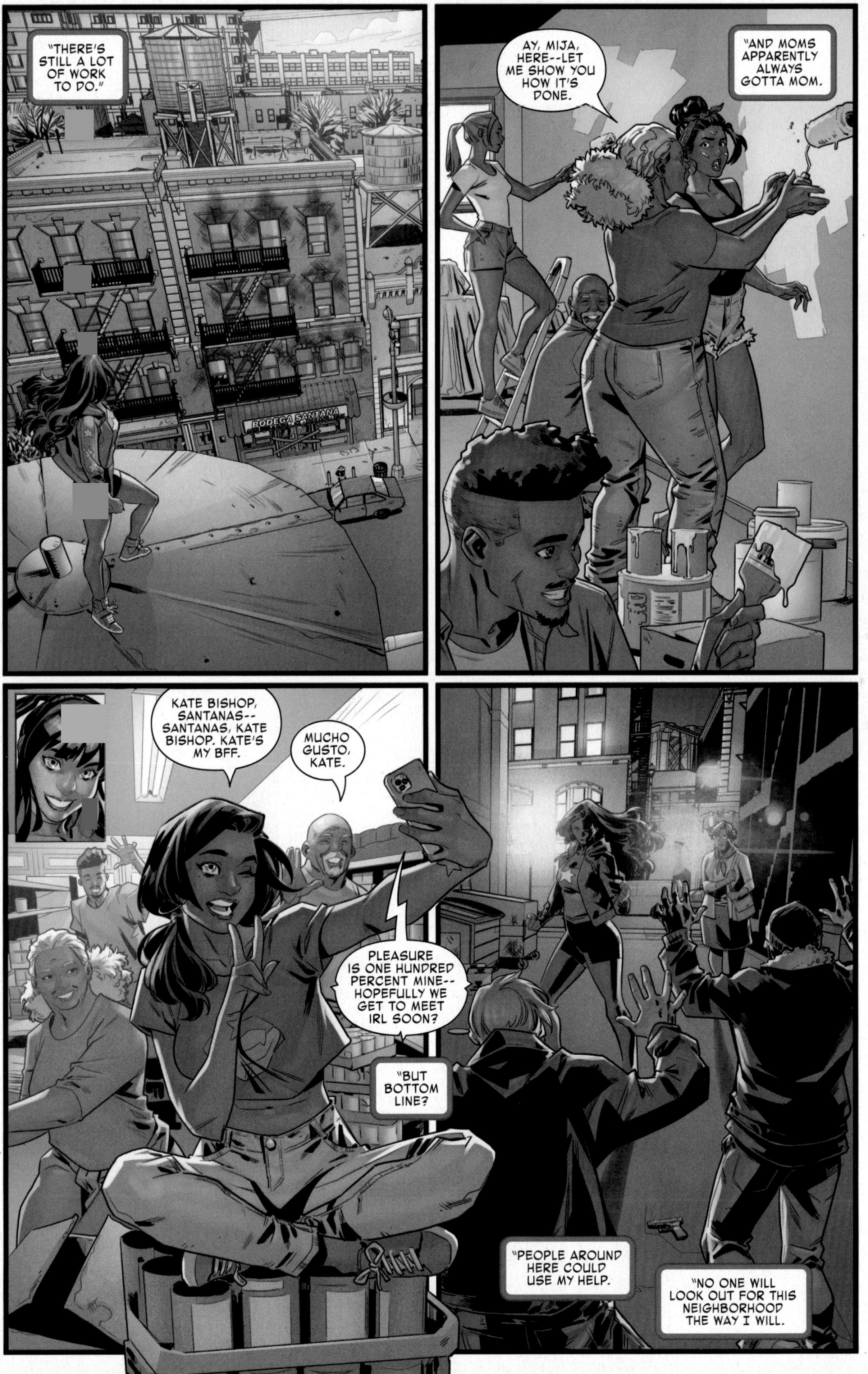
"THERE'S STILL A LOT OF WORK TO DO."
AY, MIJA, HERE--LET ME SHOW YOU HOW IT'S DONE.
"AND MOMS APPARENTLY ALWAYS GOTTA MOM.
BODEGA SANTANA
KATE BISHOP, SANTANAS--SANTANAS, KATE BISHOP. KATE'S MY BFF.
MUCHO GUSTO, KATE.
PLEASURE IS ONE HUNDRED PERCENT MINE--HOPEFULLY WE GET TO MEET IRL SOON?
"BUT BOTTOM LINE?
"PEOPLE AROUND HERE COULD USE MY HELP.
"NO ONE WILL LOOK OUT FOR THIS NEIGHBORHOOD THE WAY I WILL.

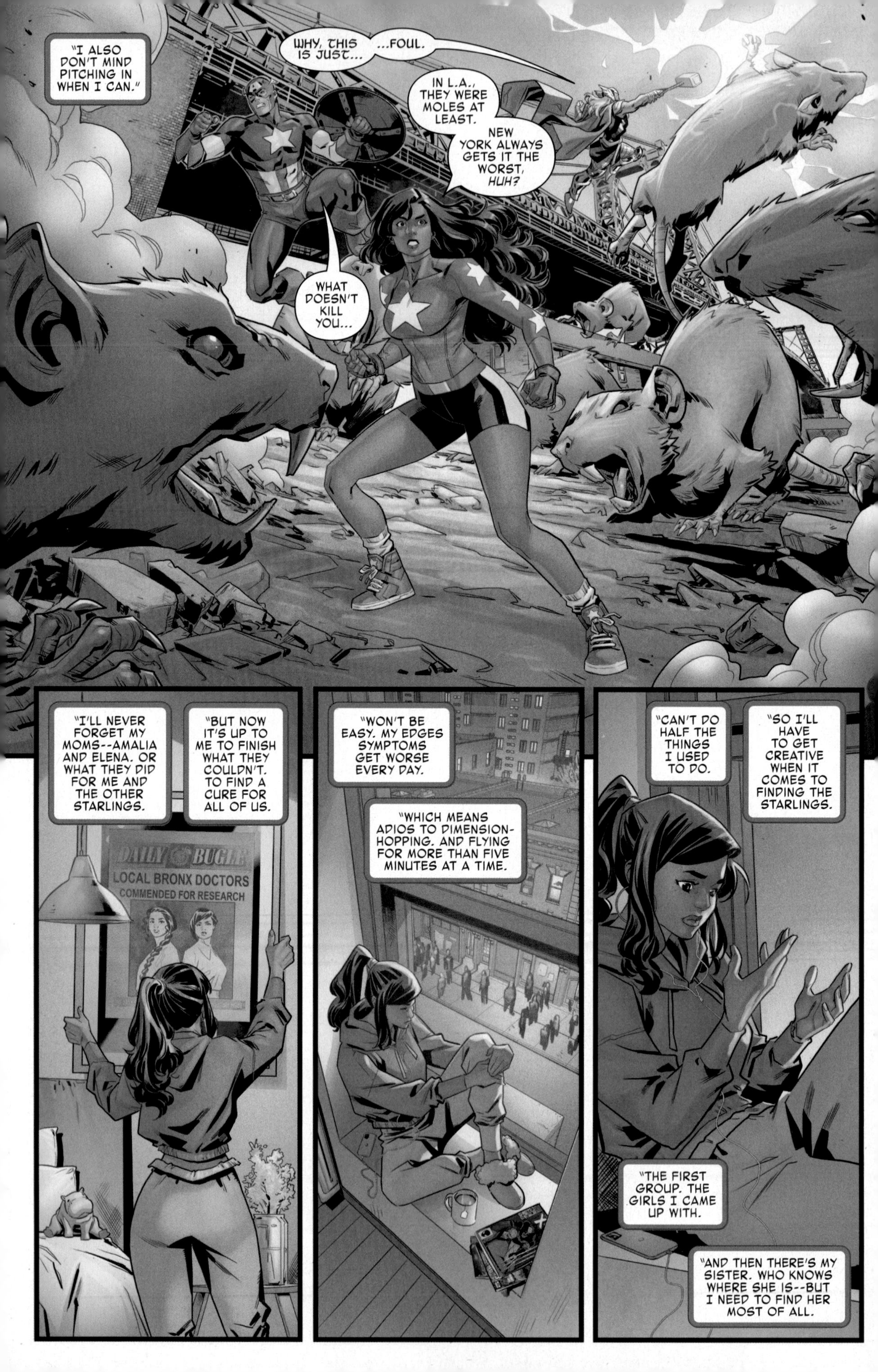

"I ALSO DON'T MIND PITCHING IN WHEN I CAN."
WHY, THIS IS JUST... ...FOUL.
IN L.A., THEY WERE MOLES AT LEAST.
NEW YORK ALWAYS GETS IT THE WORST, HUH?
WHAT DOESN'T KILL YOU...
"I'LL NEVER FORGET MY MOMS--AMALIA AND ELENA. OR WHAT THEY DID FOR ME AND THE OTHER STARLINGS.
"BUT NOW IT'S UP TO ME TO FINISH WHAT THEY COULDN'T. TO FIND A CURE FOR ALL OF US.
DAILY BUGLE
LOCAL BRONX DOCTORS
COMMENDED FOR RESEARCH
"WON'T BE EASY. MY EDGES SYMPTOMS GET WORSE EVERY DAY.
"WHICH MEANS ADIOS TO DIMENSION-HOPPING. AND FLYING FOR MORE THAN FIVE MINUTES AT A TIME.
"CAN'T DO HALF THE THINGS I USED TO DO.
"SO I'LL HAVE TO GET CREATIVE WHEN IT COMES TO FINDING THE STARLINGS.
"THE FIRST GROUP. THE GIRLS I CAME UP WITH.
"AND THEN THERE'S MY SISTER. WHO KNOWS WHERE SHE IS--BUT I NEED TO FIND HER MOST OF ALL.

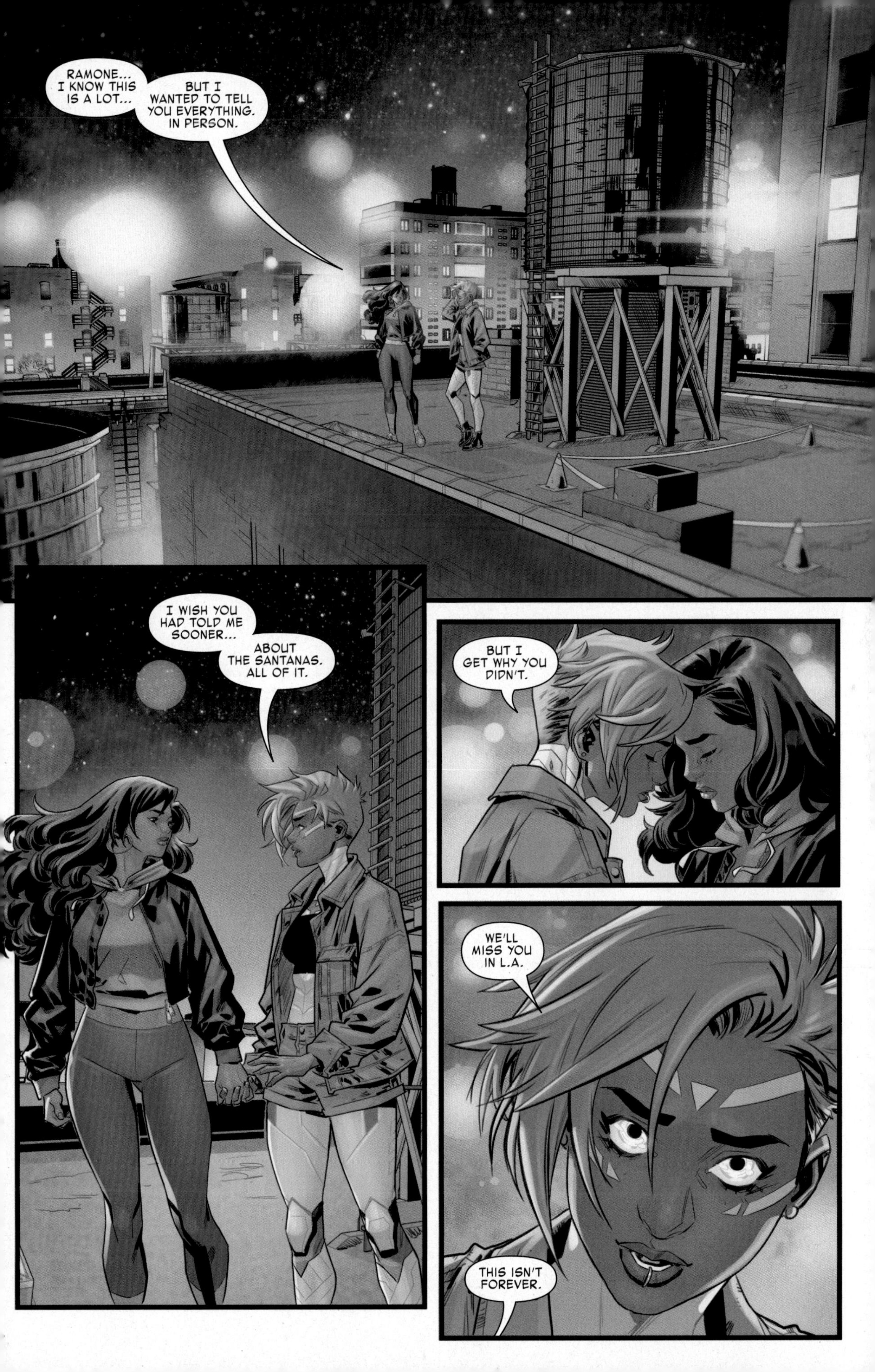
RAMONE... I KNOW THIS IS A LOT...
BUT I WANTED TO TELL YOU EVERYTHING. IN PERSON.
I WISH YOU HAD TOLD ME SOONER...
ABOUT THE SANTANAS. ALL OF IT.
BUT I GET WHY YOU DIDN'T.
WE'LL MISS YOU IN L.A.
THIS ISN'T FOREVER.

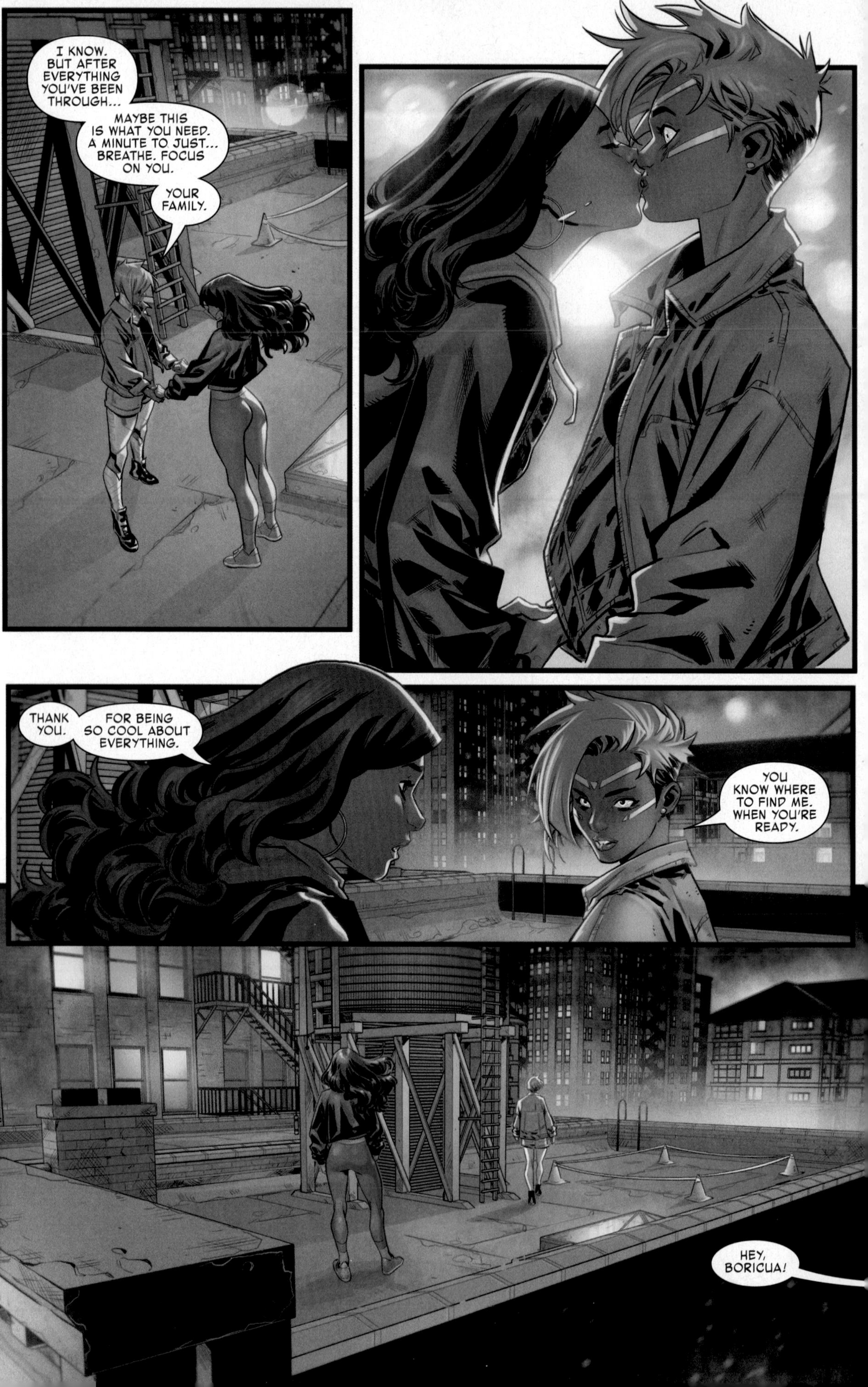
I KNOW. BUT AFTER EVERYTHING YOU'VE BEEN THROUGH...
MAYBE THIS IS WHAT YOU NEED. A MINUTE TO JUST... BREATHE. FOCUS ON YOU.
YOUR FAMILY.
THANK YOU.
FOR BEING SO COOL ABOUT EVERYTHING.
YOU KNOW WHERE TO FIND ME. WHEN YOU'RE READY.
HEY, BORICUA!

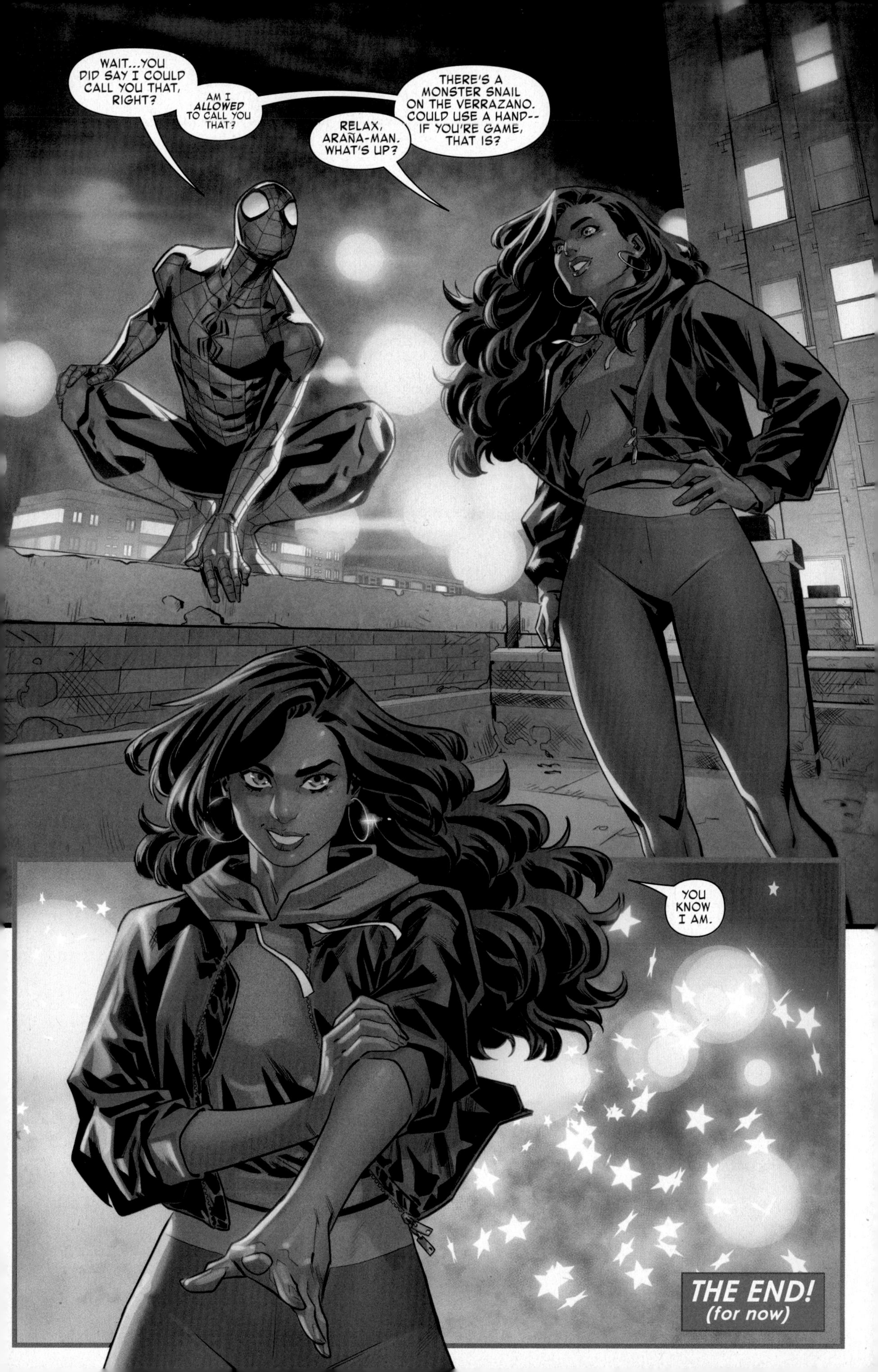
WAIT...YOU DID SAY I COULD CALL YOU THAT, RIGHT?
AM I ALLOWED TO CALL YOU THAT?
RELAX, ARAÑA-MAN. WHAT'S UP?
THERE'S A MONSTER SNAIL ON THE VERRAZANO. COULD USE A HAND-- IF YOU'RE GAME, THAT IS?
YOU KNOW I AM.
THE END! (for now)

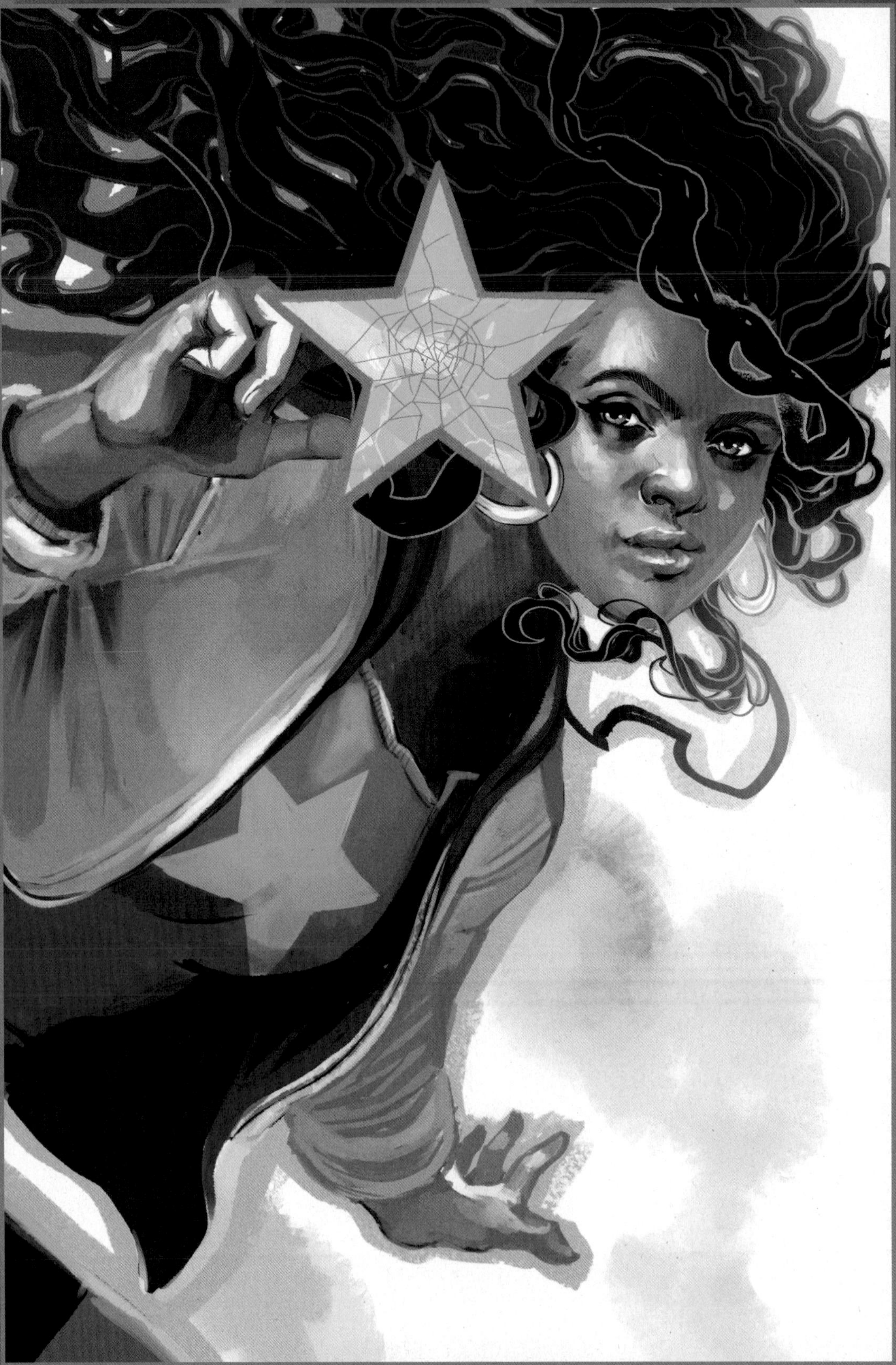

#1 VARIANT BY **Stephanie Hans**

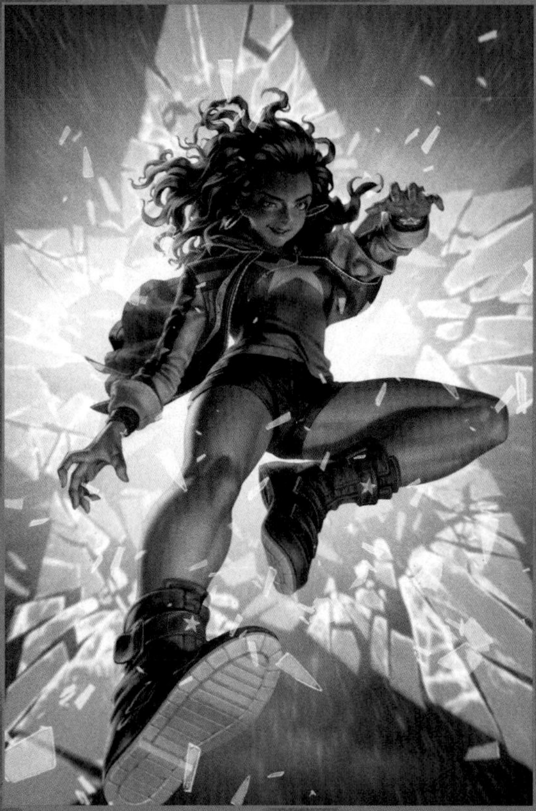

#1 VARIANT BY **Junggeun Yoon**

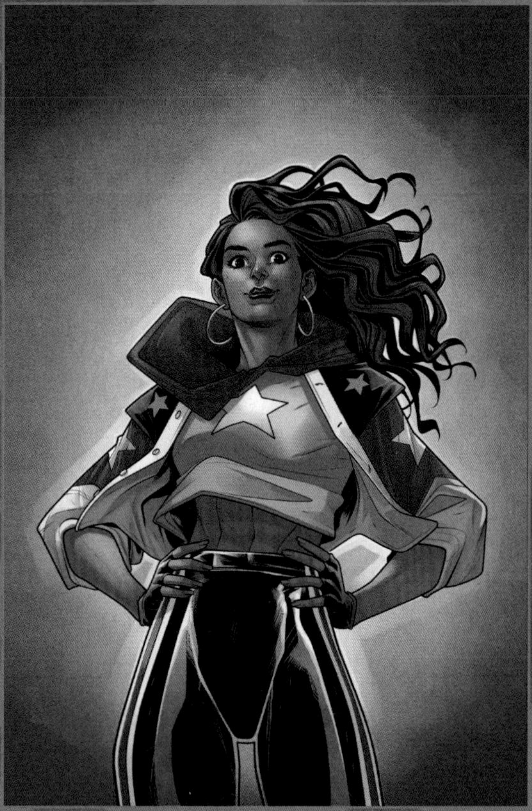

#1 VARIANT BY **Elizabeth Torque**

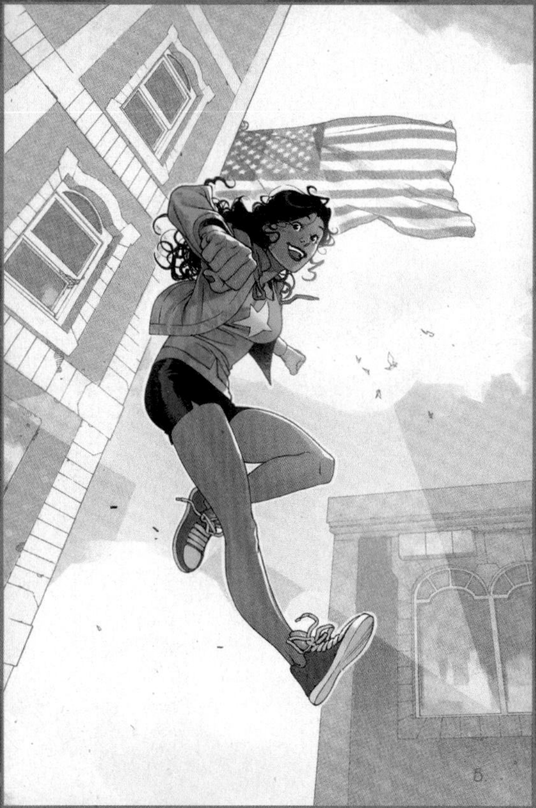

#2 VARIANT BY **Bengal**

I.R.T. SUBWAY
191 ST. ENTRANCE
NO BICYCLE RIDING IN SUBWAY

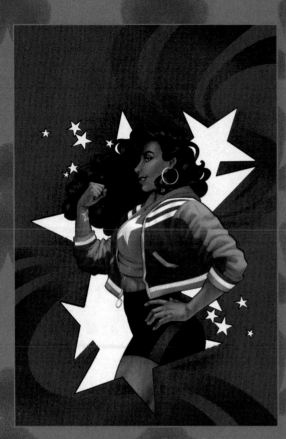

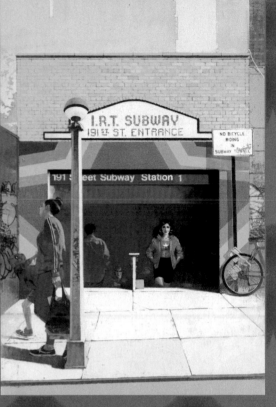

#3 VARIANT BY **Betsy Cola**

#4 VARIANT BY **Marc Aspinall**

Juan Pablo Duarte
St Nicholas

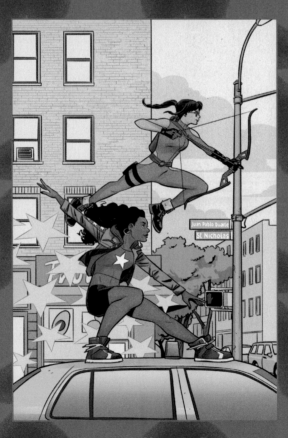

#5 VARIANT BY **Natacha Bustos**